PRAXIS
ELEMENTARY EDUCATION
0014, 5014

By: Sharon Wynne, M.S.

XAMonline, INC.
Boston

Library of Congress Cataloging-in-Publication Data

Wynne, Sharon A.
    PRAXIS Elementary Education 0014, 5014 / Sharon A. Wynne. 2nd ed
    ISBN 978-1-60787-337-2
    1. Elementary Education 0014, 5014
    2. Study Guides
    3. PRAXIS
    4. Teachers' Certification & Licensure
    5. Careers

Disclaimer:

The opinions expressed in this publication are the sole works of XAMonline and were created independently from the National Education Association, Educational Testing Service, or any State Department of Education, National Evaluation Systems or other testing affiliates.

Between the time of publication and printing, state specific standards as well as testing formats and Web site information may change and therefore would not be included in part or in whole within this product. Sample test questions are developed by XAMonline and reflect content similar to that on real tests; however, they are not former test questions. XAMonline assembles content that aligns with state standards but makes no claims nor guarantees teacher candidates a passing score. Numerical scores are determined by testing companies such as NES or ETS and then are compared with individual state standards. A passing score varies from state to state.

Printed in the United States of America   œ-1

PRAXIS Elementary Education 0014, 5014
ISBN: 978-1-60787-337-2

Table of Contents

PRAXIS

ELEMENTARY EDUCATION 0014, 5014

SECTION 1
ABOUT XAMONLINE

XAMonline—A Specialty Teacher Certification Company

Created in 1996, XAMonline was the first company to publish study guides for state-specific teacher certification examinations. Founder Sharon Wynne found it frustrating that materials were not available for teacher certification preparation and decided to create the first single, state-specific guide. XAMonline has grown into a company of over 1,800 contributors and writers and offers over 300 titles for the entire PRAXIS series and every state examination. No matter what state you plan on teaching in, XAMonline has a unique teacher certification study guide just for you.

XAMonline—Value and Innovation

We are committed to providing value and innovation. Our print-on-demand technology allows us to be the first in the market to reflect changes in test standards and user feedback as they occur. Our guides are written by experienced teachers who are experts in their fields. And our content reflects the highest standards of quality. Comprehensive practice tests with varied levels of rigor means that your study experience will closely match the actual in-test experience.

To date, XAMonline has helped nearly 600,000 teachers pass their certification or licensing exams. Our commitment to preparation exceeds simply providing the proper material for study—it extends to helping teachers **gain mastery** of the subject matter, giving them the **tools** to become the most effective classroom leaders possible, and ushering today's students toward a **successful future**.

SECTION 2
ABOUT THIS STUDY GUIDE

Purpose of This Guide

Is there a little voice inside of you saying, "Am I ready?" Our goal is to replace that little voice and remove all doubt with a new voice that says, "I AM READY. **Bring it on!**" by offering the highest quality of teacher certification study guides.

Organization of Content

You will see that while every test may start with overlapping general topics, each is very unique in the skills they wish to test. Only XAMonline presents custom content that analyzes deeper than a title, a subarea, or an objective. Only XAMonline presents content and sample test assessments along with **focus statements**, the deepest-level rationale and interpretation of the skills that are unique to the exam.

Title and field number of test

→Each exam has its own name and number. XAMonline's guides are written to give you the content you need to know for the specific exam you are taking. You can be confident when you buy our guide that it contains the information you need to study for the specific test you are taking.

Subareas

→These are the major content categories found on the exam. XAMonline's guides are written to cover all of the subareas found in the test frameworks developed for the exam.

Objectives

→These are standards that are unique to the exam and represent the main subcategories of the subareas/content categories. XAMonline's guides are written to address every specific objective required to pass the exam.

Focus statements

→These are examples and interpretations of the objectives. You find them in parenthesis directly following the objective. They provide detailed examples of the range, type, and level of content that appear on the test questions. **Only XAMonline's guides drill down to this level.**

How Do We Compare with Our Competitors?

XAMonline—drills down to the focus statement level.
CliffsNotes and REA—organized at the objective level
Kaplan—provides only links to content
MoMedia—content not specific to the state test

Each subarea is divided into manageable sections that cover the specific skill areas. Explanations are easy to understand and thorough. You'll find that every test answer contains a rejoinder so if you need a refresher or further review after taking the test, you'll know exactly to which section you must return.

How to Use This Book

Our informal polls show that most people begin studying up to eight weeks prior to the test date, so start early. Then ask yourself some questions: How much do you really know? Are you coming to the test straight from your teacher-education program or are you having to review subjects you haven't considered in ten years? Either way, take a **diagnostic or assessment test** first. Also, spend time on sample tests so that you become accustomed to the way the actual test will appear.

This guide comes with an online diagnostic test of 30 questions found online at *www.XAMonline.com*. It is a little boot camp to get you up for the task and reveal things about your compendium of knowledge in general. Although this guide is structured to follow the order of the test, you are not required to study in that order. By finding a time-management and study plan that fits your life you will be more effective. The results of your diagnostic or self-assessment test can be a guide for how to manage your time and point you toward an area that needs more attention.

After taking the diagnostic exam, fill out the **Personalized Study Plan** page at the beginning of each chapter. Review the competencies and skills covered in that chapter and check the boxes that apply to your study needs. If there are sections you already know you can skip, check the "skip it" box. Taking this step will give you a study plan for each chapter.

Week	Activity
8 weeks prior to test	Take a diagnostic test found at www.XAMonline.com
7 weeks prior to test	Build your Personalized Study Plan for each chapter. Check the "skip it" box for sections you feel you are already strong in. ✘ SKIP IT ☐
6-3 weeks prior to test	For each of these four weeks, choose a content area to study. You don't have to go in the order of the book. It may be that you start with the content that needs the most review. Alternately, you may want to ease yourself into plan by starting with the most familiar material.
2 weeks prior to test	Take the sample test, score it, and create a review plan for the final week before the test.
1 week prior to test	Following your plan (which will likely be aligned with the areas that need the most review) go back and study the sections that align with the questions you may have gotten wrong. Then go back and study the sections related to the questions you answered correctly. If need be, create flashcards and drill yourself on any area that you makes you anxious.

SECTION 3
ABOUT THE PRAXIS EXAMS

What Is PRAXIS?

PRAXIS II tests measure the knowledge of specific content areas in K-12 education. The test is a way of insuring that educators are prepared to not only teach in a particular subject area, but also have the necessary teaching skills to be effective. The Educational Testing Service administers the test in most states and has worked with the states to develop the material so that it is appropriate for state standards.

PRAXIS Points

1. The PRAXIS Series comprises more than 140 different tests in over seventy different subject areas.

2. Over 90% of the PRAXIS tests measure subject area knowledge.

3. The purpose of the test is to measure whether the teacher candidate possesses a sufficient level of knowledge and skills to perform job duties effectively and responsibly.

4. Your state sets the acceptable passing score.

5. Any candidate, whether from a traditional teaching-preparation path or an alternative route, can seek to enter the teaching profession by taking a PRAXIS test.

6. PRAXIS tests are updated regularly to ensure current content.

Often **your own state's requirements** determine whether or not you should take any particular test. The most reliable source of information regarding this is either your state's Department of Education or the Educational Testing Service. Either resource should also have a complete list of testing centers and dates. Test dates vary by subject area and not all test dates necessarily include your particular test, so be sure to check carefully.

If you are in a teacher-education program, check with the Education Department or the Certification Officer for specific information for testing and testing time-lines. The Certification Office should have most of the information you need.

If you choose an alternative route to certification you can either rely on our Web site at *www.XAMonline.com* or on the resources provided by an alternative certification program. Many states now have specific agencies devoted to alternative certification and there are some national organizations as well:

National Center for Education Information
http://www.ncei.com/Alt-Teacher-Cert.htm

National Associate for Alternative Certification
http://www.alt-teachercert.org/index.asp

Interpreting Test Results

Contrary to what you may have heard, the results of a PRAXIS test are not based on time. More accurately, you will be scored on the raw number of points you earn in relation to the raw number of points available. Each question is worth one raw point. It is likely to your benefit to complete as many questions in the time allotted, but it will not necessarily work to your advantage if you hurry through the test.

Follow the guidelines provided by ETS for interpreting your score. The web site offers a sample test score sheet and clearly explains how the scores are scaled and what to expect if you have an essay portion on your test.

Scores are usually available by phone within a month of the test date and scores will be sent to your chosen institution(s) within six weeks. Additionally, ETS now makes online, downloadable reports available for 45 days from the reporting date.

It is **critical** that you be aware of your own state's passing score. Your raw score may qualify you to teach in some states, but not all. ETS administers the test and assigns a score, but the states make their own interpretations and, in some cases, consider combined scores if you are testing in more than one area.

What's on the Test?

PRAXIS tests vary from subject to subject and sometimes even within subject area. For PRAXIS Elementary Education 0014/5014, the test can either be taken as a paper and pencil test (0014) or as a computer-delivered test (5014). The test lasts for 2 hours and consists of approximately 120 multiple-choice questions, regardless of which testing method is used. The use of scientific or four-function calculators is permitted for this test. The breakdown of the questions is as follows:

Category	Approximate Number of Questions	Approximate Percentage of the test
0014/5014: Content Knowledge		
I: Reading/Language Arts	30	25%

Table continued on next page

Category	Approximate Number of Questions	Approximate Percentage of the test
II: Mathematics	30	25%
III: Social Studies	30	25%
IV: Science	30	25%

This chart can be used to build a study plan. Thirty percent may seem like a lot of time to spend on Reading, Mathematics, Social Studies, and Science each, but when you consider that amounts to about 1 out of 3 multiple choice questions in each part of the test, it might change your perspective.

Question Types

You're probably thinking, enough already, I want to study! Indulge us a little longer while we explain that there is actually more than one type of multiple-choice question. You can thank us later after you realize how well prepared you are for your exam.

1. **Complete the Statement.** The name says it all. In this question type you'll be asked to choose the correct completion of a given statement. For example:

> The Dolch Basic Sight Words consist of a relatively short list of words that children should be able to:
>
> A. Sound out
>
> B. Know the meaning of
>
> C. Recognize on sight
>
> D. Use in a sentence

The correct answer is C. In order to check your answer, test out the statement by adding the choices to the end of it.

2. **Which of the Following.** One way to test your answer choice for this type of question is to replace the phrase "which of the following" with your selection. Use this example:

> **Which of the following words is one of the twelve most frequently used in children's reading texts:**
>
> A. There
>
> B. This
>
> C. The
>
> D. An

Don't look! Test your answer. _____ is one of the twelve most frequently used in children's reading texts. Did you guess C? Then you guessed correctly.

3. **Roman Numeral Choices.** This question type is used when there is more than one possible correct answer. For example:

> **Which of the following two arguments accurately supports the use of cooperative learning as an effective method of instruction?**
> I.   Cooperative learning groups facilitate healthy competition between individuals in the group.
> II. Cooperative learning groups allow academic achievers to carry or cover for academic underachievers.
> III. Cooperative learning groups make each student in the group accountable for the success of the group.
> IV. Cooperative learning groups make it possible for students to reward other group members for achieving.
>
> A. I and II
>
> B. II and III
>
> C. I and III
>
> D. III and IV

Notice that the question states there are **two** possible answers. It's best to read all the possibilities first before looking at the answer choices. In this case, the correct answer is D.

4. **Negative Questions.** This type of question contains words such as "not," "least," and "except." Each correct answer will be the statement that does **not** fit the situation described in the question. Such as:

> Multicultural education is **not**
>
> A. An idea or concept
>
> B. A "tack-on" to the school curriculum
>
> C. An educational reform movement
>
> D. A process

Think to yourself that the statement could be anything but the correct answer. This question form is more open to interpretation than other types, so read carefully and don't forget that you're answering a negative statement.

5. **Questions that Include Graphs, Tables, or Reading Passages.** As always, read the question carefully. It likely asks for a very specific answer and not a broad interpretation of the visual. Here is a simple (though not statistically accurate) example of a graph question:

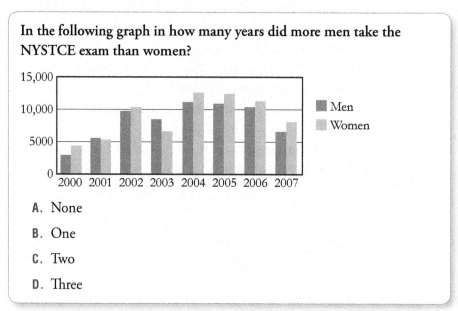

> **In the following graph in how many years did more men take the NYSTCE exam than women?**
>
> A. None
>
> B. One
>
> C. Two
>
> D. Three

It may help you to simply circle the two years that answer the question. Make sure you've read the question thoroughly and once you've made your determination, double check your work. The correct answer is C.

SECTION 4
HELPFUL HINTS

Study Tips

1. **You are what you eat.** Certain foods aid the learning process by releasing natural memory enhancers called CCKs (cholecystokinin) composed of tryptophan, choline, and phenylalanine. All of these chemicals enhance the neurotransmitters associated with memory and certain foods release memory enhancing chemicals. A light meal or snacks of one of the following foods fall into this category:

   - Milk
   - Rice
   - Eggs
   - Fish
   - Nuts and seeds
   - Oats
   - Turkey

   The better the connections, the more you comprehend!

2. **See the forest for the trees.** In other words, get the concept before you look at the details. One way to do this is to take notes as you read, paraphrasing or summarizing in your own words. Putting the concept in terms that are comfortable and familiar may increase retention.

3. **Question authority.** Ask why, why, why? Pull apart written material paragraph by paragraph and don't forget the captions under the illustrations. For example, if a heading reads *Stream Erosion* put it in the form of a question (Why do streams erode? What is stream erosion?) then find the answer within the material. If you train your mind to think in this manner you will learn more and prepare yourself for answering test questions.

4. **Play mind games.** Using your brain for reading or puzzles keeps it flexible. Even with a limited amount of time your brain can take in data (much like a computer) and store it for later use. In ten minutes you can: read two paragraphs (at least), quiz yourself with flash cards, or review notes. Even if you don't fully understand something on the first pass, your mind stores it for recall, which is why frequent reading or review increases chances of retention and comprehension.

5. **The pen is mightier than the sword.** Learn to take great notes. A by-product of our modern culture is that we have grown accustomed to getting our information in short doses. We've subconsciously trained ourselves to assimilate information into neat little packages. Messy notes fragment the flow of information. Your notes can be much clearer with proper formatting. *The Cornell Method* is one such format. This method was popularized in *How to Study in College*, Ninth Edition, by Walter Pauk. You can benefit from the method without purchasing an additional book by simply looking up the method online. Below is a sample of how *The Cornell Method* can be adapted for use with this guide.

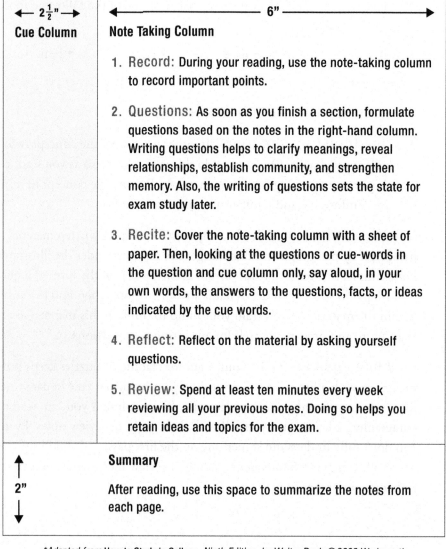

← 2½" → Cue Column	← 6" → Note Taking Column
	1. Record: During your reading, use the note-taking column to record important points.
	2. Questions: As soon as you finish a section, formulate questions based on the notes in the right-hand column. Writing questions helps to clarify meanings, reveal relationships, establish community, and strengthen memory. Also, the writing of questions sets the state for exam study later.
	3. Recite: Cover the note-taking column with a sheet of paper. Then, looking at the questions or cue-words in the question and cue column only, say aloud, in your own words, the answers to the questions, facts, or ideas indicated by the cue words.
	4. Reflect: Reflect on the material by asking yourself questions.
	5. Review: Spend at least ten minutes every week reviewing all your previous notes. Doing so helps you retain ideas and topics for the exam.
↑ 2" ↓	**Summary** After reading, use this space to summarize the notes from each page.

*Adapted from How to Study in College, Ninth Edition, by Walter Pauk, ©2008 Wadsworth

6. **Place yourself in exile and set the mood.** Set aside a particular place and time to study that best suits your personal needs and biorhythms. If you're a night person, burn the midnight oil. If you're a morning person set yourself up with some coffee and get to it. Make your study time and place as free from distraction as possible and surround yourself with what you need, be it silence or music. Studies have shown that music can aid in concentration, absorption, and retrieval of information. Not all music, though. Classical music is said to work best

7. **Get pointed in the right direction.** Use arrows to point to important passages or pieces of information. It's easier to read than a page full of yellow highlights. Highlighting can be used sparingly, but add an arrow to the margin to call attention to it.

8. **Check your budget.** You should at least review all the content material before your test, but allocate the most amount of time to the areas that need the most refreshing. It sounds obvious, but it's easy to forget. You can use the study rubric above to balance your study budget.

The proctor will write the start time where it can be seen and then, later, provide the time remaining, typically fifteen minutes before the end of the test.

Testing Tips

1. **Get smart, play dumb.** Sometimes a question is just a question. No one is out to trick you, so don't assume that the test writer is looking for something other than what was asked. Stick to the question as written and don't overanalyze.

2. **Do a double take.** Read test questions and answer choices at least twice because it's easy to miss something, to transpose a word or some letters. If you have no idea what the correct answer is, skip it and come back later if there's time. If you're still clueless, it's okay to guess. Remember, you're scored on the number of questions you answer correctly and you're not penalized for wrong answers. The worst case scenario is that you miss a point from a good guess.

3. **Turn it on its ear.** The syntax of a question can often provide a clue, so make things interesting and turn the question into a statement to see if it changes the meaning or relates better (or worse) to the answer choices.

4. **Get out your magnifying glass.** Look for hidden clues in the questions because it's difficult to write a multiple-choice question without giving away part of the answer in the options presented. In most questions you can readily eliminate one or two potential answers, increasing your chances of answering correctly to 50/50, which will help out if you've skipped a question and gone back to it (see tip #2).

5. **Call it intuition.** Often your first instinct is correct. If you've been study-ing the content you've likely absorbed something and have subconsciously retained the knowledge. On questions you're not sure about trust your instincts because a first impression is usually correct.

6. **Graffiti.** Sometimes it's a good idea to mark your answers directly on the test booklet and go back to fill in the optical scan sheet later. You don't get extra points for perfectly blackened ovals. If you choose to manage your test this way, be sure not to mismark your answers when you transcribe to the scan sheet.

7. **Become a clock-watcher.** You have a set amount of time to answer the questions. Don't get bogged down laboring over a question you're not sure about when there are ten others you could answer more readily. If you choose to follow the advice of tip #6, be sure you leave time near the end to go back and fill in the scan sheet.

Do the Drill

No matter how prepared you feel it's sometimes a good idea to apply Murphy's Law. So the following tips might seem silly, mundane, or obvious, but we're including them anyway.

1. **Remember, you are what you eat, so bring a snack.** Choose from the list of energizing foods that appear earlier in the introduction.

2. **You're not too sexy for your test.** Wear comfortable clothes. You'll be distracted if your belt is too tight or if you're too cold or too hot.

3. **Lie to yourself.** Even if you think you're a prompt person, pretend you're not and leave plenty of time to get to the testing center. Map it out ahead of time and do a dry run if you have to. There's no need to add road rage to your list of anxieties.

4. **Bring sharp number 2 pencils.** It may seem impossible to forget this need from your school days, but you might. And make sure the erasers are intact, too.

5. **No ticket, no test.** Bring your admission ticket as well as **two** forms of identification, including one with a picture and signature. You will not be admitted to the test without these things.

6. **You can't take it with you.** Leave any study aids, dictionaries, note-books, computers, and the like at home. Certain tests **do** allow a scientific or four-function calculator, so check ahead of time to see if your test does.

7. **Prepare for the desert.** Any time spent on a bathroom break **cannot** be made up later, so use your judgment on the amount you eat or drink.

8. **Quiet, Please!** Keeping your own time is a good idea, but not with a timepiece that has a loud ticker. If you use a watch, take it off and place it nearby but not so that it distracts you. And **silence your cell phone**.

To the best of our ability, we have compiled the content you need to know in this book and in the accompanying online resources. The rest is up to you. You can use the study and testing tips or you can follow your own methods. Either way, you can be confident that there aren't any missing pieces of information and there shouldn't be any surprises in the content on the test.

If you have questions about test fees, registration, electronic testing, or other content verification issues please visit *www.ets.org*.

Good luck!

Sharon Wynne
Founder, XAMonline

DOMAIN I
READING AND LANGUAGE ARTS

PERSONALIZED STUDY PLAN

KNOWN MATERIAL/ SKIP IT

PAGE	COMPETENCY AND SKILL	
3	**1:** **Foundations of Reading**	☐
	1.1: Understands the foundations of literacy and reading development	☐
	1.2: Understands the role of phonological awareness and phonics	☐
	1.3: Understands the role of fluency	☐
	1.4: Understands the role of vocabulary	☐
	1.5: Understands the role of comprehension	☐
	1.6: Understands the basic elements of fiction and nonfiction texts for children	☐
	1.7: Understands the basic elements of poetry and drama	☐
	1.8: Understands the uses of figurative language	☐
	1.9: Understands how to use resource material	☐
33	**2:** **Language in Writing**	☐
	2.1: Knows the components of written language	☐
	2.2: Knows types and traits of writing	☐
	2.3: Knows the stages of the writing process	☐
	2.4: Knows the stages of writing development	☐
	2.5: Knows sentence types and sentence structure	☐
	2.6: Knows structures and organization of writing	☐
57	**3:** **Communication Skills (Speaking, Listening, and Viewing)**	☐
	3.1: Understands different aspects of speaking	☐
	3.2: Understands different aspects of listening	☐
	3.3: Understands different aspects of viewing	☐
	3.4: Understands the role that speaking, listening, and viewing play in language acquisition for second-language learners	☐

COMPETENCY 1
FOUNDATIONS OF READING

Understands the foundations of literacy and reading development *(e.g. language acquisition, support of second-language learners, concept of print)*

During the preschool years, children acquire cognitive skills in oral language that they apply later on to reading comprehension. Reading aloud to young children is one of the most important things that an adult can do because they are teaching children how to monitor, question, predict, and confirm what they hear in stories. Reid (1988) described three metalinguistic abilities that young children acquire through early involvement in reading activities:

1. Word consciousness: Children who have access to books can first understand the story through the pictures. Gradually, they begin to understand the connection between the spoken words and the printed words. The beginning of letter and word discrimination begins in the early years.

2. Language and conventions of print: During this early stage, children learn how to hold a book, where to begin to read, left-to-right tracking, and how to continue from one line to another.

3. Functions of print: Children discover that print can be used for a variety of purposes and functions, including entertainment and information.

The typical variation in literacy that children bring to reading can make teaching more difficult. Often a teacher has to choose between focusing on the learning needs of a few students at the expense of the group or focusing on the group at the risk of leaving some students behind academically. This situation is particularly critical for diverse learners who have had less experience with reading.

> *Reading aloud to young children is one of the most important things that an adult can do because they are teaching children how to monitor, question, predict, and confirm what they hear in stories.*

KEY CONCEPTS	
Experiences with print (through reading and writing) help preschool children develop an understanding of the conventions, purpose, and functions of print.	Children learn about print from a variety of sources, and in the process, they come to realize that print carries a story. They also learn how text is structured visually (for example, in English, the text begins at the top of the page, moves from left to right, and carries over to the next page when the page is turned). Although knowledge of print conventions enables children to understand the physical structure of language, the conceptual knowledge that printed words convey a message also helps children bridge the gap between oral and written language.
Phonological awareness and letter recognition contribute to initial reading acquisition by helping children develop efficient word recognition strategies (for example, detecting pronunciations and storing associations in memory).	Phonological awareness and knowledge of print-speech relations play an important role in facilitating reading acquisition. Therefore, phonological awareness instruction should be an integral component of early reading programs. Within the emergent literacy research, viewpoints diverge on whether acquisition of phonological awareness and letter recognition are preconditions of literacy acquisition or whether they develop interdependently with literacy activities such as story reading and writing.
Story reading affects children's knowledge about, strategies for, and attitudes toward reading.	Of all the strategies intended to promote growth in literacy acquisition, none is as commonly practiced, nor as strongly supported across the emergent literacy literature, as story reading. Children in different social and cultural groups have varying degrees of access to story reading. For example, it is not unusual for a teacher to have students who have experienced thousands of hours of story-reading time along with other students who have had little or no such exposure.

Balanced Literacy

According to leading theorists, comprehension for balanced literacy is a strategic process. The reader interacts with the text and brings his or her prior knowledge and experience to it. Writing complements reading and is a mutually integrative and supportive parallel process. Hence, dividing literacy learning into reading workshops and writing workshops, using the same anchor readings or books for both, is particularly effective in teaching students.

Consider the sentence:

The test booklet was white with black print, but very scary looking.

According to the idea of constructing meaning as one reads the sentence above, readers' personal schemata (generic information stored in the mind) of tests will be activated by the author's idea that tests are scary. Readers will remember emotions they experienced during testing themselves and use this information to comprehend the author's statement. Therefore, the ultimate meaning a reader derives from the page results from the interaction of the reader's own experiences with the ideas the author presents. The reader constructs a meaning that reflects the author's intent as well as the reader's response to that intent.

Remember, also, that readings are generally fairly lengthy passages, consisting of paragraphs, which in turn consist of more than one sentence. With each successive sentence, and every new paragraph, the reader refocuses. The schemata are reconsidered, and a new meaning is constructed.

The purpose of reading is to convert visual images (letters and words) into a message. Pronouncing the words is not enough; the reader must be able to extract the meaning of the text. When people read, they utilize four sources of background information to comprehend the meaning behind the literal text:

1. **Word knowledge:** This is information about words and letters. One's knowledge of word meanings is lexical knowledge—a sort of dictionary. Knowledge of spelling patterns and pronunciations is orthographic knowledge. Poor readers do not develop a high level of automaticity in using orthographic knowledge to identify words and decode unfamiliar words.

2. **Syntax and contextual information:** When children encounter unknown words in a sentence, they rely on their background knowledge to choose a word that makes sense. Errors of younger children, therefore, are often substitutions of words in the same syntactic class. Poor readers often fail to make use of context clues to help them identify words or activate the background knowledge that would help them with comprehension. Poor readers also process sentences word by word, instead of by "chunking" phrases and clauses. This tendency results in a slow pace that focuses on decoding rather than comprehension. Poor readers also have problems answering *wh-* questions (who, what, where, when, why?) as a result of these problems with syntax.

3. **Semantic knowledge:** This encompasses the reader's background knowledge of a topic, which is combined with the text information as the reader tries to comprehend the material. New information is compared with the background information and incorporated into the reader's schema. Poor readers have problems using their background knowledge, especially with passages that require inference or cause-and-effect thinking.

4. **Text organization:** Good readers are able to differentiate types of text structure (for example, story narrative, exposition, compare-contrast, or time sequence). They use their knowledge of text to build expectations and to construct a framework of ideas on which to build meaning. Poor readers may not be able to differentiate types of text and may miss important ideas.

They may also miss important ideas and details by concentrating on lesser or irrelevant details.

Research on reading development has yielded information on the behaviors and habits of good readers versus poor readers. Some of the characteristics of good readers are:

- They think about the information they will read in the text, formulate questions they predict will be answered in the text, and confirm those predictions from the information in the text

- When faced with unfamiliar words, they attempt to pronounce them using analogies to familiar words

- Before reading, they establish a purpose for reading, anticipate possible text structure, choose a reading strategy, and make predictions about what will be in the reading

- As they read, they test and confirm their predictions, go back when something does not make sense, and make new predictions

Sample Test Questions and Rationale

(Average)

1. Which of the following represents a popular method of teaching students to read?
   I. Literacy
   II. Memorization
   III. Phonics
   IV. Whole language

   A. II and III only
   B. I and II only
   C. III and IV only
   D. I only

   Answer: C. III and IV only

   Phonics and whole language are both popular methods for teaching reading. Memorization is a different skill from reading. Literacy is the ability to read and write.

(Rigorous)

2. All of the following are true about schemata EXCEPT:

   A. Used as a basis for literary response
   B. Structures that represent concepts stored in our memories
   C. A generalization that is proven with facts
   D. Used together with prior knowledge for effective reading comprehension

   Answer: C. A generalization that is proven with facts

   Schemata are structures that represent concepts stored in our memories. When used together with prior knowledge and ideas from the printed text while reading, comprehension takes place. Schemata has nothing to do with making a generalization and proving it with facts.

SKILL
1.2 **Understands the role of phonological awareness** *(e.g., rhyming, segmenting)* **and phonics** *(e.g., decoding, letter-sound correspondence, syllabication)* **in literacy development**

Distinguishing Between Phonemic Awareness and Phonological Awareness

PHONEMIC AWARENESS is the acknowledgement of sounds and words, for example, a child's realization that some words rhyme. Onset and rhyme, for example, are skills that might help students learn that the sound of the first letter *b* in the word *bad* can be changed with the sound *d* to make it *dad*. The key in phonemic awareness is that when you teach it to children, it can be taught with the students' eyes closed. In other words, it's all about sounds, not ascribing written letters to sounds.

To be phonemically aware means that the reader and listener can recognize and manipulate specific sounds in spoken words. The majority of phonemic awareness tasks, activities, and exercises are oral.

Because the ability to distinguish between individual sounds, or **PHONEMES**, within words is a prerequisite to associating sounds with letters and manipulating sounds to blend words—a fancy way of saying "reading," teaching phonemic awareness is crucial to emergent literacy (early childhood K–2 reading instruction). Children need a strong background in phonemic awareness for phonics instruction (sound–spelling relationship–printed materials) to be effective.

As opposed to phonemic awareness, the **PHONICS** must be taught with the students' eyes open. Phonics is the connection between the sounds and letters on a page. In other words, students learning phonics might see the word *bad* and sound each letter out slowly until they recognize that they just said the word.

PHONOLOGICAL AWARENESS is the ability of the reader to recognize the sounds of spoken language. This recognition includes how these sounds can be blended together, segmented (divided up), and manipulated (switched around). This type of awareness then leads to phonics, which is a method of teaching children to read. It helps them to "sound out" words.

Development of phonological skills may begin during the pre-K years. Indeed, by the age of five, a child who has been exposed to rhyme can typically recognize another rhyme. Such a child can demonstrate phonological awareness by filling in the missing rhyming word in a familiar rhyme or rhymed picture book. It isn't unheard of for children to surprise their parents by filling in missing rhymes in a familiar nursery rhyme book at the age of four or even earlier.

PHONEMIC AWARENESS: the acknowledgement of sounds and words, for example, a child's realization that some words rhyme

To be phonemically aware means that the reader and listener can recognize and manipulate specific sounds in spoken words.

PHONEMES: the smallest unit of language capable of conveying distinction in meaning

PHONICS: method of teaching reading and spelling based on a phonetic interpretation of ordinary spelling

PHONOLOGICAL AWARENESS: the ability of the reader to recognize the sounds of spoken language

Children acquire phonological awareness when they are taught the sounds made by the letters, the sounds made by various combinations of letters, and the ability to recognize individual sounds in words.

Phonological awareness skills include:

- Rhyming and syllabification

- Blending sounds into words (such as pic-tur-bo-k)

- Identifying the beginning or starting sounds of words and the ending or closing sounds of words

- Breaking words down into sounds (also called "segmenting" words)

- Recognizing small words contained in bigger words by removing starting sounds (**hear** to *ear*)

Phonics also involves the spelling of words. Effective spelling strategies should emphasize the following principles:

- Knowledge of patterns, sounds, letter-sound association, syllables

- Memorizing sight words

- Writing those words correctly many times

- Writing the words in personal writing

Sample Test Questions and Rationale

(Average)

1. **Children are taught phonological awareness when they are taught all but which concept?**

    A. The sounds made by the letters

    B. The correct spelling of words

    C. The sounds made by various combinations of letters

    D. The ability to recognize individual sounds in words

Answer: B. The correct spelling of words

Phonological awareness happens during the pre-K years or even earlier and involves connecting letters to sounds. Children begin to develop a sense of correct and incorrect spellings of words in a transitional spelling phase that is traditionally entered in elementary school.

Sample Test Questions and Rationale (cont.)

(Easy)

2. **To decode is to:**

   A. Construct meaning

   B. Sound out a printed sequence of letters

   C. Use a special code to decipher a message

   D. None of the above

Answer: A. Construct meaning

Word analysis (phonics or decoding) is the process readers use to figure out the meaning of unfamiliar words based on written patterns. Decoding is the process of constructing the meaning of an unknown word.

SKILL **Understands the role of fluency** *(e.g., rate, accuracy)* **in literacy**
1.3 **development**

When students work on fluency, they practice reading connected pieces of text. In other words, instead of looking at a word as just a word, they might read a sentence straight through. In order for a student to comprehend what she is reading, she would need to be able to "fluently" piece words together in a sentence quickly. If a student is not fluent in reading, she would sound each letter or word out slowly and pay more attention to the phonics of each word. A fluent reader, on the other hand, might read a sentence out loud using appropriate intonations.

Fluency in reading depends on automatic word identification, which helps the student achieve comprehension of the material. Even slight difficulties in word identification can significantly increase the time it takes a student to read material, may require the student to reread some passages, and reduces the level of comprehension expected. If the student experiences reading as a constant struggle or an arduous chore, then he or she will avoid reading whenever possible and consider it a negative experience. Obviously, the ability to read for comprehension, and learning in general, will suffer if students are not assured that all aspects of reading fluency are skills that can be readily acquired with the appropriate effort.

Automatic reading (or **AUTOMATICITY**) involves the development of strong orthographic representations, which allows fast and accurate identification of whole words made up of specific letter patterns. Most young students move easily from the use of alphabetic strategies to the use of orthographic representations, which can be accessed automatically. Initially, word identification is based on the application of phonic word-accessibility strategies (letter-sound associations). These

Fluency in reading depends on automatic word identification, which helps the student achieve comprehension of the material.

AUTOMATICITY: automatic reading involves the development of strong orthographic representations, which allows fast and accurate identification of whole words made up of specific letter patterns

strategies are in turn based on the development of phonemic awareness, which is necessary to learn how to relate speech to print.

PROSODY concerns versification of text and involves such matters as which syllable of a word is accented. In terms of fluency, it is that aspect which translates reading into the same experience as listening in the reader's mind. It involves intonation and rhythm through such devices as syllable accent and punctuation.

> **PROSODY:** concerns versification of text and involves such matters as which syllable of a word is accented

The student's development of the elements necessary to automaticity continually moves through stages. Another important stage involves the automatic recognition of single graphemes as a critical first step to the development of the letter patterns that make up words or word parts. English orthography consists of four basic word types:

1. Regular, for reading and spelling (e.g., *cat, print*)

2. Regular, for reading but not for spelling (e.g., *float, brain*—could be spelled *flote* or *brane*, respectively)

3. Rule based (e.g., *canning*—doubling rule; *faking*—drop *e* rule)

4. Irregular (e.g., *beauty*)

Students must be taught to recognize all four types of words automatically in order to be effective readers. Repeated practice in pattern recognition is often necessary. True automaticity should be linked with prosody and anticipation to acquire full fluency. Such things as which syllable is accented and how word structure can be predictive are necessary to true automaticity and essential to complete fluency.

A student whose reading rate is slow, or halting and inconsistent, is exhibiting a lack of reading fluency. Some students develop accurate word pronunciation skills but read at a slow rate. They have not moved to the phase where decoding is automatic, and their limited fluency may affect performance in the following ways:

• They read less text than their peers and have less time to remember, review, or comprehend the text

• They expend more cognitive energy than their peers trying to identify individual words

• They may be less able to retain text in their memories and less likely to integrate those segments with other parts of the text

Reading fluency and comprehension involve three cueing methods: orthographic awareness, semantic cueing, and syntactic cueing. Also, sight-word and high-frequency word skills contribute to reading fluency. Teachers need to be aware of how to assess and teach those skills to enhance reading fluency.

THREE CUEING SYSTEMS	
Orthographic Awareness	The ability to perceive and recall letter strings and word forms as well as the retrieval of letters and words. Sight-word vocabulary for both reading and spelling depends on this skill. A weakness in orthographic awareness results in slow reading rates and problems with spelling. This, in turn, affects reading comprehension and writing fluency.
Syntactic Cueing	Evaluating a word for its part of speech and its place in the sentence. For example, the reader determines whether the word is a noun, verb, adjective, or other part of speech. If it is an adjective, the reader determines which word it modifies. If it is a pronoun, the reader must decide which noun it takes the place of. Syntactic cueing directly affects reading comprehension.
Semantic Cueing	Determining the meaning of a word, phrase, or sentence and determining what the passage is about.

Sample Test Question and Rationale

(Easy)

1. Which of the following indicates that a student is a fluent reader?

   A. Reads texts with expression or prosody

   B. Reads word-to-word and haltingly

   C. Must intentionally decode a majority of the words

   D. In a writing assignment, sentences are poorly organized structurally

Answer: A. Reads texts with expression or prosody

The teacher should listen to the children read aloud but there are also clues to reading levels in their writing.

SKILL
1.4 **Understands the role of vocabulary** *(e.g., affixes, root words, context clues)* **in literacy development**

Knowledge of how words are built can help students with basic and more advanced decoding. A root word is the primary base of a word. A prefix is the affix (a morpheme that attaches to a base word) that is placed at the start of a root word, but can't make a word on its own. Examples of prefixes include *re-*, *pre-*, and *un-*. A suffix follows the root word to which it attaches and appears at the end of the word. Examples of suffixes include *-s*, *-es*, *-ed*, *-ly*, and *-tion*. In the word *unlikely*, *un* is a prefix, *like* is the root word, and *ly* is a suffix.

High-Frequency and Sight Words

HIGH-FREQUENCY WORDS are the words most often used in the English language. Depending on the word list used, there are from one hundred to three hundred high-frequency words. It has been estimated that one hundred words make up 50 percent of all words used in reading. Some lists, such as the Dolch and Fry lists, use the most frequently encountered words in early childhood reading texts.

SIGHT WORDS are words that the reader learns to read spontaneously, either because of frequency or lack of conformity to orthographic rules; for example, words like *the*, *what*, and *there*, because they don't conform to rules, and words like *boy*, *girl*, and *book*, because they appear frequently in reading texts.

The National Reading Panel has released the following conclusions about vocabulary instruction:

- There is a need for direct instruction of vocabulary items required for a specific text.

- Repeated exposure to vocabulary items is important. Students should be given items that will be likely to appear in many contexts.

- Learning in rich contexts is valuable for vocabulary learning. Vocabulary words should be those that the learner will find useful in many contexts. When vocabulary items are derived from content learning materials, the learner will be better equipped to deal with specific reading matter in content areas.

- Vocabulary tasks should be restructured as necessary. It is important to be certain that students fully understand what is asked of them in the context of reading rather than to focus only on the words to be learned.

- Vocabulary learning is effective when it entails active engagement in learning tasks.

- Computer technology can be used effectively to help teach vocabulary.

HIGH-FREQUENCY WORDS: the words most often used in the English language

SIGHT WORDS: words that the reader learns to read spontaneously, either because of frequency or lack of conformity to orthographic rules

- Vocabulary can be acquired through incidental learning. Much of a student's vocabulary will have to be learned in the course of doing things rather than through explicit vocabulary learning. Repetition, richness of context, and motivation may also add to the efficacy of incidental learning of vocabulary.

- Dependence on a single vocabulary instruction method will not result in optimal learning. A variety of methods can be used effectively with emphasis on multimedia, richness of context, and repeated exposure to vocabulary words.

- The National Reading Panel found that one critical feature of effective classrooms involves utilizing lessons and activities through which students apply their vocabulary knowledge and strategies to reading and writing. Included in the activities were discussions that allowed teachers and students to talk about words, their features, and strategies for understanding unfamiliar words.

- There are many methods for directly and explicitly teaching words. The panel identified twenty-one methods that have been found effective in research projects. Many emphasize the underlying concept of a word and its connections to other words using graphics such as semantic mapping and diagrams.

- The keyword method uses words and illustrations that highlight salient features of meaning. The visualization or drawing of a picture either by the student or the teacher was found to be effective. Many words cannot be learned in this way, so effective classrooms provide multiple ways for students to learn and interact with words. The panel also found that computer-assisted activities can have a positive role in the development of vocabulary.

> *The National Reading Panel found that one critical feature of effective classrooms involves utilizing lessons and activities through which students apply their vocabulary knowledge and strategies to reading and writing.*

Spelling instruction should include learning the words that are misspelled in daily writing, generalizing spelling knowledge, and mastering objectives in progressive phases of development. The developmental stages of spelling are:

1. **Prephonemic spelling:** Children know that letters stand for a message but they do not know the relationship between spelling and pronunciation.

2. **Early phonemic spelling:** Children are beginning to understand spelling. They usually write the first letter correctly, with the rest of the word comprising consonants or long vowels.

3. **Letter-name spelling:** Children spell some words consistently and correctly. They are developing a sight vocabulary and a stable understanding of letters as representations of sounds. Long vowels are usually used accurately, but silent vowels are omitted. They spell unknown words by attempting to match the name of the letter to the sound.

4. **Transitional spelling:** Children typically enter this phase in late elementary school. They master short vowel sounds and know some spelling rules. They are developing a sense of correct and incorrect spellings.

5. Derivational spelling: This stage is usually reached between high school and adulthood. This is the stage when spelling rules are being mastered.

Sample Test Question and Rationale

(Rigorous)

1. **All of the following statements are true about vocabulary instruction EXCEPT:**

   A. There is a need for direct instruction of vocabulary items required for a specific text

   B. Vocabulary learning is effective when it entails rote memorization

   C. Computer technology can be used effectively to help teach vocabulary

   D. Vocabulary can be acquired through incidental learning

Answer: B. Vocabulary learning is effective when it entails rote memorization.

Vocabulary learning is effective when it entails active engagement in learning tasks and not rote memorization. The other three choices are also true according to the National Reading Panel.

SKILL 1.5 **Understands the role of comprehension** *(e.g., role of prior knowledge, literal and critical comprehension, metacognition)* **in literacy development**

Beginning readers must learn to recognize the conventions that create meaning and expectations in the text. For beginning readers, these literal skills include deciphering the words, punctuation, and grammar in a text. When readers achieve comprehension, they create meaning from a text. Comprehension occurs when they are able to make predictions, select main ideas, and establish significant and supporting details of the story.

A successful program of comprehension instruction should include four components:

1. Large amounts of time for actual text reading

2. Teacher-directed instruction in comprehension strategies

3. Opportunities for peer and collaborative learning

4. Occasions for students to talk to a teacher and one another about their responses to reading

Teachers can improve children's comprehension skills by providing them with opportunities and guidance in making text selections. Student choice is related to interest and motivation, both of which are related directly to learning. Teachers can encourage the rereading of texts, which, research suggests, leads to greater fluency and comprehension. Teachers can also allow time for students to read with another student, pairing students of different abilities. This provides regular opportunities for readers to discuss their reading with the teacher and with one another. Teachers can also employ guided practice strategies in which they provide feedback to the students, gradually giving them more and more responsibility for evaluating their own performances.

> *Teachers can improve children's comprehension skills by providing them with opportunities and guidance in making text selections.*

Bloom's Taxonomy

Reading comprehension skills such as generating and answering literal, inferential, and interpretive questions to demonstrate understanding of what is read in complex text are often found in the various levels of Bloom's Taxonomy. These levels, in ascending order of sophistication, are:

> *Learn more about Bloom's Taxonomy:*
>
> *http://faculty.washington.edu/krumme/guides/bloom1.html*

1. Knowledge
2. Comprehension
3. Application
4. Analysis
5. Synthesis
6. Evaluation

Higher-order cognitive questions are defined as those that ask the student to mentally manipulate bits of information previously learned in order to support an answer with logically reasoned evidence. Higher-order cognitive questions are also called open-ended, interpretive, evaluative, and inferential questions. Lower-order cognitive questions are those that ask the student merely to recall literally the material previously read or taught by the teacher.

Decoding, Word Recognition, and Spelling

WORD ANALYSIS (also called phonics or decoding) is the process readers use to figure out unfamiliar words based on written patterns. WORD RECOGNITION is the process of automatically determining the pronunciation and some degree of the meaning of an unknown word. In other words, fluent readers recognize most written words easily and correctly, without consciously decoding or breaking them down.

DECODING involves changing communication signals into messages. Reading comprehension requires that the reader learn the code in which a message is written and be able to decode it to get the message. ENCODING involves changing a message into symbols. Examples include encoding oral language into writing

WORD ANALYSIS: the process readers use to figure out unfamiliar words based on written patterns

WORD RECOGNITION: the process of automatically determining the pronunciation and some degree of the meaning of an unknown word

DECODING: changing communication signals into messages

ENCODING: changing a message into symbols

(spelling), encoding an idea into words, or encoding a mathematical or physical idea into appropriate mathematical symbols.

Although effective reading comprehension requires identifying words automatically, children do not have to be able to identify every single word or know the exact meaning of every word in a text to understand it. In fact, children can read a work with a high level of comprehension even if they do not fully know as many as 15 percent of the words in that text. Children develop the ability to decode and recognize words automatically. They can then extend their ability to decode to multisyllabic words.

Sample Test Questions and Rationale

(Rigorous)

1. **Effective reading comprehension requires:**

   A. Identifying all words automatically

   B. Knowing at least 50 percent of the words in a given text

   C. Both A and B

   D. Neither A nor B

   Answer: D. Neither A nor B

   Children do not have to be able to identify every single word or know the exact meaning of each word in a text in order to understand it, but to read with a high level of comprehension, children must be able to automatically identify and know at least 85 percent of the words in a given text. Therefore neither A nor B is a correct choice.

(Rigorous)

2. **Which of the following is NOT a strategy of teaching reading comprehension?**

   A. Summarization

   B. Utilizing graphic organizers

   C. Manipulating sounds

   D. Having students generate questions

   Answer: C. Manipulating sounds

   Comprehension simply means that the reader can ascribe meaning to text. Teachers can use many strategies to teach comprehension, including questioning, asking students to paraphrase or summarize, utilizing graphic organizers, and focusing on mental images.

SKILL 1.6 **Understands the basic elements of fiction and nonfiction texts for children**

FICTION: works that are made up by the author, or are not true

Students often misrepresent the differences between **FICTION** and **NONFICTION**. They mistakenly believe that stories are always examples of fiction. The simple truth is that stories are both fiction and nonfiction. The primary difference is that fiction is imaginary, and nonfiction is generally true (or an opinion). It is harder for students to understand that nonfiction encompasses an enormous range of material, from textbooks to true stories and newspaper articles to speeches. Fiction, on the other hand, is a fairly simple concept—imaginary stories, novels, and the like. But it is also important for students to understand that most fiction throughout history has been based on true events. In other words, authors use their own life experiences to help them create works of fiction.

> **NONFICTION:** written accounts of real people, places, objects, or events

The artistry in telling a story to convey a point is important in understanding fiction. When students see that an author's choice in a work of fiction is for the sole purpose of conveying a viewpoint, they can make better sense of the specific details.

Realizing what is truth and what is perspective is important in understanding nonfiction. Often, a nonfiction writer will present an opinion, and that opinion is quite different from a truth. Knowing the difference between the two is crucial.

> *Realizing what is truth and what is perspective is important in understanding nonfiction.*

In comparing fiction to nonfiction, students need to learn about the conventions of each genre. In fiction, students can generally expect to find plot, characters, setting, and themes. In nonfiction, students may find a plot, characters, settings, and themes, but they will also find interpretations, opinions, theories, research, and other elements.

Overall, students can begin to see patterns that distinguish fiction from nonfiction. Often, the more fanciful or unrealistic a text or story is, the more likely it is fiction.

Nonfiction comes in a variety of styles. While many students simplify nonfiction as being true (as opposed to fiction, which is make-believe), nonfiction is much deeper than that. Students should be exposed to all of the various types of nonfiction.

TYPES OF NONFICTION	
Informational Texts	These types of books explain concepts or phenomena. An informational text might explain the history of a state or the idea of photosynthesis. These types of text are usually based on research.
Newspaper Articles	These short texts rely completely on factual information and are presented in a very straightforward, sometimes choppy manner. The purpose of these texts is to present information to readers in a quick and efficient manner.
Essays	Usually, essays take an opinion (whether it is about a concept, a work of literature, a person, or an event) and describe how the opinion was arrived at or why the opinion is a good one.
Biographies	These texts describe the lives of individuals. They are usually based on extensive research.

Table continued on next page

Memoirs	In a way, a memoir is like an autobiography, but memoirs tend to be based on a specific idea, concept, issue, or event in life. For example, most presidents of the United States write memoirs about their time in office.
Letters	When letters are read and analyzed in the classroom, students are generally studying the writer's style or the writer's true opinions and feelings about certain events. Often, students will find letters of famous individuals in history reprinted in textbooks.
Journals	Like letters, journals present personal ideas. When available (most people rarely want their journals published), they give students the opportunity to see peoples' thought processes about various events or issues.

Children's Literature

> Modern educators acknowledge that introducing elementary students to a wide range of reading experiences plays an important role in their mental, social, and psychological development.

Children's literature is a genre of its own. Although it can share some of the characteristics of adult literature, it emerged as a distinct and independent form in the second half of the seventeenth century. *The Visible World in Pictures* by John Amos Comenius, a Czech educator, was one of the first printed works in existence as well as the first picture book. After its publication, educators acknowledged for the first time that children are different from adults in many respects.

Modern educators acknowledge that introducing elementary students to a wide range of reading experiences plays an important role in their mental, social, and psychological development.

COMMON FORMS OF CHILDREN'S LITERATURE	
Traditional Literature	Traditional literature opens up a world where right wins out over wrong, hard work and perseverance are rewarded, and helpless victims find vindication. These are worthwhile values that children identify with even as early as kindergarten. In traditional literature, children are introduced to fanciful beings, humans with exaggerated powers, talking animals, and heroes that will inspire them. For younger elementary children, these stories in Big Book format are ideal for providing predictable and repetitive elements that are easily grasped.
Folktales/Fairy Tales	Adventures of animals or humans and the supernatural typically characterize these stories. The hero is usually on a quest aided by other-worldly helpers. More often than not, the story focuses on good and evil and reward and punishment. Some examples of folktales and fairy tales include: "The Three Bears," "Little Red Riding Hood," "Snow White," "Sleeping Beauty," "Puss in Boots," "Rapunzel," and "Rumpelstiltskin."
Picture Books	Designed primarily for preschool children, these books tell their story with the illustrations as well as with text. The text is often limited, but can be essential. Picture books are often a child's first introduction to books and print.

Table continued on next page

Fables	Animals that act like humans are featured in these stories; the animals usually reveal human foibles or teach a lesson. Example: *Aesop's Fables*.
Myths	These stories about events from the earliest times, such as the origin of the world, are often considered true in various societies.
Legends	These are similar to myths except that they are usually about events that occurred more recently. Example: Arthurian legends.
Tall Tales	These are purposely exaggerated accounts of individuals with superhuman strength. Examples: Paul Bunyan, John Henry, and Pecos Bill.
Modern Fantasy	Many of the themes found in these stories are similar to those in traditional literature. The stories start out based in reality, which makes it easier for the reader to suspend disbelief and enter into worlds of unreality. Little people live in the walls in *The Borrowers*, and time travel is possible in *The Trolley to Yesterday*. Including some fantasy tales in the curriculum often helps elementary-grade children develop their imagination. The stories typically appeal to ideals of justice and issues related to good and evil; because children tend to identify with the characters, they are more likely to retain the message.
Science Fiction	Robots, spacecraft, mystery, and civilizations from other ages often appear in these stories. Most presume advances in science on other planets or in a future time. Most children like these stories because of their interest in space and the "what if" aspect of the stories. Examples: *Outer Space and All That Junk* and *A Wrinkle in Time*.
Modern Realistic Fiction	These stories are about real problems that real children face. By finding that their hopes and fears are shared by others, young children can find insight into their own problems. Young readers also tend to experience a broadening of interests as the result of this kind of reading. It is good for them to know that a child can be brave and intelligent and solve difficult problems.
Historical Fiction	This type of literature provides the opportunity to introduce younger children to history in a beneficial way. *Rifles for Watie* is an example of historical fiction. Presented in a historically accurate setting, it's about a sixteen-year-old boy who serves in the Union army. He experiences great hardships but discovers that his enemy is an admirable human being.
Biography	Reading about inventors, explorers, scientists, political and religious leaders, social reformers, artists, sports figures, doctors, teachers, writers, and war heroes helps children see that one person can make a difference. It also opens new vistas for children to consider when they choose a future occupation.
Informational Books	These are ways for children to learn more about something they are interested in or something that they know little about. Encyclopedias are good resources, of course, but a book like *Polar Wildlife* by Kamini Khanduri also shows pictures and facts that will capture the imaginations of young children.

Preadolescent and Adolescent Literature

The social changes post–World War II significantly affected adolescent literature. The civil rights movement, feminism, the protests of the Vietnam War era, and issues surrounding homelessness, neglect, teen pregnancy, drugs, and violence bred a new vein of contemporary fiction that helps adolescents understand and cope with the world they live in.

Popular books for preadolescents often focus on establishing relationships with members of the opposite sex (Sweet Valley High series) and learning to cope with changing bodies, personalities, or life situations (Judy Blume's *Are You There, God? It's Me, Margaret*).

Adolescents are typically interested in the fantasy and science fiction genres as well as popular juvenile fiction. Even today, middle school students still read the Little House on the Prairie series and the mysteries of the Hardy Boys and Nancy Drew. Teens also value adult literature, such as the works of Emily and Charlotte Brontë, Willa Cather, Jack London, William Shakespeare, and Mark Twain as much as those of the more modern Piers Anthony, S. E. Hinton, Madeleine L'Engle, Stephen King, and J. R. R. Tolkien.

Sample Test Questions and Rationale

(Average)

1. **Which of the following is NOT a characteristic of a fable?**

   A. Animals that feel and talk like humans

   B. Happy solutions to human dilemmas

   C. Teaches a moral or standard for behavior

   D. Illustrates specific peoples or groups without directly naming them

Answer: D. Illustrates specific people or groups without directly naming them

A fable is a short tale with animals, humans, gods, or even inanimate objects as characters. Fables often conclude with a moral, delivered in the form of an epigram (a short, witty, and ingenious statement in verse). Fables are among the oldest forms of writing in human history: They appear in Egyptian papyri of ca. 1500 BCE. The most famous fables are those of Aesop, a Greek slave living in about 600 BCE. In India, the Panchatantra appeared in the third century. The most famous modern fables are those of seventeenth-century French poet Jean de La Fontaine.

Sample Test Questions and Rationale (cont.)

(Average)

2. The children's literature genre came into its own in which century?

    A. Seventeenth century

    B. Eighteenth century

    C. Nineteenth century

    D. Twentieth century

Answer: A. Seventeenth century

In the seventeenth century, authors and their works such as Jean de La Fontaine and his *Fables*, Pierre Perreault's *Tales*, Madame d'Aulnoye's novels based on old folktales and Madame de Beaumont's *Beauty and the Beast* all created a children's literature genre. In England, Perreault's work was translated, and a work allegedly written by Oliver Smith, *The Renowned History of Little Goody Two Shoes*, also helped to establish the genre.

> **SKILL 1.7** Understands the basic elements of poetry *(e.g., mood, rhythm)* and drama *(e.g., puppetry, story theater)* for children

Poetry

People read poetry for many reasons, which are often the very same reasons poets give for writing it. Just the feeling and sounds of the words that the artistic hands and mind of a poet turn into a delightful experience is a good reason to read a poem. Good poetry constantly surprises.

The major purpose a poet has for creating his or her works of art is the sharing of an experience, a feeling, or an emotion; this is also the reason a reader turns to poetry rather than prose. Reading poetry is often a search for variety, joy, and satisfaction.

There is another important reason that poets create and that readers are drawn to their poems: Poets are interpreters of life. They feel deeply the things that others feel or even things that may be overlooked by others. Poets also have the skill and inspiration to recreate those feelings and interpret them in such a way that understanding and insight may come from the experience. They often bring understanding to life's big (or even not-so-big) questions.

Children can respond to poetry at very early ages. Elementary students are at the stage where the sounds of unusual words intrigue and entertain them. They are also very open to emotional meanings of passages. Teaching poetry to fifth graders

Teaching poetry to fifth graders can be an important introduction to seeking meaning in literature.

can be an important introduction to seeking meaning in literature. If a fifth grader enjoys reading poetry both silently and aloud, he or she may form a habit that will last a lifetime.

When we speak of structure with regard to poetry, we usually mean one of three things:

1. The pattern of the sound and rhythm

2. The visible shape it takes

3. Rhyme and free verse

The pattern of the sound and rhythm

It helps to know the background of this peculiarity of poetry. History was passed down in oral form almost exclusively until the invention of the printing press; it was often set to music. A rhymed story is much easier to commit to memory, and adding a tune makes it even easier to remember. Therefore, it is not surprising that much of the earliest literature—epics, odes, and so on, are rhymed and were probably sung.

When we speak of the pattern of sound and rhythm, we are referring to two things: verse form and stanza form. The verse form is the rhythmic pattern of a single verse. An example is any meter; blank verse, for instance, is iambic pentameter. A stanza is a group of a certain number of verses (lines) with a rhyme scheme. If the poem is written, there is usually white space between the verses (although a short poem may consist of only one stanza). If the poem is spoken, there is a pause between stanzas.

The visible shape it takes

In the seventeenth century, some poets shaped their poems on the page to reflect the theme. A good example of this is George Herbert's "Easter Wings." Since that time, poets have occasionally played with this device; however, it is generally viewed as nothing more than a demonstration of ingenuity. The rhythm, effect, and meaning are often sacrificed by being forced into the visual contours of the poem's shape.

Rhyme and free verse

Poets also use devices that underscore the meanings of their poems to establish form. One such common device is alliteration. When the poem is read (as poetry is usually intended to be), the repetition of a sound may not only underscore the meaning, but also add pleasure to the reading.

Following a strict rhyming pattern can add intensity to the meaning of the poem in the hands of a skilled and creative poet. On the other hand, the meaning can be drowned out by the steady beat-beat-beat of it. Shakespeare skillfully used the regularity of rhyme in his poetry, breaking the rhythm at certain points to effectively underscore a point. For example, in Sonnet 130, "My mistress' eyes are nothing like the sun," the rhythm is primarily iambic pentameter. It lulls the reader (or listener) to accept that the poet is following the standard conventions for love poetry, which in that day reliably used rhyme and, more often than not, iambic pentameter to express feelings of romantic love along conventional lines. However, in Sonnet 130, the last two lines sharply break from the monotonous pattern, forcing the reader or speaker to pause:

> And yet, by heaven, I think my love as rare
> As any she belied with false compare.

Shakespeare's purpose is clear: He is not writing a conventional love poem; the object of his love is not the red-and-white conventional woman written about in other poems of the period. This is a good example of a poet using form to underscore meaning.

Poets eventually began to feel constricted by rhyming conventions and began to break away and make new rules for poetry. When poetry was only rhymed, it was easy to define it. When free verse, or poetry written in a flexible form, came upon the scene in France in the 1880s, it quickly began to influence English-language poets such as T. S. Eliot, whose memorable poem, "The Wasteland," had an alarming but desolate message for the modern world. It is impossible to imagine that "The Wasteland" could have been written in the soothing, lulling rhymed verse of previous periods.

Those who first began writing in free verse in English were responding to the influence of the French *vers libre*. However, it should be noted that free verse could also be loosely applied to the poetry of Walt Whitman, writing in the mid-nineteenth century, as can be seen in the first stanza of "Song of Myself."

> I celebrate myself, and sing myself,
> And what I assume you shall assume,
> For every atom belonging to me as good belongs to you.

When poetry was no longer defined as a piece of writing arranged in verses that had a rhyme-scheme of some sort, distinguishing poetry from prose became a point of discussion. Merriam-Webster's *Encyclopedia of Literature* defines poetry as "writing that formulates a concentrated imaginative awareness of experience in language chosen and arranged to create a specific emotional response through its meaning, sound and rhythm."

A poet chooses the form of poetry deliberately, based upon the emotional response he or she hopes to evoke and the meaning he or she wishes to convey. Robert Frost, a twentieth-century poet who chose to use conventional rhyming verse to make his point, is a memorable and often-quoted modern poet. Who can forget his closing lines in "Stopping by Woods"?

> *And miles to go before I sleep,*
> *And miles to go before I sleep.*

Literary Techniques

There are a number of literary techniques that make an appearance in poetry of all forms. It is important to understand the different mechanisms that poets use in order to fully understand the meaning of a poem.

LITERARY TECHNIQUES USED IN POETRY	
Slant Rhyme	This occurs when a rhyme is not exact; often, the final consonant sounds are the same but the vowels are different. It occurs frequently in Irish, Welsh, and Icelandic verse. Examples include *green* and *gone*, *that* and *hit*, and *ill* and *shell*.
Alliteration	Alliteration occurs when the initial sounds of a word, beginning with either a consonant or a vowel, are repeated in close succession. Examples include *Athena and Apollo*, *Nate never knows*, and *people who pen poetry*. The function of alliteration, like rhyme, might be to accentuate the beauty of language in a given context, or to unite words or concepts through a kind of repetition. Alliteration, like rhyme, can follow specific patterns. Sometimes the similar-sounding consonants aren't always the initial ones (although they are generally the stressed syllables). Alliteration is less common than rhyme, but because it is less common, it can call attention to a word or line in a poem that might not have the same emphasis otherwise.
Assonance	As alliteration typically occurs at the beginning of a word, and rhyme occurs at the end, assonance takes the middle territory. Assonance occurs when the vowel sound in a word matches the sound in a nearby word, but the surrounding consonant sounds are different. *Tune* and *June* are rhymes; *tune* and *food* are assonant. The function of assonance is frequently the same as end rhyme or alliteration: All serve to give a sense of continuity or fluidity to the verse. Assonance is often especially effective when rhyme is absent, as it gives the poet more flexibility and it is not typically used as part of a predetermined pattern. Like alliteration, it does not determine the structure or form of a poem; rather, it is ornamental.
Onomatopoeia	These are words used to evoke meaning by their sounds. The early Batman television series used *pow, zap, whop, zonk,* and *eek* in an onomatopoetic way.

Table continued on next page

Rhythm	In poetry, rhythm refers to the recurrence of stresses at equal intervals. A stress (accent) is a greater amount of force given to one syllable in speaking than that given to another. For example, we put the stress on the first syllable of such words as *father*, *mother*, *daughter*, and *children*. The unstressed or unaccented syllable is sometimes called a slack syllable. All English words carry at least one stress (except articles and some prepositions such as *by*, *from*, and *at*). Indicating where stresses occur is called scansion, or scanning. Very little is gained in understanding a poem or in making a statement about it by merely scanning it. The pattern of the rhythm—the meter—should be analyzed in terms of its overall relationship to the message and impression of the poem.

Drama

Drama comes from the Greek word *dran*, meaning "to do." Therefore, drama is the acting out of a written story. Theater itself involves various elements, such as speech, gesture, dance, music, sound, and spectacle. This art form combines many of the arts into a single live performance.

Drama can involve a range of "enactments" of text or spontaneous role portrayal. Traditionally, plays (comedy, modern, or tragedy) are performed in three to five acts. Traditionalists and neoclassicists adhere to Aristotle's unities of time, place, and action. Plot development is advanced through dialogue. Literary devices include asides, soliloquies, and the chorus, which represents public opinion. Considered by many to be the greatest of all dramatists/playwrights is William Shakespeare. Other dramaturges include Ibsen, Williams, Miller, Shaw, Stoppard, Racine, Moliére, Sophocles, Aeschylus, Euripides, and Aristophanes.

It is important to expose children to character development through stories, role playing, and modeling through various teacher-guided experiences. Some experiences that are age-appropriate for the early-childhood level include puppet theater, paper dolls, character sketches, storytelling, and the retelling of stories in a student's own words. There are many plays written for children as well as adaptations of plays suitable for classroom production. Many students find a "dramatic read-aloud" of stories they are reading enhances their interest and comprehension.

- Acting: Acting requires the student to demonstrate the ability to effectively communicate using speech, movement, rhythm, and sensory awareness.

- Directing: Direction requires the management skills to produce and perform an onstage activity. This requires guiding and inspiring students as well as script and stage supervision.

- Designing: Designing involves creating and initiating the onsite management of the art of acting.

- Scriptwriting: Scriptwriting demands that a leader be able to produce original material and stage an entire production through the writing and designing of a story that has performance value.

Students can engage in acting, directing, designing, or scriptwriting in response to stories they have read or written. Acting out parts of stories can be very engaging for some students and enhance comprehension, vocabulary development, and interest in language arts.

Sample Test Questions and Rationale

(Average)

1. **Alliteration is a poetic device in which:**

   A. The words used (*pow, zap, eek*) evoke meaning by their sounds

   B. The final consonant sounds are the same, but the vowels are different

   C. The vowel sound in a word matches the vowel sound in a nearby word, but the surrounding consonant sounds are different (for example, *June* and *tune*)

   D. The initial sound of a word, beginning with either a consonant or a vowel, is repeated in succession (for example, *p*eople who *p*en *p*oetry)

   Answer: D. The initial sound of a word, beginning with either a consonant or a vowel, is repeated in succession (for example, *p*eople who *p*en *p*oetry)

   Alliteration is the repetition of a consonant or a vowel sound.

(Average)

2. **Assonance is a poetic device in which:**

   A. The vowel sound in a word matches the sound in a nearby word, but the surrounding consonant sounds are different

   B. The initial sounds of a word, beginning either with a consonant or a vowel, are repeated in close succession

   C. The words used evoke meaning by their sounds

   D. The final consonant sounds are the same, but the vowels are different

   Answer: A. The vowel sound in a word matches the sound in a nearby word, but the surrounding consonant sounds are different

   Assonance takes the middle territory of rhyming so that the vowel sounds are similar, but the consonant sounds are different: *Tune* and *food* are assonant. Repeating in close succession words that have the same initial sound (*puppies who pant pathetically*) is alliteration. Using the sounds of words to evoke meaning (*zip, pow, pop*) is onomatopoeia. When the final consonant sounds are the same and the vowels are different, an author has used a different kind of alliteration.

Understands the uses of figurative language *(e.g., types of resources, graphic organizers)* **in reading and language arts**

Figurative language is often called by a more familiar term: figures of speech. Poets and writers use figures of speech to sharpen the effect and meaning of their work and to help readers see things in ways they have never seen them before. Marianne Moore observed that a fir tree has "an emerald turkey-foot at the top." Her poem makes us aware of something we probably had never noticed before. The sudden recognition of the likeness yields pleasure in the reading.

Figurative language allows for the statement of truths that more literal language cannot convey. Skillfully used, a figure of speech will help the reader to see more clearly and to focus upon particulars. Figures of speech add many dimensions of richness to the reading and understanding of a poem; they also provide many opportunities for analysis. The approach to analyzing a poem on the basis of its figures of speech is to ask pertinent questions:

- What do they do for the poem?

- Do they underscore meaning?

- Do they intensify understanding?

- Do they increase the intensity of our response?

Types of Figurative Language

Most of us are aware of a number of types of figures of speech; in fact, if all of them were listed, it would be a very long list! For the purpose of analyzing poetry or literature, the following list is fairly comprehensive.

Simile

A direct comparison of two things, often using the term *like* or *as* to foster the comparison. A common example is, "My love is like a red, red rose."

Metaphor

An indirect comparison of two things. Metaphor is the use of a word or phrase denoting one kind of object or action in place of another. Poets use metaphors extensively, but they are also essential to understanding everyday speech. For example, chairs are said to have "legs" and "arms," even though they are typically unique to humans and other animals.

Parallelism

The arrangement of ideas into phrases, sentences, and paragraphs that balance one element with another of equal importance and similar wording. An example from Francis Bacon's *Of Studies* is, "Reading maketh a full man, conference a ready man, and writing an exact man."

Personification

The attribution of human characteristics to an inanimate object, an abstract quality, or an animal. For example, John Bunyan wrote characters named Death, Knowledge, Giant Despair, Sloth, and Piety in *Pilgrim's Progress*. The metaphor of the "arm" of a chair is also a form of personification.

Euphemism

The substitution of an agreeable or inoffensive term for one that might offend or suggest something unpleasant. Many euphemisms are used to refer to death, including "passed away," "crossed over," or even simply "passed."

Hyperbole

A deliberate exaggeration for effect. This passage from Shakespeare's *The Merchant of Venice* is an example:

> *Why, if two gods should play some heavenly match*
> *And on the wager lay two earthly women,*
> *And Portia one, there must be something else*
> *Pawned with the other, for the poor rude world*
> *Hath not her fellow.*

Climax

A number of phrases or sentences arranged in ascending order of rhetorical forcefulness. This passage from Melville's *Moby Dick* is an example:

> *All that most maddens and torments; all that stirs up the lees of things; all truth with malice in it; all that cracks the sinews and cakes the brain; all the subtle demonisms of life and thought; all evil, to crazy Ahab, were visibly personified and made practically assailable in Moby Dick.*

Bathos

A ludicrous attempt to portray pathos—that is, to evoke pity, sympathy, or sorrow. It may result from inappropriately dignifying the commonplace, using elevated language to describe something trivial, or greatly exaggerating pathos.

Oxymoron

A contradiction in terms deliberately employed for effect. It is usually seen in a qualifying adjective whose meaning is contrary to that of the noun it modifies, such as "wise folly." For example, a fairly common oxymoron is "jumbo shrimp."

Irony

The expression of something other than, and particularly the opposite of, the literal meaning, such as words of praise when blame is intended. In poetry, irony is often used as a sophisticated or resigned awareness of contrast between what is and what ought to be; it expresses a controlled pathos without sentimentality. It is a form of indirectness that avoids overt praise or censure. An early example is the Greek comic character Eiron, a clever underdog who, by his wit, repeatedly triumphs over the boastful character Alazon.

Alliteration

The repetition of consonant sounds in two or more neighboring words or syllables. In its simplest form, alliteration reinforces one or two consonant sounds. For example, notice the repetition in Shakespeare's Sonnet 12:

> When I do count the clock that tells the time.

Some poets have used more complex patterns of alliteration by creating similar consonant sounds both at the beginning of words and at the beginning of stressed syllables within words. For example, hear the sounds in Shelley's "Stanzas Written in Dejection Near Naples":

> The City's voice itself is soft like Solitude's

Onomatopoeia

The naming of a thing or action by a vocal imitation of the sound associated with it, such as *buzz* or *hiss*. It is marked by the use of words whose sound suggests the sense. One good example is from "The Brook" by Tennyson:

> I chatter over stony ways,
> In little sharps and trebles,
> I bubble into eddying bays,
> I babble on the pebbles.

Malapropism

A verbal blunder in which one word is replaced by another that is similar in sound but different in meaning. The term itself comes from Sheridan's Mrs. Malaprop in *The Rivals* (1775). Thinking of the geography of contiguous countries, she spoke of the "geometry" of "contagious countries."

Sample Test Question and Rationale

(Average)

1. A euphemism is:

   A. A direct comparison of two things

   B. An indirect comparison of two things

   C. A deliberate exaggeration for effect

   D. The substitution of an agreeable term for one that might offend

Answer: D. The substitution of an agreeable term for one that might offend

A euphemism substitutes a more pleasant term for one that might suggest something unpleasant. For example, one might say that a relative "passed on" instead of "died." The other choices are definitions of other types of figurative language.

SKILL 1.9 **Understands how to use resource material** *(e.g., types of resources, graphic organizers)* **in reading and language arts**

Core resources for teaching reading and writing are books in all shapes and forms. All printed material can be used in creative ways. Magazines and newspapers, textbooks, and book club selections are all valuable. Encyclopedias, online databases, reference texts, and many other sources are also useful in the literacy process.

Examples of other resources teachers can use to teach reading and writing include graphic organizers, reading journals, and techniques like the spelling-pattern word wall.

Examples of resources teachers can use to teach reading and writing include graphic organizers, reading journals, and techniques like the spelling-pattern word wall.

Graphic Organizers

Graphic organizers solidify, in chart format, a visual relationship among various reading and writing ideas. The content of a graphic organizer may include sequence, timelines, character traits, fact and opinion, main idea and details, and differences and likenesses (generally done using a Venn diagram of interlocking circles, a KWL chart, and so on). These charts and formats are essential for providing scaffolding for instruction through activating pertinent prior knowledge.

KWL charts

KWL charts are exceptionally useful for reading comprehension, as they outline what children **k**now, what they **w**ant to know, and what they've **l**earned after reading. Students are asked to activate prior knowledge of a topic and further develop their knowledge of a topic using this organizer. Teachers often opt to display and maintain KWL charts throughout a text to continually record pertinent information about students' reading.

SPIDER KWL		
What I know	**What I want to know**	**What I have learned**
•	•	•
•	•	•
•	•	•
The most interesting fact I learned was: _____ _____		

When the teacher first introduces the KWL strategy, children should be allowed sufficient time to brainstorm what they all actually know about the topic. The children should have a three-column KWL worksheet template for their journals, and there should be a chart to record the responses from class or group discussion. The children can write in each column in their own journal; they should also help the teacher with notations on the chart. This strategy gives the children experience in note taking and a concrete record of new information gleaned from the passage.

Depending on the grade level of the participating children, the teacher may want to ask them to consider categories of information they hope to learn from the expository passage. For instance, they may be reading a book on animals to find out more about the animals' habitats during the winter or about the animals' mating habits.

When children are working on the middle section of their KWL chart (the "What do I want to know?" section), the teacher may want to give them a chance to share what they would like to learn further about the topic and help them express it in question format.

KWL can even be introduced as early as second grade with extensive teacher discussion support. It not only serves to support children's comprehension of a particular expository text, but it also models a format for note taking. Additionally, when the teacher wants to introduce report writing, the KWL format provides excellent outlines and question introductions for at least three paragraphs of a report.

Cooper (2004) recommends this strategy for use with thematic units and with reading chapters in required science, social studies, or health textbooks. KWL also provides the teacher with a concrete format to assess how well children have absorbed pertinent new knowledge within a passage (by looking at the third, L, section). Ultimately it is hoped that students will learn to use this strategy, not only under explicit teacher direction with templates of KWL sheets, but also on their own by informally writing questions they want to find out about in their journals and then going back to their own questions and answering them after the reading.

Reading Journals

Keeping a reading journal can facilitate the tracking of reading activities by elementary children. Simply listing the books and authors they read, their responses to those books and authors, and a little about each book (a synopsis) can help students monitor their progress. It also provides an opportunity to write about reading, developing comprehension and thinking skills as well as encouraging writing. For some students, their reading journal becomes a place to write about more than the books they read; it turns into a journal about their love of reading and what the process is like for them.

Spelling-Pattern Word Wall

In your classroom create a spelling-pattern word wall. Wylie and Durrell have identified spelling patterns that are in their classic thirty-seven "dependable" rhymes. The spelling-pattern word wall can be created by stapling a piece of 3-by-5-inch butcher block paper to the bulletin board. Then attach spelling-pattern cards around the border with thumbtacks so the cards can be easily removed to use at the meeting area.

Once you decide on a spelling pattern for instruction, remove the corresponding card from the word wall. Then take a 1-by-3-inch piece of a contrasting color of butcher block paper and tape the card to the top end of a sheet the children will use for their investigation. Next, read one of Wylie and Durrell's short rhymes with the children and have them identify the pattern.

After the pattern is identified, the children can try to come up with other words that have the same spelling pattern. Write these on the spelling-pattern sheet, using a different color marker to highlight the spelling pattern in the word. The children should add to the list until the sheet is full, which might take two days or more.

After the sheet is full, the completed spelling pattern is attached to the wall.

COMPETENCY 2
LANGUAGE IN WRITING

Conventions for language that appear in print have developed over several centuries; they change somewhat from generation to generation but compared to the use of language in electronic media, they are fairly static. On the other hand, language use in radio and television has undergone rapid changes. Listening to a radio show from the thirties is a step back in time. The intonation had its own peculiar qualities. Even in its own time, it would not have been recognized as a conversation between two people.

Listening to President Franklin Delano Roosevelt's "fireside chats" also takes us back in time, not only because of the content of the speeches, but also in the way they were delivered. Declamation is a good term for the radio presentation style of that day, and, to some extent, even the style of public speeches. Declamation was notable for rhetorical effect or display. Television followed in the style of the radio shows. It was declamatory in nature and sounded more like an announcement than a conversation. Listening to early television news shows—broadcasters such as Edward R. Murrow, for example—reminds us instantly of an earlier time.

Radio and television speech nowadays is much more conversational in tone. In fact, on many of the news shows, two or more newspeople carry on a conversation before, after, and between the news stories. This would have seemed peculiar to earlier listeners.

Because so many aspects of language change while others stay the same, teachers must be familiar with the proper rules and conventions of punctuation, capitalization, and spelling in the modern oral and written language. Competency exams are designed to ensure this by testing the ability to apply advanced language skills.

To aid in meeting the expectations of the competency exams, a limited number of the more frustrating rules are presented here. Rules should be applied according to the American style of English (that is, spelling *theater* instead of *theatre* and placing terminal marks of punctuation almost exclusively within other marks of punctuation). The most common conventions are discussed below.

Syntax

SYNTAX refers to the rules or patterned relationships that correctly create phrases and sentences from words. When readers develop an understanding of syntax, they begin to understand the structure of how sentences are built, and eventually the beginning of grammar.

> Example: *"I am going to the movies."*
>
> *This statement is syntactically and grammatically correct.*
>
> Example: *"They am going to the movies."*
>
> *This statement is syntactically correct since all the words are in their correct place, but it is grammatically incorrect with the use of the word "They" rather than "I."*

Spelling

Concentration in this section will be on spelling plurals and possessives. The multiplicity and complexity of spelling rules based on phonics, letter doubling, and exceptions to rules that are not mastered by adulthood should be replaced by a good dictionary. As spelling mastery is also difficult for adolescents, the recommendation is the same: Learning the use of a dictionary and thesaurus will be a more rewarding use of time.

Most plurals of nouns that end in hard consonant sounds followed by a silent e are made by adding s. Some words ending in vowels also only add an *s*.

> *fingers, numerals, banks, bugs, riots, homes, gates, radios, bananas*

For nouns that end in the soft consonant sounds *s*, *j*, *x*, *z*, *ch*, and *sh*, add *es* to make them plural. Some nouns ending in *o* also add *es*.

> *dresses, waxes, churches, brushes, tomatoes, potatoes*

Nouns ending in *y* preceded by a vowel are pluralized by just adding *s*.

> *boys, alleys*

For nouns ending in *y* preceded by a consonant, change the *y* to *i* and add *es* to make them plural.

> *babies, corollaries, frugalities, poppies*

Some noun plurals are formed irregularly or remain the same.

> *sheep, deer, children, leaves, oxen*

Some nouns derived from foreign words, especially Latin, may make their plurals in two different ways. Sometimes, the meanings are the same; other times, the two plurals are used in slightly different contexts. It is always wise to consult the dictionary.

> appendices, appendixes   criterion, criteria
>
> indexes, indices   crisis, crises

Make the plurals of closed (solid) compound words in the usual way except for words ending in *ful*, which make their plurals on the root word.

> timelines, hairpins, cupsful

Make the plurals of open or hyphenated compounds by adding the change in inflection to the word that changes in number.

> fathers-in-law, courts-martial, masters of art, doctors of medicine

Make the plurals of letters, numbers, and abbreviations by adding *s*.

> fives and tens, IBMs, 1990s, ps and qs

Sentence Completeness

Avoid fragments and run-on sentences. Recognizing sentence elements necessary to make a complete thought, properly using independent and dependent clauses, and using proper punctuation will correct such errors.

Capitalization

Capitalize all proper names of persons (including specific organizations or agencies of government); places (countries, states, cities, parks, and specific geographical areas); things (political parties, structures, historical and cultural terms, and calendar and time designations); and religious terms (any deity, revered person or group, sacred writings).

> Percy Bysshe Shelley, Argentina, Mount Rainier National Park, Grand Canyon, League of Nations, Sears Tower, Birmingham, Lyric Theater, Americans, Midwesterners, Democrats, Renaissance, Boy Scouts of America, Easter, God, Bible, Dead Sea Scrolls, Koran

Capitalize proper adjectives and titles used with proper names.

> California gold rush, President John Adams, French fries, Homeric epic, Romanesque architecture, Senator John Glenn

Note: Some words that represent titles and offices are not capitalized unless used with a proper name.

Capitalized	Not Capitalized
Congressman McKay	the congressman from Florida
Commander Alger	commander of the Pacific Fleet
Queen Elizabeth	the queen of England

Capitalize all main words in titles of works of literature, art, and music.

(See "Italics" in the "Punctuation" section)

Punctuation

In a quoted statement that is either declarative or imperative, place the period inside the closing quotation marks.

> *"The airplane crashed on the runway during takeoff."*

If the quotation is followed by other words in the sentence, place a comma inside the closing quotations marks and a period at the end of the sentence.

> *"The airplane crashed on the runway during takeoff," said the announcer.*

In most instances in which a quoted title or expression occurs at the end of a sentence, the period is placed before either the single or double quotation marks.

> *"The middle school readers were unprepared to understand Bryant's poem 'Thanatopsis.'"*
>
> *Early book-length adventure stories like Don Quixote and The Three Musketeers were known as "picaresque novels."*

There is an instance in which the final quotation mark would precede the period: If the content of the sentence were about a speech or quote, and the meaning would be obscured by the placement of the period.

> *The first thing out of his mouth was "Hi, I'm home."*
>
> but
>
> *The first line of his speech began "I arrived home to an empty house".*

In sentences that are interrogatory or exclamatory, the question mark or exclamation point should be positioned outside the closing quotation marks if the quote itself is a statement or command or cited title.

> *Who decided to lead us in the recitation of the "Pledge of Allegiance"?*
>
> *Why was Tillie shaking as she began her recitation, "Once upon a midnight dreary..."?*
>
> *I was embarrassed when Mrs. White said, "Your slip is showing"!*

In sentences that are declarative but the quotation is a question or an exclamation, place the question mark or exclamation point inside the quotation marks.

> *The hall monitor yelled, "Fire! Fire!"*
>
> *"Fire! Fire!" yelled the hall monitor.*
>
> *Cory shrieked, "Is there a mouse in the room?" (In this instance, the question supersedes the exclamation.)*

Commas

Separate two or more coordinate adjectives that modify the same word and three or more nouns, phrases, or clauses in a list.

> *It was a dank, dark day.*
>
> *Maggie's hair was dull, dirty, and lice-ridden.*
>
> *Dickens portrayed the Artful Dodger as a skillful pickpocket, loyal follower of Fagin, and defender of Oliver Twist.*
>
> *Ellen daydreamed about getting out of the rain, taking a shower, and eating a hot dinner.*
>
> *In Elizabethan England, Ben Johnson wrote comedy, Christopher Marlowe wrote tragedies, and William Shakespeare composed both.*

Use commas to separate antithetical or complementary expressions from the rest of the sentence.

> *The veterinarian, not his assistant, would perform the delicate surgery.*
>
> *The more he knew about her, the less he wished he had known.*
>
> *Randy hopes to, and probably will, get an appointment to the Naval Academy.*
>
> *His thorough, though esoteric, scientific research could not easily be understood by high school students.*

Semicolons

Use semicolons to separate independent clauses when the second clause is introduced by a transitional adverb. (These clauses may also be written as separate sentences, preferably by placing the adverb within the second sentence.)

> *The Elizabethans modified the rhyme scheme of the sonnet; thus, it was called the English sonnet.*
>
> or
>
> *The Elizabethans modified the rhyme scheme of the sonnet. Thus, it was called the English sonnet.*

Use semicolons to separate items in a series that are long and complex or have internal punctuation.

> The Italian Renaissance produced masters in the fine arts: Dante Alighieri, author of the Divine Comedy; Leonardo da Vinci, painter of The Last Supper; and Donatello, sculptor of the Quattro Coronati, the four saints.

> The leading scorers in the WNBA were Zheng Haixia, averaging 23.9 points per game; Lisa Leslie, 22; and Cynthia Cooper, 19.5.

Colons

Place a colon at the beginning of a list of items. (Note its use in the sentence about Renaissance Italians in the previous section.)

> The teacher directed us to compare Faulkner's three symbolic novels: Absalom, Absalom; As I Lay Dying; and Light in August.

Do not use a colon if the list is preceded by a verb.

> Three of Faulkner's symbolic novels are Absalom, Absalom; As I Lay Dying; and Light in August.

Subject-Verb Agreement

A verb should always agree in number with its subject. Making them agree relies on the ability to properly identify the subject.

> One of the boys was playing too rough.

> No one in the class, not the teacher nor the students, was listening to the message from the intercom.

> The candidates, including a grandmother and a teenager, are debating some controversial issues.

If two singular subjects are connected by *and*, the verb must be plural.

> A man and his dog were jogging on the beach.

If two singular subjects are connected by *or* or *nor*, a singular verb is required.

> Neither Dot nor Joyce has missed a day of school this year.

> Either Fran or Paul is missing.

If one singular subject and one plural subject are connected by *or* or *nor*, the verb agrees with the subject nearest to the verb.

> Neither the coach nor the players were able to sleep on the bus.

If the subject is a collective noun, its sense of number in the sentence determines the verb: singular if the noun represents a group or unit, and plural if the noun represents individuals.

> *The House of Representatives has adjourned for the holidays.*
>
> *The House of Representatives have failed to reach agreement on the subject of adjournment.*

Verbs (Tense)

Present tense is used to express that which is currently happening or is always true.

> *Randy is playing the piano.*
> *Randy plays the piano like a pro.*

Past tense is used to express action that occurred in a past time.

> *Randy learned to play the piano when he was six years old.*

Future tense is used to express action or a condition of future time.

> *Randy will probably earn a music scholarship.*

Present perfect tense is used to express action or a condition that started in the past and is continued to or completed in the present.

> *Randy has practiced piano every day for the last ten years.*
> *Randy has never been bored with practice.*

Past perfect tense expresses action or a condition that occurred as a precedent to some other action or condition.

> *Randy had considered playing clarinet before he discovered the piano.*

Future perfect tense expresses action that started in the past or the present and will conclude at some time in the future.

> *By the time he goes to college, Randy will have been an accomplished pianist for more than half of his life.*

Verbs (Mood)

Indicative mood is used to make unconditional statements; subjunctive mood is used for conditional clauses or wish statements that pose untrue conditions. Verbs in subjunctive mood are plural with both singular and plural subjects.

> *If I were a bird, I would fly.*
> *I wish I were as rich as Donald Trump.*

Conjugation of verbs

The conjugation of verbs follows the patterns used in the discussion of tense above. However, the most frequent problems in verb use stem from the improper formation of past and past participial forms.

> Regular verb: *believe, believed, (have) believed*
>
> Irregular verbs: *run, ran, run; sit, sat, sat; teach, taught, taught*

Other problems stem from the use of verbs that are the same in some tenses but have different forms and different meanings in other tenses.

> *I lie on the ground. I lay on the ground yesterday. I have lain down.*
>
> *I lay the blanket on the bed. I laid the blanket there yesterday. I have laid the blanket every night.*
>
> *The sun rises. The sun rose. The sun has risen. He raises the flag. He raised the flag. He had raised the flag.*
>
> *I sit on the porch. I sat on the porch. I have sat in the porch swing.*
>
> *I set the plate on the table. I set the plate there yesterday. I had set the table before dinner.*

Two other common verb problems stem from misusing the preposition *of* for the verb auxiliary *have* and misusing the verb ought (now rare).

> Incorrect: *I should of gone to bed.*
>
> Correct: *I should have gone to bed.*
>
> Incorrect: *He hadn't ought to get so angry.*
>
> Correct: *He ought not to get so angry.*

Pronouns

A pronoun used as a subject of predicate nominative is in nominative case.

> *She was the drum majorette. The lead trombonists were Joe and he. The band director accepted whoever could march in step.*

A pronoun used as a direct object, indirect object, or object of a preposition is in objective case.

> *The teacher praised him. She gave him an A on the test. Her praise of him was appreciated. The students whom she did not praise will work harder next time.*

Some common pronoun errors occur from the misuse of reflexive pronouns:

Singular:	*myself, yourself, herself, himself, itself*
Plural:	*ourselves, yourselves, themselves*
Incorrect:	*Jack cut hisself shaving.*
Correct:	*Jack cut himself shaving.*
Incorrect:	*They backed theirselves into a corner.*
Correct:	*They backed themselves into a corner.*

Adjectives

An adjective should agree with its antecedent in number.

Those apples are rotten. This one is ripe. These peaches are hard.

Comparative adjectives end in *-er* and superlatives in *-est*, with some exceptions like *worse* and *worst*. Some adjectives that cannot easily make comparative inflections are preceded by *more* and *most*.

Mrs. Carmichael is the better of the two basketball coaches.

That is the hastiest excuse you have ever contrived.

Avoid double comparisons.

Incorrect:	*This is the worstest headache I ever had.*
Correct:	*This is the worst headache I ever had.*

When comparing one thing to others in a group, exclude the thing under comparison from the rest of the group.

Incorrect:	*Joey is larger than any baby I have ever seen. (Since you have seen him, he cannot be larger than himself.)*
Correct:	*Joey is larger than any other baby I have ever seen.*

Include all the words necessary to make a comparison clear in meaning.

I am as tall as my mother. I am as tall as she (is).

My cats are better behaved than those of my neighbor.

Sample Test Questions and Rationale

(Rigorous)

1. Which sentence is NOT punctuated correctly?

   A. The more he knew about her, the less he wished he had known.

   B. Ellen daydreamed about getting out of the rain, taking a shower and eating a hot dinner.

   C. The veterinarian, not his assistant, would perform the delicate surgery.

   D. His thorough, though esoteric, scientific research could not easily be understood by high school students.

   Answer: B. Ellen daydreamed about getting out of the rain, taking a shower and eating a hot dinner.

   B is incorrectly punctuated because the three phrases are not all separated by a comma. The rule is to separate three or more nouns, phrases, or clauses in a list by commas. The correct punctuation would be "…getting out of the rain, taking a shower, and eating a hot dinner."

(Rigorous)

2. The following words are made plural correctly EXCEPT:

   A. Radios

   B. Bananas

   C. Poppies

   D. Tomatos

   Answer: D. Tomatos

   Words that end in *o* with a consonant before it require adding an *es* for the plural form. *Radio* does not have a consonant before the *o* and therefore only takes the *s* ending to avoid three vowels in a row.

> **SKILL 2.2** **Knows types** *(e.g., narrative, persuasive, journaling)* **and traits** *(e.g., tone, purpose, audience)* **of writing**

Types of Writing

Most nonfiction writing falls into one of four different forms: narrative, descriptive, expository, and persuasive.

Persuasive writing

PERSUASIVE WRITING is a piece of writing, a poem, a play, or a speech whose purpose is to change the minds of the audience members or to get them to do something. This is achieved in many ways:

> **PERSUASIVE WRITING:** a piece of writing, a poem, a play, or a speech whose purpose is to change the minds of the audience members or to get them to do something

1. The credibility of the writer/speaker might lead the listeners/readers to a change of mind or a recommended action.

2. Reasoning is important in persuasive discourse. No one wants to believe that he or she accepts a new viewpoint or goes out and takes action just because he or she likes and trusts the person who recommended it. Logic comes into play in reasoning that is persuasive.

3. The third and most powerful force that leads to acceptance or action is emotional appeal. Even if audience members have been persuaded logically and reasonably that they should believe something different, they are unlikely to act on it unless moved emotionally. A person with resources might be convinced that people suffered in New Orleans after Hurricane Katrina, but that person will not be likely to do anything about it until he or she feels a deeper emotional connection to the disaster. Sermons are good examples of persuasive discourse.

Expository writing

In contrast to persuasion, the only purpose of **EXPOSITION** is to inform. Expository writing is not interested in changing anyone's mind or getting anyone to take a certain action. Its purpose is to give information. Some examples include directions to a particular place or the directions for putting together a toy that arrives unassembled. The writer doesn't care whether you do or don't follow the directions. He or she only wants to be sure you have the information in case you decide to use it.

> **EXPOSITION:** in contrast to persuasion, the only purpose of exposition is to inform

Narrative writing

NARRATION is discourse that is arranged chronologically—something happened, and then something else happened, and then something else happened. It is also called a story. News reports are often narrative in nature, as are records of trips or experiences.

> **NARRATION:** discourse that is arranged chronologically—something happened, and then something else happened

Descriptive writing

DESCRIPTIVE WRITING has the purpose of making an experience available through one of the five senses—seeing, smelling, hearing, feeling (as with the fingers), and tasting. Descriptive words are used to make it possible for readers to "see" with their own mind's eye, hear through their own mind's ear, smell through their own mind's nose, taste with their own mind's tongue, and feel with their own mind's fingers. This is how language moves people. Only by experiencing an event can the emotions become involved. Poets are experts in descriptive language. Descriptive writing is typically used to make sure the point is established emotionally.

> **DESCRIPTIVE WRITING:** has the purpose of making an experience available through one of the five senses—seeing, smelling, hearing, feeling (as with the fingers), and tasting

Traits of Writing

In both fiction and nonfiction, authors portray ideas in very subtle ways through their skillful use of language. Style, tone, and point-of-view are the most basic of ways in which authors do this.

Style

STYLE: is the artful adaptation of language to meet various purposes

STYLE is the artful adaptation of language to meet various purposes. Authors can modify their word choice, sentence structure, and organization in order to convey certain ideas. For example, an author may write on a topic (such as the environment) in many different styles. In an academic style, the author uses long, complex sentences, advanced vocabulary, and structured paragraphing. However, in an informal explanation in a popular magazine, the author may use a conversational tone with simple words and simple sentence structures.

Tone

TONE: the attitude an author takes toward his or her subject

TONE is the attitude an author takes toward his or her subject. That tone is exemplified in the language of the text. For example, consider the topic of the environment. One author may dismiss the idea of global warming; the tone may be one of derision against environmentalists. A reader might notice this through the style (such as word choice), the details the author decides to present, and the order in which the details are presented. Another author may be angry about global warming and therefore use harsh words and other tones that indicate anger. Finally, yet another author may not care about the issue of the environment one way or the other. Let's say this author is a comedian who likes to poke fun at political activists. His or her tone may be humorous; therefore, he or she will adjust the language used accordingly. In this example, all types of tones are about the same subject—they simply reveal, through language, different opinions and attitudes about the subject.

Point of view

POINT OF VIEW: perspective

Finally, POINT OF VIEW is perspective. While most of us think of point-of-view in terms of first or third person in fiction (or even the points of view of various characters in stories), point of view also helps to explain much of language and the presentation of ideas in nonfiction texts. The environmentalism example above proves this. Three points of view are represented, and each creates a different style of language.

Students need to learn that language and text are changed dramatically by tone, style, and point of view. They can practice these concepts in everything they read. Doing so takes little time for each nonfiction or fiction text students read in class, and it goes a long way in helping them to comprehend text at a more advanced level.

Sample Test Questions and Rationale

(Rigorous)

1. Which is NOT a true statement concerning an author's literary style?

   A. Style can be modified through word choice

   B. Style may vary across genres

   C. Style can be affected by sentence structure

   D. Style is the expression of the author's attitude toward his or her subject

   Answer: D. Style is the expression of the author's attitude toward his or her subject.

   Style does not express an author's attitude but involves the adaptation of language to meet various writing purposes that the author may have. An author who is changing his or her word choice or sentence structures is adapting the language for different purposes. An author's style will vary across genres because a dissertation on the history of fashion will require different words and sentence structures than an article on fashion in a fashion magazine, even if both are written by the same author.

(Easy)

2. A student has written a paper with the following characteristics: written in first person; characters, setting, and plot; some dialogue; and events organized in chronological sequence with some flashbacks. In what genre has the student written?

   A. Expository writing

   B. Narrative writing

   C. Persuasive writing

   D. Technical writing

   Answer: B. Narrative writing

   These are all characteristics of narrative writing. Expository writing is intended to give information such as an explanation or directions; in it, the information is logically organized. Persuasive writing gives an opinion in an attempt to convince the reader that this point of view is valid. It also tries to persuade the reader to take a specific action. The goal of technical writing is to clearly communicate a select piece of information to a targeted reader or group of readers.

SKILL 2.3 Knows the stages of the writing process *(e.g., draft, edit, publish)*

Writing is an iterative process. As students engage in the various stages of writing, they develop and improve not only their writing skills, but their thinking skills as well. Students must understand that writing is a process and typically involves many steps when producing quality work. No matter the level of writer, students should be experienced in the following stages of the writing process.

Prewriting

Students gather ideas before writing. Prewriting may include clustering, listing, brainstorming, mapping, free writing, and charting. Providing many ways for a student to develop ideas on a topic will increase his or her chances for success.

Remind students that as they prewrite, they need to consider their audience.

Common prewriting strategies

Prewriting strategies assist students in a variety of ways. Listed below are the most common prewriting strategies students can use to explore, plan, and write on a topic. It is important to remember when teaching these strategies that not all prewriting must eventually produce a finished piece of writing. In fact, in the initial lesson of teaching prewriting strategies, it might be more effective to have students practice prewriting strategies without the pressure of having to write a finished product.

- Keep an idea book so students can jot down ideas that come to mind.

- Write in a daily journal.

- Write down whatever comes to mind; this is called free writing. Students do not stop to make corrections or interrupt the flow of ideas.

Focused free writing

A variation of this technique is focused free writing—writing on a specific topic—to prepare for an essay.

- Make a list of all ideas connected with their topic; this is called brainstorming.

- Make sure students know that this technique works best when they let their minds work freely. After completing the list, students should analyze the list to see if a pattern or way to group the ideas emerges.

- Ask the questions: Who? What? When? Where? and How? Help the writer approach a topic from several perspectives.

- Create a visual map on paper to gather ideas. Cluster circles and lines to show connections between ideas. Students should try to identify the relationship that exists between their ideas. If they cannot see the relationships, have them pair up, exchange papers, and have their partners look for some related ideas.

- Observe details of sight, hearing, taste, touch, and smell.

- Visualize by making mental images of something and write down the details in a list.

After students have practiced each of these prewriting strategies, ask them to pick out the ones they prefer and ask them to discuss how they might use the techniques to help them with future writing assignments. It is important to remember that they can use more than one prewriting strategy at a time. Also, they may find that different writing situations may suggest certain techniques.

Drafting

Students compose the first draft. Students should follow their notes/writing plan from the prewriting stage.

Writing introductions

It is important to remember that in the writing process, the introduction should be written last. Until the body of the paper has been determined—the thesis as well as its development—it is difficult to make strategic decisions regarding the introduction.

The Greek rhetoricians called this part of a discourse *exordium*, meaning "leading into." The basic purpose of the introduction, then, is to lead the audience into the discourse. It can let the reader know what the purpose of the discourse is and it can condition the audience to be receptive to what the writer wants to say. It can be very brief or it can take up a large percentage of the total word count. Aristotle said that the introduction could be compared to the flourishes that flute players make before their performance—an overture in which the musicians display what they can play best in order to gain the favor and attention of the audience for the main performance.

In order to do this, we must first know what we are going to say; who the readership is likely to be; what the social, political, and/or economic climate is; what preconceived notions the audience is likely to have regarding the subject; and how long the discourse is going to be.

There are many ways to introduce a topic in the introduction. The following list provides many options:

- Show that the subject is important

- Show that although the points being presented may seem improbable, they are true

- Show that the subject has been neglected, misunderstood, or misrepresented in the past

- Explain an unusual mode of development

- Forestall any misconception of the purpose

- Apologize for a deficiency

> *It is important to remember that in the writing process, the introduction should be written last.*

- Arouse interest in the subject with an anecdotal lead-in

- Ingratiate oneself with the readership

- Establish one's own credibility

THESIS: the point or purpose of the paper

The introduction often ends with the **THESIS**: the point or purpose of the paper. However, this is not set in stone; the thesis may open the body of the discussion, or it may conclude the discourse. The most important thing to remember is that the purpose and structure of the introduction should be deliberate if it is to serve the purpose of "leading the reader into the discussion."

Writing conclusions

It is easier to write a conclusion after the decisions regarding the introduction have been made.

It is easier to write a conclusion after the decisions regarding the introduction have been made. Aristotle taught that the conclusion should strive to do five things:

1. Inspire the reader with a favorable opinion of the writer

2. Amplify the force of the points made in the body of the paper

3. Reinforce the points made in the body

4. Arouse appropriate emotions in the reader

5. Restate in a summary way what has been said in the paper

RECAPITULATION: a brief restatement of the main points or certainly of the thesis

The conclusion can be short or it can be long, depending on its purpose in the paper. **RECAPITULATION**, a brief restatement of the main points or certainly of the thesis, is the most common form of effective conclusions. A good example is the closing argument in a court trial.

Revision and Editing

Revise comes from the Latin word *revidere*, meaning, "to see again." Revision is probably the most important step for the writer in the writing process. The students examine their work and make changes in wording, details, and ideas. So many times, students write a draft and then feel they're done. On the contrary, students must be encouraged to develop, change, and enhance their writing as they go, as well as once they've completed a draft.

As you discuss revision, begin with discussing the definition of *revise*. Also, state that all writing must be revised to improve it. After students have revised their writing, it is time for the final editing and proofreading.

Both teachers and students should be aware of the difference between these two writing processes. Revising typically entails making substantial changes to a written draft, and it is during this process that the look, idea, and feel of a draft may be altered, sometimes significantly. Like revising, editing continues to make changes to a draft. However the changes made during the editing process do more to enhance the ideas in the draft, rather than change or alter them. Finally, proofreading is the stage where grammatical and technical errors are addressed.

Training students to revise and edit

Effective teachers realize that revision and editing go hand in hand and students often move back and forth between these stages during the course of one written work. Also, these stages must be practiced in small groups, pairs, and/or individually. Students must learn to analyze and improve their own work as well as the work of their peers. Some methods to use include:

- Students, working in pairs, analyze sentences for variety

- Students work in pairs or groups to ask questions about unclear areas in the writing or to help other students add details, more information, and so on

- Students perform final edit

Students need to be trained to become effective at proofreading, revising, and editing strategies. Begin by training them using both desk-side and scheduled conferences. Listed below are some strategies to guide students through the final stages of the writing process:

- Provide some guide sheets or forms for students to use for peer responses.

- Allow students to work in pairs and limit the agenda.

- Model the use of the guide sheet or form for the entire class.

- Give students a time limit or a number of written pieces to be completed in a specific amount of time.

- Have the students read their partners' papers and ask at least three *who*, *what*, *when*, *why*, *how* questions. The students answer the questions and use them as a place to begin discussing the piece.

- At this point in the writing process, a mini-lesson that focuses on some of the problems your students are having would be appropriate.

To help students revise, provide them with a series of questions that will assist them in revising their writing:

- Do the details give a clear picture? Add details that appeal to more than just the sense of sight.

- How effectively are the details organized? Reorder the details if necessary.

- Are the thoughts and feelings of the writer included? Add personal thoughts and feelings about the subject.

> *Effective teachers realize that revision and editing go hand in hand and students often move back and forth between these stages during the course of one written work.*

Teaching grammar

Grammar needs to be taught in the context of the students' own work. Listed below is a series of classroom practices that encourage meaningful context-based grammar instruction, combined with occasional mini-lessons and other language strategies that can be used on a daily basis.

- Connect grammar with the students' own writing while emphasizing grammar as a significant aspect of effective writing.

- Emphasize the importance of editing and proofreading as an essential part of classroom activities.

- Provide students with an opportunity to practice editing and proofreading cooperatively.

- Give instruction in the form of fifteen- to twenty-minute mini-lessons.

- Emphasize the sound of punctuation by connecting it to pitch, stress, and pause.

- Involve students in all facets of language learning including reading, writing, listening, speaking, and thinking. Good use of language comes from exploring all forms of it on a regular basis.

There are a number of approaches that involve grammar instruction in the context of the writing.

- Sentence combining: Try to use the students' own writing as much as possible. The theory behind combining ideas and the correct punctuation should be emphasized.

- Sentence and paragraph modeling: Provide students with the opportunity to practice imitating the style and syntax of professional writers.

- Sentence transforming: Give students an opportunity to change sentences from one form to another, i.e., from passive to active, inverting the sentence order, changing forms of the words used.

- Daily language practice: Introduce or clarify common errors using daily language activities. Use actual student examples whenever possible. Correct and discuss the problems with grammar and usage.

Proofreading

Students proofread their drafts for punctuation and mechanical errors. There are a few key points to remember when helping students learn to edit and proofread their work.

- It is crucial that students are not taught grammar in isolation, but in the context of the writing process

- Ask students to read their writing and check for specific errors such as whether or not every sentence starts with a capital letter and has the correct punctuation at the end

- Provide students with a proofreading checklist to guide them as they edit their work

Publishing

Students may have their work displayed on a bulletin board, read aloud in class, or printed in a literary magazine or school anthology.

It is important to realize that these steps are iterative: They are repeated as a student engages in each aspect of the writing process. The students may begin with prewriting, then write, revise, write, revise, edit, and publish. They do not engage in this process in a lockstep manner; it is more circular.

Sample Test Questions and Rationale

(Average)

1. The most important step for the writer in the writing process is:

   A. Prewriting

   B. Researching

   C. Drafting

   D. Revising

   Answer: D. Revising

   During the revision process, students examine their work and make changes in wording, details, and ideas. While all steps of the writing process must be completed, teachers should encourage activities to help students learn to analyze and improve their work.

(Average)

2. All of the following are true about writing an introduction EXCEPT:

   A. It should be written last

   B. It should lead the audience into the discourse

   C. It is the point of the paper

   D. It can take up a large percentage of the total word count

   Answer: C. It is the point of the paper

   The thesis is the point of the paper, not the introduction. The rest of the statements about an introduction are true.

(Average)

3. Which of the following is NOT a technique of prewriting?

   A. Clustering

   B. Listing

   C. Brainstorming

   D. Proofreading

   Answer: D. Proofreading

   Proofreading cannot be a method of prewriting, since it is done only on texts that have already been written.

SKILL 2.4 **Knows the stages of writing development** *(e.g., picture, scribble, letter for words)*

Young children develop writing in stages just as they do reading. As with reading, writing development is not a linear progression, but rather an overlapping one. Though many label the scribbling that children start out with as prewriting, it is actually one of the stages of writing development.

Each writing stage has unique characteristics involving the areas of spelling, penmanship, print/mechanics concepts, and content. The following table explains the requisite skill for each stage and area.

	Spelling	Penmanship	Print/Mechanics Concepts	Content
Role-Play Writer	Scribbles and uses writing-like behavior; scribbles to represent word; no phonetic association	Develops pencil position and traces words and letters	Develops awareness of environmental print	Uses pictures and scribble writing
Emergent Writer	Writes initial consonants; correlates some letter/sounds; each syllable has a letter	Can write on line; incorrectly mixes upper- and lowercase letters	Makes some letters and words; attempts to write name	Copies words and uses pattern sentences
Developing Writer	Left/right correspondence; invented spelling with initial/final consonants; few vowels	Correctly uses upper- and lowercase letters	Directional writing and one-to-one writing/reading words; writes word patterns	Uses invented spelling and simple sentences
Beginning Writer	Correct spelling for most words; uses resources and decoding for spelling	Sentence structure; only focuses on one writing component at a time, i.e., spelling or punctuation	Chooses personally significant topics for writing assignments	Organizes paragraphs using complete sentences
Expanding Writer	Edits for mechanics during and after writing	Varies writing components based on writing task	Uses organization and variety of word choices	Writes in a variety of formats: poetry, stories, reports

Sample Test Question and Rationale

(Rigorous)

1. Which stage of writing development would most accurately describe the following text?

   "Bobbie n me playd games at hr moms house. We ate sereal n toest."

   A. Emergent writer

   B. Developing writer

   C. Beginning writer

   D. Expanding writer

Answer: B. Developing writer

The basic structure of sentences, the correct use of upper- and lowercase letters, and the invented spelling all suggest a developing writer.

SKILL **Knows sentence types** *(e.g., declarative, imperative)* **and sentence**
2.5 **structure** *(e.g., simple, compound, complex)*

Types of Sentences

Sentences are made up of two parts: the subject and the predicate. The subject is the "do-er" of an action or the element that is being joined. Any adjectives describing this do-er or element are also part of the subject. The predicate is made up of the verb and any other adverbs, adjectives, pronouns, or clauses that describe the action of the sentence.

A simple sentence contains one independent clause (which contains one subject and one predicate).

In the following examples, the subject is underlined once and the predicate is underlined twice.

The dancer bowed.
Nathan skied down the hill.

A compound sentence is made up of two independent clauses that are joined by a conjunction, a correlative conjunction (e.g., *either-or*, *neither-nor*), or a semicolon. Both of these independent clauses are able to stand on their own, but for sentence variety, authors will often combine two independent clauses.

In the following examples, the subjects of each independent clause are underlined once, and the predicates of each independent clause are underlined twice. The conjunction is in bold.

> Samantha ate the cookie, **and** she drank her milk.
>
> Mark is excellent with computers; he has worked with them for years.
>
> **Either** Terry runs the project **or** I will not participate.

A complex sentence is made up of one independent clause and at least one dependent clause. In the following examples, the subjects of each clause are underlined once, and the predicates are underlined twice. The independent clause is in plain text, and the dependent clause is in italics.

> When *Jody saw how clean the house was,* she was happy.
>
> Brian loves *taking diving lessons, which he has done for years.*

Sample Test Question and Rationale

(Average)

1. A sentence that contains one independent clause with one subject and one predicate best describes a:

    A. Simple sentence

    B. Compound sentence

    C. Complex sentence

    D. Compound complex sentence

Answer: A. Simple sentence

Simple sentences contain one independent clause, and each independent clause contains one subject and one predicate. The other choices have more than one independent clause, a dependent clause, or both types of clauses within the sentence.

SKILL 2.6 **Knows structures** *(e.g. description, definition, examples)* **and organization** *(e.g., descriptive comparison/contrast, persuasion)* **of writing**

Organization of Text

In studies of professional writers and how they produce their successful works, it has been revealed that writing is a process that can be clearly defined (although in practice, it must have enough flexibility to allow for creativity). The teacher must be able to define the various stages that a successful writer goes through in order to make a statement that has value.

First, there must be a discovery stage when ideas, materials, and supporting details are deliberately collected. These may come from many possible sources: the writer's own experience and observations, research of written sources, interviews, television presentations, or the Internet.

The next stage is the organization, during which the purpose, thesis, and supporting points are determined. Most writers will put forth more than one possible thesis; in the next stage, the writing of the paper, they will settle on one through the process of trial and error.

Once the paper is written, the editing stage is necessary. This is probably the most important stage. This is not just about polishing the paper; at this point, decisions must be made regarding whether the reasoning is cohesive: Does it hold together? Is the arrangement the best possible one or should the points be rearranged? Are there holes that need to be filled in? What form will the introduction take? Does the conclusion lead the reader out of the discourse, or is it inadequate or too abrupt?

Patterns of organization

Various conventions of writing serve the purpose of making comprehension easier for readers. Those conventions include: good paragraphing; transitions between paragraphs, ideas, and sentences; topic sentences; concluding sentences; appropriate vocabulary; and sufficient context.

1. Good paragraphing entails dividing up ideas into bite-sized chunks. A good paragraph typically includes a topic sentence that explains the content of the paragraph. A good paragraph also includes a sufficient explanation of that topic sentence. Thus, if a topic sentence suggests that the paragraph will be about the causes of the Civil War, the rest of the paragraph should actually explain specific causes of the Civil War.

2. As writers transition from one paragraph to another—or from one sentence to another—they usually provide transitional phrases that give signposts to readers about what is coming next. Words like *however*, *furthermore*, *although*, and *likewise* are good ways of communicating intention to readers. When ideas are thrown together on a page, it is hard to tell what the writer is actually doing with those ideas. Therefore, students need to become familiar with using transitional phrases.

3. As mentioned above, topic sentences are used at the beginning of paragraphs to provide structure for the information that the paragraph will contain. Topic sentences help both readers and writers in communicating and understanding.

4. Concluding sentences are often unnecessary; however, when done right, they provide a nice "farewell" or closing to a piece of writing. Students should be warned to not always use concluding sentences in paragraphs to avoid overexposure. However, they should also be alerted to their potential benefits.

5. When writers use appropriate vocabulary, they are sensitive to the audience and the purpose of what they are writing. For example, if writing an essay on a scientific concept to a group of nonscientists, it would not be a good idea to use specialized vocabulary to explain concepts. However, if writing for a group of scientists, not using that vocabulary may make the writer appear less credible. Vocabulary depends on what the writer intends with the piece of writing. Therefore, students need to learn early on that all writing has a purpose and that because of that purpose, good writers will make conscious decisions about how to arrange their texts, which words to use, and which examples and metaphors to include.

6. When writers provide sufficient context, they ensure that readers do not have to extensively question the text to figure out what is going on. Again, this has a lot to do with knowing the audience. Using the scientific concept example from above, the writer would need to provide more context if the audience were a group of nonscientists than if the audience were scientists. In other words, it would be necessary to provide more background so that the nonscientists could understand the basic concepts.

Sample Test Questions and Rationale

(Rigorous)

1. **All of the following statements are true about the topic sentence of a paragraph EXCEPT:**

   A. It is more general than the other sentences

   B. It usually covers one single idea

   C. In question form, all the other sentences answer it

   D. It could be in any position in the paragraph

Answer: B. It usually covers one single idea

Topic sentences are general, cover many things, and look at the big picture and not one single idea. Detail sentences are more specific and cover a single part of an idea. Topic sentences can also be in any position in the paragraph and can be answered by all the other sentences.

Sample Test Questions and Rationale (cont.)

(Average)

2. Topic sentences, transition words, and appropriate vocabulary are used by writers to:

   A. Meet various purposes

   B. Organize a multiparagraph essay

   C. Express an attitude on a subject

   D. Explain the presentation of ideas

Answer: B. Organize a multiparagraph essay

Correctly organizing an essay allows a writer to clearly communicate his or her ideas. To organize, a writer needs topic sentences, transition words, and appropriate vocabulary. Meeting a purpose, expressing an attitude, and explaining ideas are all done by an author in a piece of writing, but they are separate elements.

COMPETENCY 3
COMMUNICATION SKILLS (SPEAKING, LISTENING, AND VIEWING)

> **SKILL 3.1** **Understands different aspects of speaking** *(e.g., purpose, audience, tone)*

There are a number of factors that must be taken into consideration when giving a speech. Here is a detailed list of tips to keep in mind:

- Voice: Many people fall into one of two traps when speaking: talking in a monotone or talking too fast. These are both typically caused by anxiety. A monotone restricts your natural inflection but can be remedied by releasing tension in the upper and lower body muscles. Talking too fast, on the other hand, is not necessarily a bad thing if the speaker is exceptionally articulate. However, if the speaker is not articulate, or if he or she is talking about very technical things, it becomes far too easy for the audience to become lost.

If you talk too fast and begin tripping over your words, it is important to consciously pause after every sentence. Don't be afraid of brief silences. The audience needs time to absorb what you are saying.

- **Volume:** Problems with volume, whether too soft or too loud, can usually be addressed with practice. If you tend to speak too softly, have someone stand in the back of the room and give you a signal when your volume is strong enough. If possible, have someone in the front of the room as well to make sure you're not overcompensating with excessive volume. In this same vein, if you have a problem with speaking too loudly, have the person in the front of the room signal you when your voice is soft enough and check with the person in the back to make sure it is still loud enough to be heard. In both cases, note your volume level for future reference. Don't be shy about asking your audience, "Can you hear me in the back?" Suitable volume is beneficial for both you and the audience.

- **Pitch:** Pitch refers to the length, tension, and thickness of a person's vocal bands. As your voice gets higher, the pitch gets higher. In an oral performance, pitch reflects upon the emotional arousal level. More variation in pitch typically corresponds to more emotional arousal, but can also be used to convey sarcasm or to highlight specific words.

- **Posture:** Maintain a straight but not stiff posture. Instead of shifting weight from hip to hip, point your feet directly at the audience and distribute your weight evenly. Keep shoulders oriented toward the audience. If you have to turn your body to use a visual aid, turn forty-five degrees and continue speaking in the direction of the audience.

- **Movement:** Instead of staying glued to one spot or pacing back and forth, stay within four to eight feet of the front row of your audience; take maybe a step or half step to the side every once in a while. If you are using a lectern, feel free to move to the front or side of it to engage your audience more. Avoid distancing yourself from the audience. You want them to feel involved and connected.

- **Gestures:** Gestures are a great way to keep a natural atmosphere when speaking in public. Use them just as you would when speaking to a friend. They shouldn't be exaggerated, but they should be utilized for added emphasis. Avoid keeping your hands in your pockets or locked behind your back, wringing your hands, fidgeting nervously, or keeping your arms crossed.

- **Eye contact:** Many people are intimidated by using eye contact when speaking to large groups. Interestingly, eye contact usually *helps* the speaker to overcome speech anxiety by allowing him or her to connect with the attentive audience and by easing feelings of isolation. Instead of looking at a spot on the back wall or at your notes, scan the room and make eye contact for one to three seconds with various people.

Appropriate Communication Styles

In public speaking, not all speeches deserve the same type of speaking style. For example, when making a humorous speech, it is important to utilize body language that accents the humorous moments. However, when giving instructions, it is extremely important to speak clearly and slowly, carefully noting the mood of the audience, so that if there is general confusion on peoples' faces, you can go back and review something. In group discussions, it is important to ensure that you are listening to others carefully and tailoring your message so that what you say fits into the general mood and location of the discussion at hand. When giving an oral presentation, the mood should be both serious and friendly; you should focus on ensuring that the content is covered, while also relating to audience members as much as possible.

It used to be that we thought of speaking and communication only in terms of what is effective and what is not effective. Today, we realize that there is more to communication than just good and bad. We must adjust our communication styles for various audiences.

While we should not stereotype audiences, we can still recognize that certain methods of communication are more appropriate with certain people than with others. Age is an easy one to consider: Adults know that when they talk to children, they should come across as pleasant and nonthreatening, and they should use vocabulary that is simple for children to understand. On the other hand, teenagers realize that they should not speak to their grandmothers the way they speak with their peers. When dealing with communication between cultures and genders, people must be sensitive, considerate, and appropriate.

How do teachers help students to understand these "unspoken" rules of communication? These rules are not easy to communicate in regular classroom lessons. Instead, teachers must model these behaviors, and they must have high expectations for students (clearly communicated, of course) inside and outside the classroom walls.

Teachers must model "unspoken" rules of communication for students.

Teachers must also consider these aspects as they interact with colleagues, parents, community members, and even students. They must realize that all communication should be tailored so that it conveys appropriate messages and tones to listeners.

Informal versus formal language

The differences between informal and formal language are distinctions made on the basis of the occasion as well as the audience. At a "formal" occasion (for example, a meeting of executives or government officials), even conversational exchanges are likely to be formal. At a cocktail party or a golf game, the language is likely to be much more informal. Formal language uses fewer or no contractions, less slang, longer sentences, and more organization in longer segments. Speeches delivered to executives, college professors, or government officials are likely to be formal. Speeches made to fellow employees are likely to be informal. Sermons tend to be formal; Bible lessons tend to be informal.

Sample Test Question and Rationale

(Rigorous)

1. **Students should practice all of the following when speaking orally EXCEPT:**

    A. Students should look at a spot on the back wall or at notes

    B. Students should vary the pitch of their voice

    C. Students should maintain a straight but not stiff posture

    D. Students should use gestures they would use when speaking to a friend

Answer: A. Students should look at a spot on the back wall or at notes

Eye contact helps the speaker overcome speech anxiety by allowing him or her to connect with the audience, so students should look at the audience and not at a spot on the wall. Varying pitch reflects emotion; using gestures keeps the atmosphere natural; and maintaining a straight but not stiff posture keeps the speaker facing the audience. All of these techniques should be practiced during oral speaking.

SKILL 3.2 Understands different aspects of listening *(e.g., following directions, responding to questions appropriately, focusing on the speaker)*

Listening is a very specific skill for very specific circumstances. There are two aspects of listening that warrant attention: comprehension and purpose. Comprehension is simply understanding what someone says, the purpose behind the message, and the context in which it is said. Purpose comes in to play when considering that while someone may completely understand a message, they must also know what to do with it. Are they expected to just nod and smile? Go out and take action?

While listening comprehension is a significant skill in itself—one that deserves a lot of focus in the classroom (in the same way that reading comprehension does), we will focus on purpose here. Often, when we understand the purpose of listening in various contexts, comprehension is much easier. Furthermore, when we know the purpose of listening, we can better adjust our comprehension strategies.

The Purpose of Listening

When complex or new information is provided to us orally, we must analyze and interpret that information. What is the author's most important point? How do the figures of speech affect meaning? How can we arrive at conclusions? Often, making sense of this information can be difficult for oral presentations—first, because we have no way to go back and review material already stated; second, because oral language is so much less predictable than written language. However, when we focus on extracting the meaning, message, and speaker's purpose, rather than just "listening" and waiting for things to make sense for us—in other words, when we are more "active" in our listening—we have greater success in interpreting speech.

When we are more "active" in our listening, we have greater success in interpreting speech.

Listening to literature read aloud

Listening is often done for the purpose of enjoyment. We like to listen to stories, we enjoy poetry, and we like radio dramas and theater. Listening to literature can also be a great pleasure. The problem today is that students have not learned how to extract great pleasure from simply listening. Perhaps that is because we have not done a good enough job of showing students how listening to literature, for example, can be more interesting than television or video games.

In the classrooms of exceptional teachers, we often find that students are captivated by the reading aloud of good literature. It is refreshing and enjoyable to just sit and soak in the language, story, and poetry of literature being read aloud. Therefore, we must teach students *how* to listen and enjoy such work. We do this by making it fun and providing many possibilities and alternatives to capture the wide array of interests in each classroom.

In the classrooms of exceptional teachers, we often find that students are captivated by the reading aloud of good literature.

Listening in conversations and discussions

Let us consider listening in large and small group conversations. The difference here is that conversation requires more than just listening: It involves feedback and active involvement. This can be particularly challenging, as in our culture, we are trained to move conversations along, to discourage silence in a conversation, and to always get the last word in. This poses significant problems for the art of listening.

In a discussion, for example, when we are preparing our next response—rather than listening to what others are saying—we do a large disservice to the entire discussion. Students need to learn how listening carefully to others in discussions actually promotes better responses on the part of subsequent speakers. One way teachers can encourage this in both large and small group discussions is to expect students to respond directly to the previous student's comments before moving ahead with their new comments. This will encourage them to frame their new comments in light of the comments that came just before them.

Making Sense of Oral Language

Many of the skills and strategies that help us in reading comprehension can help us in listening comprehension.

Oral speech can also be much less structured than written language. Yet, aside from rereading, many of the skills and strategies that help us in reading comprehension can help us in listening comprehension. For example, as soon as we start listening to something new, we should tap into our prior knowledge in order to attach new information to what we already know. This will not only help us to understand the new information more quickly, but it will also assist us in remembering the material.

Transitions between ideas

We can also look for transitions between ideas. Sometimes this is simple, such as when voice tone or body language changes; as listeners, we have access to the animation that comes along with live speech. Human beings have to try very hard to be completely nonexpressive in their speech. Listeners should pay attention to how the speaker changes character and voice in order to signal a transition of ideas.

Nonverbal cues

Listeners can also better comprehend the underlying intent of the author when they notice nonverbal cues. In oral speech, unlike written text, elements like irony are not indicated by the actual words, but rather by the speaker's tone and nonverbal cues. Simply looking to see the expression on the face of a speaker can often do more to communicate irony than trying to extract irony from actual words.

Note taking

One good way to follow oral speech is to take notes and outline major points. Because oral speech can be more circular than written text, it can be helpful to keep track of an author's message. Students can learn this strategy in many ways in the classroom: They can take notes during the teacher's presentations as well as other students' presentations and speeches.

Other classroom methods can also be used to help students learn good listening skills. For example, teachers can have students practice following complex directions. They can also have students orally retell stories—or retell (in writing or in oral speech) oral presentations of stories or other materials. These activities give students direct practice in the very important skills of listening. They provide students with outlets in which they can slowly improve their abilities to comprehend oral language and take decisive action based on oral speech.

Analyzing the speech of others

Analyzing the speech of others is an excellent technique for helping students improve their own public speaking abilities. In most circumstances, students cannot view themselves as they give speeches and presentations; however, when they get the opportunity to critique, question, and analyze others' speeches, they begin to learn what works and what doesn't work in effective public speaking.

However, an important word of warning: *Do not* have students critique each others' public speaking skills. It could be very damaging to a student to have his or her peers point out what did not work in a speech. Instead, video is a great tool teachers can use. Any appropriate source of public speaking can be used in the classroom for students to analyze and critique.

Sample Test Question and Rationale

(Average)

1. **Which of the following methods will help students learn good listening skills?**

   A. Have students write down questions to ask the speaker

   B. Have students critique the speaker's public speaking skills

   C. Have students participate in a discussion

   D. Have students practice following complex directions

Answer: D. Have students practice following complex directions

Writing down questions, critiquing speaking skills, and participating in a discussion will distract from a student's listening. Following a set of complex directions will help students practice listening well.

> SKILL **Understands different aspects of viewing** (*e.g., interpreting images,*
> 3.3 *evaluating media techniques, understanding the message*)

Maintaining a visually stimulating classroom helps students understand language by adding the dimension of nonverbal communication.

Our world is rich with both print and nonprint images. Children, especially, are used to seeing multicolored, rapidly changing images as part of their daily world. Maintaining a visually stimulating classroom helps students understand language by adding the dimension of nonverbal communication. Utilizing images in texts as well as in art, signage, posters, or online can be useful in teaching core communication skills.

Using Illustrations in a Text

Illustrations can be key supports for emergent and early readers. Teachers should not only use wordless stories (books that tell their narratives through pictures alone), but can also make targeted use of Big Books for read-alouds, so that young children become habituated to the use of illustrations as an important component for constructing meaning. The teacher should model for the child how to reference an illustration for help in identifying a word in the text the child does not recognize.

Children can also go on a picture walk with the teacher as part of a mini-lesson or guided reading and anticipate the story (narrative) using the pictures alone to construct meaning.

Sample Test Question and Rationale

(Average)

1. Which of the following would NOT be useful in developing students' ability to view images to enhance their literacy skills?

    A. Describing a picture in a book in great detail

    B. Cutting out pictures in magazines to tell a story

    C. Drawing self-portraits

    D. Identifying billboards in their environment that reflect a certain theme

Answer: C. Drawing self-portraits

Although making self-portraits can be a productive teaching activity, it is not particularly linked to the development of literacy and communication skills.

> **SKILL 3.4** **Understands the role that speaking, listening, and viewing play in language acquisition for second-language learners**

In learning a second language, which is often English for students who come from homes where another language is spoken, having many opportunities for speaking, hearing, and seeing language and print in the classroom in various contexts is important. These multifaceted opportunities enhance the process of learning a second language and create greater comprehension.

Word Walls

A word wall is an organized collection of words displayed on a classroom wall to support students in correctly spelling high-frequency words. The words should include the words students encounter in their daily reading and writing as well as words they frequently misspell. Word-wall words can be arranged alphabetically, by spelling patterns, or by themes. Activities with a word wall could include clapping out the letters in a word, solving mystery words, making word cards, and organizing them (i.e., by parts of speech, by letters, or by subjects/themes).

A word wall is a great teaching tool for words in isolation and with writing. Each of the letters of the alphabet is displayed, with words under each letter that begin with that letter. Students are able to find the letter on the wall and read the words under each one.

Labeling

Labeling items in the classroom takes word walls to another level. Labels provide students with another everyday visual of additional words that are commonly encountered in a classroom. Labeling can also be done in multiple languages to promote diversity in the classroom. Images as well as words can be included.

Displays

Teachers should display the students' work throughout the room. Children can be encouraged to dictate a title for their own artwork and "stories." The students' work should be placed at the children's eye level for the other students to read, recognize, and enjoy.

Classroom Libraries

Students need many opportunities to read and comprehend a wide assortment of books and other texts. Classroom libraries should offer students a variety of

> *Classroom libraries should offer students a variety of reading materials, and the teacher should attempt to build a collection with various genres of children's literature.*

reading materials, and the teacher should attempt to build a collection with various genres of children's literature. The reading difficulty should vary to include multiple levels of reading. That is, a number of the books should be easy to read, while others are more challenging and of increasing difficulty and complexity. Libraries should include a variety of topics to interest all students, and a diversity of books and themes.

Encouraging Effective Communication

While it is important to expose children to numerous opportunities throughout the day to read and interact with print, it is equally important for students to have the opportunity to express themselves and communicate with each other. "Teacher-talk" is often one sided and limited. Instead, teachers should provide opportunities for students to develop and expand their vocabularies.

Encouraging more than single-word answers, inviting descriptive language, and modeling descriptive phrases are all strategies teachers can utilize to help students become more effective communicators.

Encouraging more than single-word answers, inviting descriptive language, and modeling descriptive phrases are all strategies teachers can utilize to help students become more effective communicators. Tying these skills into the way students interact with print and the types and quality of literature to which they are exposed will also help students develop in this area.

For students for whom English is not their native language, it is important for teachers to encourage and provide significant examples of descriptive language. It is through these descriptions that these students can build a foundation upon which they can build comprehension. In the case of second-language learners, the cliché of a picture being worth a thousand words cannot be truer. Whenever the teacher can tie a picture with descriptive language, it is more powerful for all learners.

It is also important to sometimes limit the language required for those students learning English. Students may have understanding of complex concepts well beyond their understanding of English. Limiting the language they need to use in a response, allows them to become more active participants within the classroom, builds their self-confidence, and demonstrates to peers the wealth of knowledge they have to share.

Sample Test Question and Rationale

(Average)

1. Ms. Chomski is presenting a new story to her class of first graders. In the story, a family visits their grandparents, where they all gather around a record player and listen to music. Many students do not understand what a record player is, especially some children for whom English is not their first language. Which of the following things should Ms. Chomski do?

    A. Discuss what a record player is with her students

    B. Compare a record player with a CD player

    C. Have students look up *record player* in a dictionary

    D. Show the students a picture of a record player

Answer: D. Show the students a picture of a record player

The most effective method of ensuring adequate comprehension is through direct experience. Sometimes this cannot be achieved and therefore it is necessary to utilize pictures or other visual aids to provide students with experience in another form besides oral language.

DOMAIN II
MATHEMATICS

PERSONALIZED STUDY PLAN

KNOWN
MATERIAL/
SKIP IT

COMPETENCY 4
MATHEMATICAL PROCESSES

> ### SKILL 4.1 Understands mathematical processes (e.g., representation, problem solving, making connections)

Representation

Mathematical operations include addition, subtraction, multiplication, and division.

Addition can be indicated by the following expressions: *sum, greater than, and, more than, increased by, added to.*

Subtraction can be expressed by: *difference, fewer than, minus, less than, decreased by.*

Multiplication is shown by: *product, times, multiplied by, twice.*

Division is indicated by: *quotient, divided by, ratio.*

Examples:

7 added to a number	$n + 7$
a number decreased by 8	$n - 8$
12 times a number divided by 7	$12n \div 7$
28 less than a number	$n - 28$
4 times the sum of a number and 21	$4(n + 21)$

Mathematical operations can be shown using manipulatives, or drawings.

Multiplication can be shown using arrays.

3×4

□ □ □ □
□ □ □ □
□ □ □ □

Addition and subtraction can be demonstrated with symbols.

ψψψ ζζζζ
$3 + 4 = 7$
$7 - 3 = 4$

Fractions can be clarified using pattern blocks, fraction bars, or paper folding.

To read a bar graph or a pictograph, read the explanation of the scale that was used in the legend. Compare the length of each bar with the dimensions on the axes and calculate the value each bar represents. On a pictograph, count the number of pictures used in the chart and calculate the value of all the pictures.

To read a circle graph, find the total of the amounts represented on the entire graph. To determine the amount that each sector of the graph represents, multiply the percentage in a sector by the number representing the total amount.

To read a chart, read the row and column headings on the table. Use this information to evaluate the given information in the chart.

Problem Solving

DEDUCTIVE THINKING is the process of arriving at a conclusion based on other statements that are all known to be true, such as theorems, axioms, or postulates. Conclusions found by deductive thinking based on true statements will *always* be true.

> **DEDUCTIVE THINKING:** the process of arriving at a conclusion based on other statements that are all known to be true, such as theorems, axioms, or postulates

INDUCTIVE THINKING is the process of finding a pattern from a group of examples. The pattern is the conclusion that a set of examples seemed to indicate. It may be a correct conclusion or it may be an incorrect conclusion, as other examples may not follow the predicted pattern.

> **INDUCTIVE THINKING:** the process of finding a pattern from a group of examples

Example:
Suppose:

   On Monday Mr. Peterson eats breakfast at McDonald's.
   On Tuesday Mr. Peterson eats breakfast at McDonald's.
   On Wednesday Mr. Peterson eats breakfast at McDonald's.
   On Thursday Mr. Peterson eats breakfast at McDonald's.

Conclusion:

   On Friday Mr. Peterson will eat breakfast at McDonald's again.

This is a conclusion based on inductive reasoning. Based on several days' observations, you conclude that Mr. Peterson will eat at McDonald's. This may or may not be true, but it is a valid inductive conclusion.

A VALID ARGUMENT is a deductive argument in which the conclusion necessarily follows from the premises. That is to say, for a valid argument, if the premises of the argument are all true, then the conclusion must also be true.

> **VALID ARGUMENT:** a deductive argument in which the conclusion necessarily follows from the premises

Consider the conclusion of an example argument, "The sum of two odd numbers is always even." The argument might include the following reasoning.

"An even number is divisible by two, but an odd number is not (dividing an odd number by two leaves a remainder of magnitude one). Define positive integers $m = 2a + 1$ and $n = 2b + 1$ as some odd numbers. Then:

$$\frac{m}{2} = a + \frac{1}{2} \quad and \quad \frac{n}{2} = b + \frac{1}{2}$$

In this case, a and b are both positive integers, and the remainder from the division becomes the added term of $\frac{1}{2}$. Next, add m and n and divide by two:

$$\frac{m+n}{2} = \frac{m}{2} + \frac{n}{2} = \left(a + \frac{1}{2}\right) + \left(b + \frac{1}{2}\right) = a + b + 1$$

The result of dividing the sum of m and n by two is $a + b + 1$; this is an integer value. As a result, the sum of m and n is divisible by two. The same reasoning works for negative odd numbers (simply subtract $\frac{1}{2}$ instead of adding $\frac{1}{2}$ in the above expressions) or with one negative odd number and one positive odd number, so the sum of two odd numbers is even."

By following the reasoning of the argument and showing that each step is legitimate, it is possible to demonstrate that the argument is valid. In this case, because the premises of the argument are true, the argument is both valid and sound.

Problem analysis

Conditional statements are frequently written in if-then form. The *if* clause of the conditional is known as the hypothesis, and the then clause is called the conclusion. In a proof, the hypothesis is the information that is assumed to be true, while the conclusion is what is to be proven true. A conditional is considered to be of the form:

> If p, then q.
> P is the hypothesis and q is the conclusion.

Conditional statements can be diagrammed using a **VENN DIAGRAM**. This is a diagram used to represent logical relations between sets. A conditional statement is represented by a circle drawn inside another circle. The inner circle represents the hypothesis. The outer circle represents the conclusion. If the hypothesis is taken to be true, then you are located inside the inner circle. If you are located in the inner circle then you are also inside the outer circle, so that proves the conclusion is true.

VENN DIAGRAM: a diagram used to represent logical relations between sets

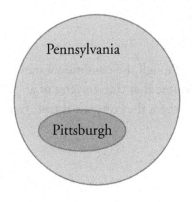

Example: If you are in Pittsburgh, then you are in Pennsylvania.
In this statement, "you are in Pittsburgh" is the hypothesis.
In this statement, "you are in Pennsylvania" is the conclusion.

Example: If an angle has a measure of 90 degrees, then it is a right angle.
In this statement, "an angle has a measure of 90 degrees" is the hypothesis.
In this statement, "it is a right angle" is the conclusion.

Conditional: **If p, then q.**

P is the hypothesis and q is the conclusion.

Inverse: **If ~p, then ~q.**

Negate both the hypothesis (If not p) and the conclusion (then not q) from the original conditional.

Converse: **If q, then p.**

Reverse the two clauses. The original hypothesis (p) becomes the conclusion. The original conclusion (q) then becomes the new hypothesis.

Contrapositive: **If ~q, then ~p.**

Reverse the two clauses. The original hypothesis (p) becomes the conclusion. The original conclusion (q) then becomes the new hypothesis. *Then* negate both the new hypothesis and the new conclusion.

Example:
Given the conditional:
If an angle measures 60 degrees, then it is an acute angle.

Its inverse, in the form "If ~p, then ~q," would be:
If an angle doesn't measure 60 degrees, then it is not an acute angle.

Notice that the inverse is not true, even though the conditional statement was true.

Its converse, in the form "If q, then p," would be:
If an angle is an acute angle, then it measures 60 degrees.

Notice that the converse is not necessarily true, even though the conditional statement was true. It is a common logical mistake to assume that the converse of a given statement is true. There are times (see below) where the converse is true, but in general it does not have to be true.

Its contrapositive, in the form "If ~q, then ~p," would be:
If an angle isn't an acute angle, then it doesn't measure 60 degrees.

Notice that the contrapositive is true, assuming the original conditional statement was true.

Examples: Find the inverse, converse, and contrapositive of the following conditional statements. Also determine whether each of the statements is true or false.

Conditional: If $x = 5$, then $x^2 - 25 = 0$. TRUE
Inverse: If $x \neq 5$, then $x^2 - 25 \neq 0$. FALSE, x could be -5
Converse: If $x^2 - 25 = 0$, then $x = 5$. FALSE, x could be -5
Contrapositive: If $x^2 - 25 \neq 0$, then $x \neq 5$. TRUE

Conditional: If $x = 5$, then $6x = 30$. TRUE
Inverse: If $x \neq 5$, then $6x \neq 30$. TRUE
Converse: If $6x = 30$, then $x = 5$. TRUE
Contrapositive: If $6x \neq 30$, then $x \neq 5$. TRUE

Sometimes, as in these examples, all four statements can be true; however, the only statement that will always be logically equivalent to the original conditional is the contrapositive.

Conditional statements can also be diagrammed using a Venn diagram.

Suppose that these statements are given to you, and you are asked to try to reach a conclusion. The statements are:

> All swimmers are athletes.
> All athletes are scholars.

In "if-then" form, these would be:

> If you are a swimmer, then you are an athlete.
> If you are an athlete, then you are a scholar.

Clearly, if you are a swimmer, then you are also an athlete. This includes you in the group of scholars.

> **Tip:** *If you are asked to pick a statement that is logically equivalent to a given conditional, look for the contrapositive. The inverse and converse are not always logically equivalent to every conditional. The contrapositive is always logically equivalent.*

COMPETENCY 5
NUMBER SENSE AND NUMERATION

> **SKILL 5.1** **Understands prenumeration concepts** *(e.g., informal counting, meaning of number, patterns)*

Place Value

PLACE VALUE SYSTEM: one in which the position of a digit in a number determines its value

Place value is the basis of our entire number system. A **PLACE VALUE SYSTEM** is one in which the position of a digit in a number determines its value. In the standard system, called base ten, each place represents ten times the value of the place to its right. You can think of this as making groups of ten of the smaller unit and combining them to make a new unit.

Base ten

Ten ones make up one of the next larger unit—tens. Ten of those units make up one of the next larger unit—hundreds. This pattern continues for greater values (ten hundreds = one thousand, ten thousands = one ten thousand, etc.), and lesser, decimal values (ten tenths =1, ten hundredths = one tenth, etc.).

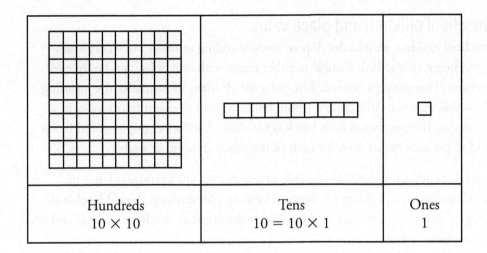

Hundreds	Tens	Ones
10 × 10	10 = 10 × 1	1

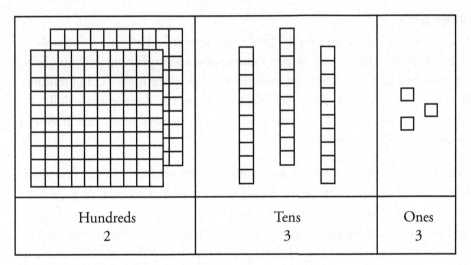

Hundreds	Tens	Ones
2	3	3

In standard form, the number modeled above is 233.

Teaching place value

A place-value chart is a way to make sure digits are in the correct places. The value of each digit depends on its position or place. A great way to see the place-value relationships in a number is to model the number with actual objects (place-value blocks, bundles of craft sticks, etc.), write the digits in the chart, and then write the number in the usual, or standard form.

Place value is vitally important to all later mathematics. Without it, keeping track of greater numbers rapidly becomes impossible. (Can you imagine trying to write 999 with only ones?) A thorough mastery of place value is essential to learning the operations with greater numbers. It is the foundation for regrouping ("borrowing" and "carrying") in addition, subtraction, multiplication, and division.

Preschool children and place value

Preschool children should develop an understanding of one-to-one correspondence, being able to link a single number name with one object, and only one, at a time. This concept is needed in order for children to formalize the meaning of a whole number. An example would be for a child to count four blocks in a row, saying the number as each block is touched. Another example would be for a child to get a carton of milk for each of the other children at a table.

Preschool children should also be able to use one-to-one correspondence to compare the size of a group of objects. For example, students should be able to compare the number of cars they have with the number another child has and say, "I have more…or less."

Number sense

Number sense develops into the further understanding of place value and how numbers are related. This involves identifying and explaining how numbers can be grouped into tens, ones and eventually hundreds or more. Using trading games, place value mats, and base ten blocks students can develop these skills. These activities will progress until the student understands that the one in sixteen represents ten, not simply one.

Children first learn to count using the counting numbers (1, 2, 3 . . .). Preschool children should be able to recite the names of the numerals in order or sequence (rote counting). This might be accomplished by singing a counting song. This should progress to being able to attach a number name to a series of objects. A preschool child should understand that the last number spoken when counting a group of objects represents the total number of objects.

In kindergarten, children should learn to read the numbers 0 through 10, and in first grade, they should be able to read through the number 20. At first, this could involve connecting a pictorial representation of the number with a corresponding number of items. This exercise may or may not involve assistive technology. As students advance, they should be able to read the numbers as sight words.

Naming procedure

Students should be taught that there is a naming procedure for our number system. The numbers 0, 1 . . . 12 all have unique names. The numbers 13, 14 . . . 19 are the "teens." These names are a combination of earlier names, with the ones place named first. For example, fourteen is short for "four ten" which means "ten plus four." The numbers 20, 21 . . . 99 are also combinations of earlier names, but the tens place is named first. For example, 48 is "forty-eight," which means "four tens plus eight." The numbers 100, 101 . . . 999 are combinations of hundreds

> *Preschool children should develop an understanding of one-to-one correspondence, being able to link a single number name with one object, and only one, at a time.*

> *In kindergarten, children should learn to read the numbers 0 through 10, and in first grade, they should be able to read through the number 20.*

and previous names. Once a number has more than three digits, groups of three digits are usually set off by commas.

Real-life application of numbers

As students gain an understanding of numbers and are able to read them, they should be taught to apply these concepts to everyday life applications. For example, once children can read the numbers 1 through 12, they can begin to learn how to tell time. At the very basic level, if shown a clock or a diagram of a clock, a child needs to understand that the big hand represents minutes and the little hand represents hours. The child begins to recognize that when the big hand is on the twelve and the little hand is on the two, it is 2 o'clock. As the child learns to count by fives, the concept may be expanded so that the child understands that the distance between two consecutive numbers is an interval of five minutes. The child then begins to recognize by counting by fives that when the big hand is on the 4 and the little hand is on the 2, it is twenty minutes after the hour of 2 o'clock.

As students gain an understanding of numbers and are able to read them, they should be taught to apply these concepts to everyday life applications.

Money

Another real-life application is money. In kindergarten, students learn to recognize a penny, nickel, dime, quarter, and one-dollar bill. In first grade, they learn how different combinations of coins have equivalent values, for example, that 10 pennies are the same as 1 dime and 10 dimes are the same as 1 dollar. Teaching children that money has value can start with a simple exercise of counting pennies to understand their monetary value. From here, students can advance to counting nickels, dimes, and so on. The next step might be to have students combine different coins and compute the value of the combination. As students advance in their understanding of the value of money, shopping math can be introduced where students see that money has value in exchange for goods. They can also learn to make change and count change.

Teaching children that money has value can start with a simple exercise of counting pennies to understand their monetary value.

Sample Test Questions and Rationale

(Easy)

1. 4,087,361: What number represents the ten-thousands place?

   A. 4

   B. 6

   C. 0

   D. 8

Answer: D. 8

The ten-thousands place is the number 8 in this problem.

SKILL **Understands basic number systems** *(e.g., whole numbers, integers,*
5.2 *fractions, decimals)*

Number Systems

The real number system includes all rational and irrational numbers.

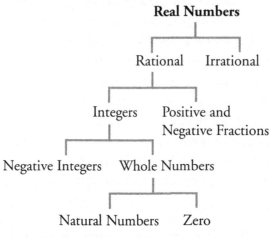

Real Numbers

RATIONAL NUMBERS:
can be expressed as the ratio of two integers, $\frac{a}{b}$, where b ≠ 0

RATIONAL NUMBERS can be expressed as the ratio of two integers, $\frac{a}{b}$, where b ≠ 0. For example: $\frac{2}{3}$, $-\frac{4}{5}$, $\frac{5}{1}$ = 5.

The rational numbers include integers, fractions and mixed numbers, and terminating and repeating decimals. Every rational number can be expressed as a repeating or terminating decimal and can be shown on a number line.

INTEGERS: the positive and negative whole numbers and zero

INTEGERS are the positive and negative whole numbers and zero.
...-6, -5, -4, -3, -2, -1, 0, 1, 2, 3, 4, 5, 6,...

WHOLE NUMBERS are the natural numbers and zero.
0, 1, 2, 3, 4, 5, 6...

WHOLE NUMBERS: the natural numbers and zero

NATURAL NUMBERS are the counting numbers.
1, 2, 3, 4, 5, 6...

NATURAL NUMBERS:
the counting numbers

IRRATIONAL NUMBERS are real numbers that cannot be written as the ratio of two integers. They are infinite, nonrepeating decimals.

Examples:

IRRATIONAL NUMBERS:

DECIMAL: a number written with a whole-number part, a decimal point, and a decimal part

PERCENT = per 100 (written with the symbol %). Thus 10% = $\frac{10}{100}$ = $\frac{1}{10}$.

DECIMALS = deci = part of ten. To find the decimal equivalent of a fraction, use the denominator to divide the numerator as shown in the following examples.

Example: Find the decimal equivalent of $\frac{7}{10}$.

$$\begin{array}{r} .7 \\ 10\overline{)7.0} \\ \underline{70} \\ 00 \end{array}$$

Since 10 cannot divide into 7 evenly, put a decimal point in the answer row on top; put a 0 behind 7 to make it 70. Continue the division process. If a remainder occurs, put a 0 by the last digit of the remainder and continue the division.

Thus $\frac{7}{10} = 0.7$

It is a good idea to write a 0 before the decimal point so that the decimal point is emphasized.

Example: Find the decimal equivalent of $\frac{7}{125}$.

$$\begin{array}{r} .056 \\ 125\overline{)7.000} \\ \underline{625} \\ 750 \\ \underline{750} \\ 0 \end{array}$$

Example: Convert 0.056 to a fraction.

Multiplying 0.056 by $\frac{1000}{1000}$ to get rid of the decimal point:

$$0.056 \times \frac{1000}{1000} = \frac{56}{1000} = \frac{7}{125}$$

Example: Find 23% of 1000.

$$= \frac{23}{100} \times \frac{1000}{1} = 23 \times 10 = 230$$

Example: Convert 6.25% to a fraction.

$$6.25\% = 0.0625 = 0.0625 \times \frac{10000}{10000} = \frac{625}{10000} = \frac{1}{16}$$

A decimal can be converted to a percent by multiplying by 100, or merely moving the decimal point two places to the right. A percent can be converted to a decimal by dividing by 100, or moving the decimal point two places to the left.

A decimal can be converted to a percent by multiplying by 100, or merely moving the decimal point two places to the right. A percent can be converted to a decimal by dividing by 100, or moving the decimal point two places to the left.

Examples:

$0.375 = 37.5\%$	$84\% = 0.84$
$0.7 = 70\%$	$3\% = 0.03$
$0.04 = 4\%$	$60\% = 0.6$
$3.15 = 315\%$	$110\% = 1.1$
	$\frac{1}{2}\% = 0.5\% = 0.005$

A percent can be converted to a fraction by placing it over 100 and reducing to simplest terms.

Examples:

$32\% = \frac{32}{100} = \frac{8}{25}$

$6\% = \frac{6}{100} = \frac{3}{50}$

$111\% = \frac{111}{100} = 1\frac{11}{100}$

Common equivalents

COMMON EQUIVALENTS				
$\frac{1}{2}$	=	0.5	=	50%
$\frac{1}{3}$	=	0.33	=	$33\frac{1}{3}\%$
$\frac{1}{4}$	=	0.25	=	25%
$\frac{1}{5}$	=	0.2	=	20%
$\frac{1}{6}$	=	0.17	=	$16\frac{2}{3}\%$

Table continued on next page

$\frac{1}{8}$	=	0.125	=	$12\frac{1}{2}\%$
$\frac{1}{10}$	=	0.1	=	10%
$\frac{2}{3}$	=	0.67	=	$66\frac{2}{3}\%$
$\frac{5}{6}$	=	0.83	=	$83\frac{1}{3}\%$
$\frac{3}{8}$	=	0.375	=	$37\frac{1}{2}\%$
$\frac{5}{8}$	=	0.625	=	$62\frac{1}{2}\%$
$\frac{7}{8}$	=	0.875	=	$87\frac{1}{2}\%$
1	=	1.0	=	100%

Decimal values have been rounded off to the hundredths place.

CARDINAL NUMBERS are also known as "counting" numbers because they indicate quantity. Examples of cardinal numbers are 1, 2, and 10.

ORDINAL NUMBERS indicate the order of things in a set; for example, 1st, 2nd, 10th. They do not show quantity, only position.

	WORD NAME	STANDARD NUMERAL	PICTORIAL MODE
Decimal	Three-tenths	0.3	
Fraction	One-half	$\frac{1}{2}$	
Integer or Whole Number	Three	3	

CARDINAL NUMBERS: also known as "counting" numbers because they indicate quantity

ORDINAL NUMBERS: indicate the order of things in a set

Sample Test Question and Rationale

(Rigorous)

1. Which of the following is an irrational number?

   A. .36262626262...

   B. 4

   C. 8.2

   D. –5

Answer: A. .362626262626...

Irrational numbers are numbers that cannot be made into a fraction. This number cannot be made into a fraction so it must be irrational.

(Average)

2. Which of the following terms most accurately describes the set of numbers below?

$$\{3, \sqrt{16}, \pi^{\circ}, 6, \tfrac{28}{4}\}$$

A. Rationals

B. Irrationals

C. Complex

D. Whole numbers

Answer: D. Whole numbers

Let's simplify the set of numbers as follows:

$$\{3, 4, 1, 6, 7\}$$

Note that this set of numbers can be described as real numbers, rationals, integers, and whole numbers, but they are best described as whole numbers.

SKILL 5.3 Understands basic four operations *(e.g., addition, subtraction, multiplication, and division)* **and their properties** *(e.g., commutativity, order of operations)*

Mathematical operations

MATHEMATICAL OPERATIONS include addition, subtraction, multiplication, and division. Addition can be indicated by these expressions: sum, greater than, and, more than, increased by, added to. Subtraction can be expressed by difference, fewer than, minus, less than, and decreased by. Multiplication is shown by product, times, multiplied by, and twice. Division is expressed by quotient, divided by, and ratio.

Recognition and understanding of the relationships between concepts and topics is of great value in mathematical problem solving and the explanation of more complex processes.

For instance, multiplication is simply repeated addition. This relationship explains the concept of variable addition. We can show that the expression $4x + 3x = 7x$ is true by rewriting 4 times x and 3 times x as repeated addition, yielding the expression $(x + x + x + x) + (x + x + x)$. Thus, because of the relationship between multiplication and addition, variable addition is accomplished by coefficient addition.

PROPERTIES are rules that apply for addition, subtraction, multiplication, or division of real numbers. These properties are:

MATHEMATICAL OPERATIONS: include addition, subtraction, multiplication, and division

PROPERTIES: rules that apply for addition, subtraction, multiplication, or division of real numbers

Commutative	You can change the order of the terms or factors as follows.
	For addition: $\qquad a + b = b + a$
	For multiplication: $\qquad ab = ba$
	This rule does not apply for division and subtraction.
	Example: 5 + 8 = 8 + 5 = 13
	Example: 2 × 6 = 6 × 2 = 12
Associative	You can regroup the terms as you like.
	For addition: $\qquad a + (b + c) = (a + b) + c$
	For multiplication: $\qquad a(bc) = (ab)c$
	This rule does not apply for division and subtraction.
	Example: (2 + 7) + 5 = 2 + (7 + 5) $\qquad\quad$ *9 + 5 = 2 + 12 = 14*
	Example: (3 × 7) × 5 = 3 × (7 × 5) $\qquad\quad$ *21 × 5 = 3 × 35 = 105*
Identity	Finding a number so that when added to a term results in that number (additive identity); finding a number such that when multiplied by a term results in that number (multiplicative identity).
	For addition: $\qquad a + 0 = a$ (zero is additive identity)
	For multiplication: $\quad a \times 1 = a$ (one is multiplicative identity)
	Example: 17 + 0 = 17
	Example: 34 × 1 = 34
	The product of any number and one is that number.
Inverse	Finding a number such that when added to the number it results in zero; or when multiplied by the number results in 1.
	For addition: $\qquad a - a = 0$
	For multiplication: $\qquad a \times \left(\frac{1}{a}\right) = 1$
	$(-a)$ is the additive inverse of a; $\left(\frac{1}{a}\right)$, also called the reciprocal, is the multiplicative inverse of a.
	Example: 25 − 25 = 0
	Example: $5 \times \frac{1}{5} = 1$
	The product of any number and its reciprocal is one.

Table continued on next page

Distributive	This technique allows us to operate on terms within parentheses without first performing operations within the parentheses. This is especially helpful when terms within the parentheses cannot be combined.
	$a(b + c) = ab + ac$
	Example: $6 \times (4 + 9) = (6 \times 4) + (6 \times 9)$ $6 \times 13 = 24 + 54 = 78$
	To multiply a sum by a number, multiply each addend by the number, then add the products.

Addition of Whole Numbers

Example: At the end of a day of shopping, a shopper had $24 remaining in his wallet. He spent $45 on various goods. How much money did the shopper have at the beginning of the day?

The total amount of money the shopper started with is the sum of the amount spent and the amount remaining at the end of the day.

$$\begin{array}{r} \$\ 24 \\ +\ 45 \\ \hline \$\ 69 \end{array}$$ The original total was $69.

Example: A race took the winner 1 hr. 58 min. 12 sec. on the first half of the race and 2 hr. 9 min. 57 sec. on the second half of the race. How much time did the entire race take?

1 hr 58 min 12 sec	
+ 2 hr 9 min 57 sec	Add these numbers.
3 hr 67 min 69 sec	
+ 1 min − 60 sec	Change 60 sec to 1 min.
3 hr 68 min 9 sec	
+ 1 hr − 60 min	Change 60 min to 1 hr.
4 hr 8 min 9 sec	Final answer.

Subtraction of Whole Numbers

Example: At the end of his shift, a cashier has $96 in the cash register. At the beginning of his shift, he had $15. How much money did the cashier collect during his shift?

The total collected is the difference between the ending amount and the starting amount.

$ 96
−15
$ 81   The total collected was $81.

Multiplication of Whole Numbers

Multiplication is one of the four basic number operations. In simple terms, multiplication is the addition of a number to itself a certain number of times. For example, 4 multiplied by 3 is equal to $4 + 4 + 4$ or $3 + 3 + 3 + 3$. Another way of conceptualizing multiplication is to think in terms of groups. For example, if we have 4 groups of 3 students, the total number of students is 4 multiplied by 3. We call the solution to a multiplication problem the PRODUCT.

The basic algorithm for whole number multiplication begins with aligning the numbers by place value, with the number containing more places on top.

172
× 43   Note that we placed 172 on top because it has more places than 43 does.

Next, we multiply the ones place of the bottom number by each place value of the top number sequentially.

(2)
172   {$3 × 2 = 6, 3 × 7 = 21, 3 × 1 = 3$}
× 43   Note that we had to carry a 2 to the hundreds column
516   because $3 × 7 = 21$. Note also that we add carried numbers to the product.

Next, we multiply the number in the tens place of the bottom number by each place value of the top number sequentially. Because we are multiplying by a number in the tens place, we place a zero at the end of this product.

(2)
172
× 43   {$4 × 2 = 8, 4 × 7 = 28, 4 × 1 = 4$}
516
6880

Finally, to determine the final product, we add the two partial products.

172
× 43
516
+ 6880
7396   The product of 172 and 43 is 7396.

> Another way of conceptualizing multiplication is to think in terms of groups.

> **PRODUCT:** the answer to a multiplication problem

Example: A student buys 4 boxes of crayons. Each box contains 16 crayons. How many total crayons does the student have?

The total number of crayons is 16×4.

$$
\begin{array}{r}
16 \\
\times\ 4 \\
\hline
64
\end{array}
$$ The total number of crayons equals 64.

Division of Whole Numbers

Division, the inverse of multiplication, is another of the four basic number operations. When we divide one number by another, we determine how many times we can multiply the divisor (number divided by) before we exceed the number we are dividing (dividend). For example, 8 divided by 2 equals 4 because we can multiply 2 four times to reach 8 ($2 \times 4 = 8$ or $2 + 2 + 2 + 2 = 8$). Using the grouping conceptualization we used with multiplication, we can divide 8 into 4 groups of 2 or 2 groups of 4. We call the answer to a division problem the QUOTIENT.

QUOTIENT: the answer to a division problem

If the divisor does not divide evenly into the dividend, we express the leftover amount either as a remainder or as a fraction with the divisor as the denominator. For example, 9 divided by 2 equals 4 with a remainder of 1, or $4\frac{1}{2}$.

The basic algorithm for division is long division. We start by representing the quotient as follows.

$14\overline{)293}$ → 14 is the divisor and 293 is the dividend. This represents $293 \div 14$.

Next, we divide the divisor into the dividend, starting from the left.

$\dfrac{2}{14\overline{)293}}$ → 14 divides into 29 two times with a remainder.

Next, we multiply the partial quotient by the divisor, subtract this value from the first digits of the dividend, and bring down the remaining dividend digits to complete the number.

$$
\begin{array}{r}
2 \\
14\overline{)293} \\
-\,28\downarrow \\
\hline
13
\end{array}
$$ → $2 \times 14 = 28$, $29 - 28 = 1$, and bringing down the 3 yields 13.

Finally, we divide again (the divisor into the remaining value) and repeat the preceding process. The number left after the subtraction represents the remainder.

$$
\begin{array}{r}
20 \\
14\overline{)293} \\
-28 \\
\hline
13 \\
-\ 0 \\
\hline
13 \rightarrow
\end{array}
$$

The final quotient is 20 with a remainder of 13. We can also represent this quotient as $20\frac{13}{14}$.

Example: Each box of apples contains 24 apples How many boxes must a grocer purchase to supply a group of 252 people with one apple each?

The grocer needs 252 apples. Because he must buy apples in groups of 24, we divide 252 by 24 to determine how many boxes he needs to buy.

$$
\begin{array}{r}
10 \\
24\overline{)252} \\
-24 \\
\hline
12 \rightarrow \\
-\ 0 \\
\hline
12
\end{array}
$$

The quotient is 10 with a remainder of 12.

Thus, the grocer needs 10 boxes plus 12 more apples. Therefore, the minimum number of boxes the grocer can purchase is 11.

Example: At his job, John gets paid $20 for every hour he works. If John made $940 in a week, how many hours did he work?

This is a division problem. To determine the number of hours John worked, we divide the total amount made ($940) by the hourly rate of pay ($20). Thus, the number of hours worked equals 940 divided by 20.

$$
\begin{array}{r}
47 \\
20\overline{)940} \\
-80 \\
\hline
140 \\
-140 \\
\hline
0 \rightarrow
\end{array}
$$

20 divides into 940 a total of 47 times with no remainder. John worked 47 hours.

Addition and Subtraction of Decimals

When adding and subtracting decimals, we align the numbers by place value as we do with whole numbers. After adding or subtracting each column, we bring the decimal down, placing it in the same location as in the numbers added or subtracted.

When adding and subtracting decimals, we align the numbers by place value as we do with whole numbers.

Example: Find the sum of 152.3 and 36.342.

$$152.300$$
$$+\ 36.342$$
$$\overline{188.642}$$

Note that we placed two zeros after the final place value in 152.3 to clarify the column addition.

Example: Find the difference of 152.3 and 36.342.

$$2\ 9\ 10 \qquad (4)11(12)$$
$$152.\cancel{300} \qquad 1\cancel{52.300}$$
$$-\ 36.342 \qquad -\ 36.342$$
$$\overline{\quad\ 58} \qquad \overline{115.958}$$

Note how we borrowed to subtract from the zeros in the hundredths and thousandths places of 152.300.

Sample Test Questions and Rationale

(Average)

1. The order of mathematical operations is done in the following order:

   A. Simplify inside grouping characters such as parentheses, brackets, square root, fraction bar, etc.; multiply out expressions with exponents; do multiplication or division, from left to right; do addition or subtraction, from left to right

   B. Do multiplication or division, from left to right; simplify inside grouping characters such as parentheses, brackets, square root, fraction bar, etc.; multiply out expressions with exponents; do addition or subtraction, from left to right

   C. Simplify inside grouping characters such as parentheses, brackets, square root, fraction bar, etc.; do addition or subtraction, from left to right; multiply out expressions with exponents; do multiplication or division, from left to right

   D. None of the above

Answer: A. Simplify inside grouping characters such as parentheses, brackets, square root, fraction bar, etc.; multiply out expressions with exponents; do multiplication or division, from left to right; do addition or subtraction, from left to right. The mnemonic used to remember this is PEMDAS (Parentheses, Exponent, Multiplication, Division, Addition, Subtraction).

When facing a mathematical problem that requires all mathematical properties to be performed first, you do the math within the parentheses, brackets, square roots, or fraction bars. Then you multiply out expressions with exponents. Next, you do multiplication or division. Finally, you do addition or subtraction.

Sample Test Questions and Rationale (cont.)

(Average)

2. Calculate the value of the following expression.

$$\left(\frac{6}{3} + 1 \times 5\right)^2 \times \left(\frac{1}{7}\right) + (3 \times 2 - 1)$$

A. 6

B. 10

C. 12

D. 294

Answer: C. 12

Apply the correct order of operations to get the correct result: first, calculate all terms in parentheses, followed by exponents, division and multiplication, and addition and subtraction (in that order).

$(2 + 5)^2 \times \left(\frac{1}{7}\right) + (6 - 1) = 7^2 \times \frac{1}{7} + 5 = 49 \times \frac{1}{7} + 5 = 7 + 5 = 12$

SKILL 5.4 **Understands basic concepts of number theory** *(e.g., factors, multiples, prime and composite)*

Greatest Common Factor

GCF is the abbreviation for **GREATEST COMMON FACTOR**. The GCF is the largest number that is a factor of all the numbers given in a problem. The GCF can be no larger than the smallest number given in the problem. If no other number is a common factor, then the GCF will be the number 1.

> **GREATEST COMMON FACTOR:** the largest number that is a factor of all the numbers in a problem

To find the GCF, list all possible factors of the smallest number (include the number itself). Starting with the largest factor (which is the number itself), determine if that factor is also a factor of all the other given numbers. If so, that factor is the GCF. If that factor doesn't divide evenly into the other given numbers, try the same method on the next smaller factor. Continue until a common factor is found. That factor is the GCF.

> *Note: There can be other common factors besides the GCF.*

Example: Find the GCF of 12, 20, and 36.
The smallest number in the problem is 12. The factors of 12 are 1, 2, 3, 4, 6 and 12. 12 is the largest of these factors, but it does not divide evenly into 20. Neither does 6. However, 4 will divide into both 20 and 36 evenly. Therefore, 4 is the GCF.

Example: Find the GCF of 14 and 15.
The factors of 14 are 1, 2, 7 and 14. 14 is the largest factor, but it does not divide evenly into 15. Neither does 7 or 2. Therefore, the only factor common to both 14 and 15 is the number 1, the GCF.

Least Common Multiple

LCM is the abbreviation for **LEAST COMMON MULTIPLE**. The least common multiple of a group of numbers is the smallest number that all of the given numbers will divide into. The LCM will always be the largest of the given numbers or a multiple of the largest number.

Example: Find the LCM of 20, 30, and 40.
The largest number given is 40, but 30 will not divide evenly into 40. The next multiple of 40 is 80 (2 × 40), but 30 will not divide evenly into 80 either. The next multiple of 40 is 120. 120 is divisible by both 20 and 30, so 120 is the LCM.

Example: Find the LCM of 96, 16, and 24.
The largest number is 96. 96 is divisible by both 16 and 24, so 96 is the LCM.

Sample Test Questions and Rationale

(Rigorous)

1. **What is the LCM of 6, 7, and 9?**

   A. 14
   B. 42
   C. 126
   D. 378

   Answer: C. 126

   The LCM is the smallest number for which the numbers given above are factors. We can approach this problem in one of several ways. One possibility is to list multiples of each number until we come across a multiple common to all three, or we can determine the prime factors of each number and use those to determine an LCM.

6:	6, 12, 18, 24, 30, 36, 42, 48…
7:	7, 14, 21, 28, 35, 42, 49…
9:	9, 18, 27, 36, 45, 54, 63, 72…

As yet, the lists above do not show any common multiples. Let's try multiplying the prime factors of each number until we find a common multiple.

6 = 2 × 3   7 = 7   9 = 3 × 3

2 × 3 × 7 = 42 (not a common multiple)
2 × 3 × 3 × 7 = 126 (LCM)

If you continued the lists of multiples, which was our first attempt, you will eventually find that 126 is the first (and least) common multiple.

Sample Test Questions and Rationale (cont.)

(Easy)

2. **What is the greatest common factor of 16, 28, and 36?**

   A. 2

   B. 4

   C. 8

   D. 16

Answer: B. 4

The smallest number in this set is 16; its factors are 1, 2, 4, 8, and 16. The largest factor is 16, but it does not divide into 28 or 36. Neither does 8. The answer is 4, which does factor into both 28 and 36.

SKILL 5.5 Understands how to solve problems *(e.g., modeling, estimation, algorithms)* **and recognize the reasonableness of results**

Estimation and approximation may be used to check the reasonableness of answers.

Example: Estimate the answer.

$$\frac{58 \times 810}{1989}$$

58 becomes 60, 810 becomes 800, and 1989 becomes 2000.

$$\frac{60 \times 800}{2000} = 24$$

For word problems, an estimate may sometimes be all that is needed to find the solution.

Example: Janet goes into a store to purchase a CD that is on sale for $13.95. While shopping, she sees two pairs of shoes priced at $19.95 and $14.50. She only has $50. Can she purchase everything?

Solve by rounding:

$19.95 \rightarrow $20.00

$14.50 \rightarrow $15.00

$13.95 \rightarrow $14.00

$49.00   Yes, she can purchase the CD and the shoes.

Sample Test Question and Rationale

(Easy)

1. The mass of a cookie is closest to:

    A. 0.5 kilograms

    B. 0.5 grams

    C. 15 grams

    D. 1.5 grams

Answer: C. 15 grams

A common estimation of mass used in elementary schools is that a paper clip has a mass of approximately one gram, which eliminates choices B and D, as they are very close to one gram. A common estimation is that one liter of water has the mass of one kilogram. Half of one liter of water is still much more than one cookie, eliminating choice A. Therefore, the best estimation of the mass of one cookie is narrowed to 15 grams.

SKILL 5.6 Understands how to make, describe, and explore numerical patterns and engage in mathematical investigations

The unit cost for purchasing an item is its price divided by the number of pounds (or ounces, etc.) in the item. The item with the lowest unit cost has the lowest price.

Example: Find the item with the best unit cost.

$1.79 for 10 ounces

$1.89 for 12 ounces

$5.49 for 32 ounces

$\frac{1.79}{10}$ .179 per ounce $\frac{1.89}{12}$ .1575 per ounce $\frac{5.49}{32}$ .172 per ounce

$1.89 for 12 ounces is the best price.

A second way to find the better buy is to make a proportion, for example, with the price over the number of ounces. Cross-multiply the proportion, writing the products above the numerator that is used. The better price will have the smaller product.

Example: Find the better buy: $8.19 for forty pounds or $4.89 for twenty-two pounds. Find the unit costs.

$$\frac{40}{8.19} = \frac{1}{x}$$
$$40x = 8.19$$
$$x = .20475$$

$$\frac{22}{4.89} = \frac{1}{x}$$
$$22x = 4.89$$
$$x = .222\overline{27}$$

Since $.20475 < .222\overline{27}$, $8.19 is the lower price and a better buy.

To find the amount of sales tax on an item, change the percentage of sales tax into an equivalent decimal number. Then multiply the decimal number by the price of the object to find the sales tax. The total cost of the item will be the price of the item plus the sales tax.

Example: A guitar costs $120.00 plus 7% sales tax. How much are the sales tax and the total cost?

$7\% = .07$ as a decimal

$(.07)(120) = \$8.40$ sales tax

$\$120.00 + \$8.40 = \$128.40 \leftarrow$ total price

Example: A suit costs $450.00 plus $6\frac{1}{2}$% sales tax. How much are the sales tax and the total cost?

$6\frac{1}{2}\% = .065$ as a decimal

$(.065)(450) = \$29.25$ sales tax

$\$450.00 + \$29.25 = \$479.25 \leftarrow$ total price

Examining the change in area or volume of a given figure requires you first to find the existing area, given the original dimensions, and then the new area, given the increased dimensions.

Example: Given the rectangle below, determine the change in area if the length is increased by 5 and the width is increased by 7.

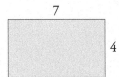

7

4

Draw and label a sketch of the new rectangle.

Find the areas.

Area of original = LW	Area of enlarged shape = LW
= (7)(4)	= (12)(11)
= 28 units²	= 132 units²

The change in area is $132 - 28 = 104$ units².

Ratios, Proportions, Percentages

Proportions can be used to solve word problems whenever relationships are compared. Some situations include scale drawings and maps, similar polygons, speed, time and distance, cost, and comparison shopping.

Example: Which is the better buy, six items for $1.29 or eight items for $1.69?

Find the unit costs.

$$6x = 1.29 \qquad\qquad 8x = 1.69$$
$$x = 0.215 \qquad\qquad x = 0.21125$$

Thus, eight items for $1.69 is the better buy.

Example: A car travels 125 miles in two and a half hours. How far will it go in six hours?

Write a proportion comparing the distance and time.

Let x represent distance in miles. Then,

$\frac{125}{2.5} = \frac{x}{6}$	Set up the proportion.
$2.5x = 6 \times 125$	Cross-multiply.
$2.5x = 750$	Simplify.
$2.5x = \frac{750}{2.5}$	Divide both sides of the equation by 2.5.
$x = 300$ miles	Simplify.

Example: The scale on a map is one inch = 6 miles. What is the actual distance between two cities if they are 2 inches apart on the map?

Write a proportion comparing the scale to the actual distance.

$\frac{1}{6} = \frac{2}{x}$; Cross-multiplying, x = 12.

Thus, the actual distance between the cities is twelve miles.

Word problems involving percentages can be solved by writing the problem as an equation, then solving the equation. Keep in mind that *of* means multiplication and *is* means equals.

> Word problems involving percentages can be solved by writing the problem as an equation, then solving the equation.

Example: The ski club has eighty-five members; 80% of the members are able to attend the meeting. How many members attended the meeting?

Restate the problem:	What is 80% of 85?
Write an equation:	$n = 0.8 \times 85$
Solve:	$n = 68$

Sixty-eight members attended the meeting.

Example: There are sixty-four dogs in the kennel. Forty-eight are collies. What percentage are collies?

Restate the problem:	48 is what percentage of 64?
Write an equation:	$48 = n \times 64$
Solve:	$48 \div 64 = n$
	$n = .75$

Seventy-five percent of the dogs are collies.

Example: The auditorium was filled to 90% capacity. There were 558 seats occupied. What is the capacity of the auditorium?

Restate the problem:	90% of what number is 558?
Write an equation:	$0.9n = 558$
Solve:	$n = \frac{558}{.9}$
	$n = 620$

The capacity of the auditorium is 620 people.

Example: Shoes cost $42.00. Sales tax is 6%. What is the total cost of the shoes?

Restate the problem:	What is 6% of 42?
Write an equation:	$n = 0.06 \times 42$
Solve:	$n = 2.52$
Add the sales tax:	$42.00 + $2.52 = $44.52

The total cost of the shoes, including sales tax, is $44.52.

Sample Test Questions and Rationale

(Average)

1. An item that sells for $375.00 is put on sale at $120.00. What is the percentage of decrease?

    A. 25%

    B. 28%

    C. 68%

    D. 34%

    Answer: C. 68%

    In this problem you must set up a cross-multiplication problem. You begin by placing $\frac{x}{100}$ to represent the variable you are solving for (the percentage) and then you place $\frac{(375 - 120)}{375} = \frac{255}{375}$ to represent the decrease in price over the original price. Once you cross-multiply you will get 68, which is the percentage decrease the item is selling for.

(Average)

2. The final cost of an item (with sales tax) is $8.35. If the sales tax is 7%, what was the pretax price of the item?

    A. $7.80

    B. $8.00

    C. $8.28

    D. $8.93

    Answer: A. $7.80

    We can solve this problem by constructing a proportionality expression. Let's call the pretax price of the item x; then, if we add 7% of x to this price, we get a final cost of $8.35.

    $$x + 0.07x = \$8.35$$
    $$1.07x = \$8.35$$
    $$x = \frac{\$8.35}{1.07} = \$7.80$$

    Thus, the initial price of the item was $7.80. You can also determine this answer by multiplying each option by 1.07; the correct answer is the one that yields a product of $8.35.

COMPETENCY 6
ALGEBRAIC CONCEPTS

**SKILL Understands basic algebraic methods and representations
6.1**

A relationship between two quantities can be shown using a table, graph, or rule. In this example, the rule $y = 9x$ describes the relationship between the total amount earned, y, and the total number of $9.00 sunglasses sold, x.

A table using these data would appear as:

number of sunglasses sold	1	5	10	15
total dollars earned	9	45	90	135

Each (x,y) relationship between a pair of values is called the coordinate pair that can be plotted on a graph. The coordinate pairs (1,9), (5,45), (10,90), and (15,135) are plotted on the graph below.

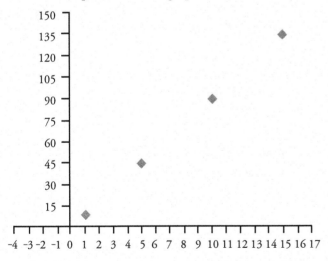

The graph above shows a linear relationship. A **LINEAR RELATIONSHIP** is a relationship in which two quantities are proportional to each other. Doubling x also doubles y. On a graph, a straight line depicts a linear relationship.

Another type of relationship is a **NONLINEAR RELATIONSHIP**. This is a relationship in which change in one quantity does not affect the other quantity to the same extent. Nonlinear graphs have a curved line, as in the graph below.

LINEAR RELATIONSHIP: a relationship in which two quantities are proportional to each other

NONLINEAR RELATIONSHIP: a relationship in which change in one quantity does not affect the other quantity to the same extent

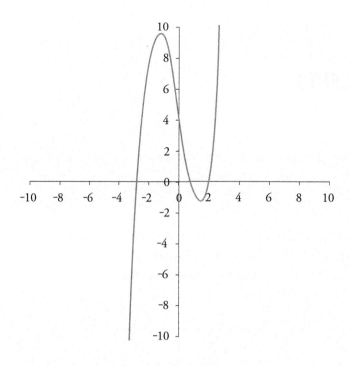

Sample Test Question and Rationale

(Average)

1. Find the coordinates of the intersection point for the lines described by the equations below.

$y = 3x - 7$ $\qquad$ $y = -2x + 1$

A. $(1, 2)$

B. $(-1.6, 2.2)$

C. $(1.6, 2)$

D. $(1.6, -2.2)$

Answer: D. (1.6, -2.2)

The point of intersection for two functions is the point (x, y) at which the two functions are equal. Thus, we can start solving this problem by setting the two expressions equal and then solving for x.

$$3x - 7 = -2x + 1$$
$$3x + 2x = 1 + 7$$
$$5x = 8$$
$$x = \frac{8}{5} = 1.6$$

Because the two equations are equal at $x = 1.6$, we can use either one to find the y coordinate.

$$y = 3x - 7 = 3(1.6) - 7 = 4.8 - 7 = -2.2$$

We can check the result by calculating the y value using the other equation as well.

$$y = -2x + 1 = -2(1.6) + 1 = -3.2 + 1 = -2.2$$

SKILL 6.2 Understands the associative, commutative, and distributive properties

Field Properties

Real numbers exhibit the following addition and multiplication properties, where a, b, and c are real numbers.

Note: Multiplication is implied when there is no symbol between two variables. Thus,

$a \times b$ can be written ab.

Multiplication can also be indicated by a raised dot · as in $(a \cdot b)$.

Closure

$a + b$ is a real number.

Example: Since 2 and 5 are both real numbers, 7 is also a real number.

ab is a real number.

Example: Since 3 and 4 are both real numbers, 12 is also a real number.

The sum or product of two real numbers is a real number.

Denseness

The set of rational numbers is dense. Between any pair of rational numbers, there is at least one rational number. The set of natural numbers is *not* dense because, between two consecutive natural numbers, there may not exist another natural number.

Example: Between 7.6 and 7.7, there is the rational number 7.65 in the set of real numbers.

Between 3 and 4 there exists no other natural number.

Commutative

$a + b = b + a$

Example:

$5 + \text{-}8 = \text{-}8 + 5 = \text{-}3$

$ab = ba$

Example:

-2 × 6 = 6 × -2 = -12

The order of the addends or factors does not affect the sum or product.

Associative

$(a + b) + c = a + (b + c)$

Example:

(-2 + 7) + 5 = -2 + (7 + 5)

5 + 5 = -2 + 12 = 10

$(ab) c = a (bc)$

Example:

(3 × -7) × 5 = 3 × (-7 × 5)

-21 × 5 = 3 × -35 = -105

The grouping of the addends or factors does not affect the sum or product.

Distributive

$a (b + c) = ab + ac$

Example:

6 × (-4 + 9) = (6 × -4) + (6 × 9)

6 × 5 = -24 + 54 = 30

To multiply a sum by a number, multiply each addend by the number, then add the products.

Sample Test Questions and Rationale

(Rigorous)

1. What is the value of the following expression?

$$\frac{15 - 24(1 - 0.8)}{-5 + 8}$$

A. -24.6

B. -3.6

C. 3.4

D. 13.4

Answer: C. 3.4

The fraction line is equivalent to parentheses and indicates that the numerator is to be simplified first. Then use the standard order of operations. The denominator (-5 + 8, or 3) divides the entire numerator, not just one of the terms.

Sample Test Questions and Rationale (cont.)

(Average)

2. **Which property justifies the following manipulation?**

$x^2 - 3y \rightarrow -3y + x^2$

A. Associative

B. Commutative

C. Distributive

D. None of the above

Answer: B. Commutative

The commutative property tells us that $a + b = b + a$; thus, the manipulation of the algebraic expression in the problem statement can be justified by the commutative property.

SKILL 6.3 Understands additive and multiplicative inverses

Additive Identity (Property of Zero)

$a + 0 = a$

Example:

$17 + 0 = 17$

The sum of any number and zero is that number.

Multiplicative Identity (Property of One)

$a \times 1 = a$

Example:

$-34 \times 1 = -34$

The product of any number and one is that number.

Additive Inverse (Property of Opposites)

$a + -a = 0$

Example:

$25 + -25 = 0$

The sum of any number and its opposite is zero.

Multiplicative Inverse (Property of Reciprocals)

$a \times \frac{1}{5} = 1$

Example:

$5 \times \frac{1}{5} = 1$

The product of any number and its reciprocal is one.

Sample Test Questions and Rationale

(Rigorous)

1. An equation in the form $\frac{a}{b} x = c$ is solved by multiplying both sides by $\frac{b}{a}$. Which of the following statements explains why?

   I.   The product of multiplicative inverses is 1

   II. The solution must be in the form $1x =$ some number

   III. Use of the multiplicative inverse cancels the factor $\frac{a}{b}$ to zero

   A. I and II

   B. II and III

   C. I and III

   D. I, II, and III

   Answer: A. I and II

   The solution must be expressed in the form $1x =$ some number. By definition, the product of multiplicative inverses is 1: $\frac{a}{b} \times \frac{b}{a} = 1$.

(Average)

2. Which of the following is an example of a multiplicative inverse?

   A. $x^2 - x^2 = 0$

   B. $(y - 3)^0 = 1$

   C. $\frac{1}{e^{3z}} e^{3z} = 1$

   D. $f^2 = \frac{1}{g}$

   Answer: C. $\frac{1}{e^{3z}} e^{3z} = 1$

   A multiplicative inverse has the form

   $a \times \frac{1}{a} = 1$

   Thus, answer C best fits this definition.

SKILL 6.4 Understands the special properties of zero and one

See Skills 6.2 and 6.3

Sample Test Question and Rationale

(Rigorous)

1. Which of the following statements are always true?

   I. The square of a negative number is a whole number

   II. The quotient of two integers is a rational number

   III. Fractions are rational numbers

   IV. Decimals are rational numbers

   A. I

   B. II and III

   C. II and IV

   D. II, III, and IV

Answer: B. II and III

A rational number is a number that can be expressed as the ratio of two integers $\frac{a}{b}$ where b is nonzero. The square of a negative fraction may be a positive fraction. Decimals may be irrational numbers.

SKILL 6.5 Understands equalities and inequalities

Word problems can sometimes be solved by using a system of two equations in two unknowns. This system can then be solved using substitution, the addition-subtraction method, or graphing.

Example: Ms. Winters bought four dresses and six pairs of shoes for $340.00. Ms. Summers went to the same store and bought three dresses and eight pairs of shoes for $360.00. If all of the dresses were the same price and all of the shoes were the same price, find the price charged for a dress and the price for a pair of shoes.

Let x = the price of a dress

Let y = the price of a pair of shoes

Ms. Winters's equation would be:　　　　　$4x + 6y = 340$

Ms. Summers's equation would be:　　　　$3x + 8y = 360$

To solve by addition-subtraction:

Multiply the first equation by 4:　　　　$4(4x + 6y = 340)$

Multiply the other equation by –3:　　　$-3(3x + 8y = 360)$

By doing this, the equations can be added to each other to eliminate one variable and to solve for the other variable.

$$16x + 24y = 1360$$
$$\underline{-9x - 24y = -1080}$$
$$7x = \quad 280$$
$$x = 40 \leftarrow \text{The price of a dress was \$40.}$$

Solving for y, $y = 30 \leftarrow$ The price of a pair of shoes was $30.

Example: Aardvark Taxi charges $4.00 initially, plus $1.00 for every mile traveled. Baboon Taxi charges $6.00 initially, plus $.75 for every mile traveled. Determine when it is cheaper to ride with Aardvark Taxi and when it is cheaper to ride with Baboon Taxi.

Aardvark Taxi's equation:　　　$y = 1x + 4$

Baboon Taxi's equation:　　　　$y = .75x + 6$

Using substitution:　　　　　　$.75x + 6 = 1x + 4$

Multiplying by 4:　　　　　　　$3x + 24 = 4x + 16$

Solving for x:　　　　　　　　$8 = x$

This tells you that at eight miles, the total charge for the two companies is the same. If you compare the charge for one mile, Aardvark charges $5.00 and Baboon charges $6.75. Therefore, Aardvark is cheaper for distances up to eight miles, but Baboon Taxi is cheaper for distances greater than eight miles.

This problem can also be solved by graphing the two equations.

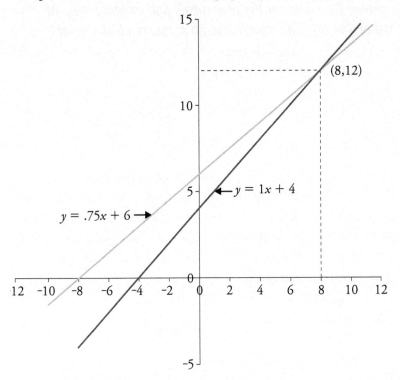

The lines intersect at (8,12); therefore at eight miles, both companies charge $12.00. At values of less than eight miles, Aardvark Taxi charges less (the graph is below Baboon). At values greater than eight miles, Aardvark charges more (the graph is above Baboon).

Some word problems can be solved using a system of equations or inequalities. Watch for phrases like *greater than, less than, at least*, or *no more than*, as they indicate the need for inequalities.

Example: The YMCA wants to sell raffle tickets to raise at least $32,000. If they must pay $7,250 in expenses and prizes out of the money collected from the tickets, how many $25 tickets must they sell?

Since they want to raise *at least* $32,000, that means they would be happy to get 32,000 *or more*. This requires an inequality.

Let x = number of tickets sold

Then $25x$ = total amount of money collected for x tickets

The total amount of money minus expenses is greater than $32,000.

$25x - 7,250 \geq 32,000$

$25x \geq 39,250$

$x \geq 1,570$

If they sell 1,570 tickets or more, they will raise at least $32,000.

TEACHER CERTIFICATION STUDY GUIDE

Example: The Simpsons went out for dinner. All four of them ordered the aardvark steak dinner. Bert paid for the four meals and included a tip of $12.00 for a total of $84.60. How much was an aardvark steak dinner?

Let x = the price of one aardvark dinner

So $4x$ = the price of four aardvark dinners

$4x + 12 = 84.60$

$4x = 72.60$

$x = \$18.15$ for each dinner

Example: Sharon's Bike Shoppe can assemble a three-speed bike in thirty minutes and a ten-speed bike in sixty minutes. The profit on each bike sold is $60.00 for a three-speed and $75.00 for a ten-speed bike. How many of each type of bike should they assemble during an eight-hour day (480 minutes) to make the maximum profit? Total daily profit must be at least $300.00.

Let x = number of three-speed bikes

y = number of ten-speed bikes

Since there are only 480 minutes in each day, $30x + 60y \leq 480$ is the first inequality.

Since the total daily profit must be at least $300.00, $60x + 75y \geq 300$ is the second inequality.

$30x + 60y \leq 480$ solves to $y \leq 8 - \frac{x}{2}$

$60x + 75y \geq 300$ solves to $y \geq 4 - \frac{4x}{5}$

Graph these two inequalities:

$y \leq 8 - \frac{x}{2}$

$y \geq 4 - \frac{4x}{5}$

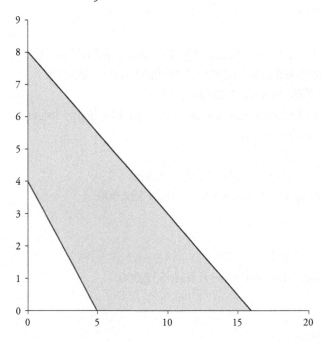

Note that $x \geq 0$ and $y \geq 0$, since the number of bikes assembled cannot be a negative number. Graph these as additional constraints on the problem.

The number of bikes assembled must always be an integer value, so points within the shaded area of the graph must have integer values. The maximum profit will occur at or near a corner of the shaded portion of this graph. Those points occur at (0,4), (0,8), (16,0), and (5,0).

Since profits are $60/three-speed and $75/ten-speed, the profits for these four points would be:

(0, 4)	$60(0) + 75(4) = 300$
(0, 8)	$60(0) + 75(8) = 600$
(16, 0)	$60(16) + 75(0) = 960$ ← Maximum profit
(5, 0)	$60(5) + 75(0) = 300$

The maximum profit will occur if 16 three-speed bikes are made daily.

Sample Test Question and Rationale

(Average)

1. **What is the solution set of the following inequality?**

    $-5(2x - 1) \geq 6x - 5$

    A. $x \leq 0$

    B. $x \geq 0$

    C. $x \leq \frac{5}{8}$

    D. $x \geq \frac{5}{8}$

Answer: C. $x \leq \frac{5}{8}$

Apply the distributive property on the left. Remember to reverse the sign of inequality when you multiply by a negative number.

$-5(2x - 1) \geq 6x - 5$
$-10x + 5 \geq 6x - 5$
$-10x - 6x \geq -5 - 5$
$-16x \geq -10$
$x \leq \frac{10}{16}$ or $\frac{5}{8}$

SKILL 6.6 Understands the appropriate application of formulas

An algebraic formula is an equation that describes a relationship among variables. While it is not often necessary to derive the formula, one must know how to rewrite a given formula in terms of a desired variable.

Example: Given that the relationship of voltage, V, applied across a material with electrical resistance, R, when a current, I, is flowing through the material is represented by the formula V = IR, find the resistance of the material when a current of 10 milliamps is flowing, when the applied voltage is 2 volts.

$V = IR$ Solve for R.

$IR = V;\ R = \dfrac{V}{I}$ Divide both sides by I.

When $V = 2$ volts; $I = 10 \times 10^{-3}$ amps;

$R = \dfrac{2}{10^1 \times 10^{-3}}$

$R = \dfrac{2}{10^{-2}}$ Substituting $R = \dfrac{V}{I}$, we get,

$R = 2 \times 10^2$

$R = 200$ ohms

Sample Test Questions and Rationale

(Rigorous)

1. **Two farmers are buying feed for animals. One farmer buys eight bags of grain and six bales of hay for $105.00, and the other farmer buys three bags of grain and nine bales of hay for $69.75. How much is a bag of grain?**

    A. $4.50

    B. $9.75

    C. $14.25

    D. $28.50

Answer: B. $9.75

Let x be the price of a bag of grain, and let y be the price of a bale of hay. We can then write two equations based on the information provided in the problem.

Farmer 1: $8x + 6y = \$105.00$

Farmer 2: $3x + 9y = \$69.75$

We want to find x, the price of a bag of grain. One approach to solving this problem is to solve either the first or second equation for y and then substitute the result into the other equation and solve for y. Another approach involves subtraction. Let's multiply both sides of the second equation by $\frac{2}{3}$.

$\frac{2}{3}(3x + 9y) = \$69.76$

$2x + 6y = \$46.50$

Now, subtract this from the first equation.

$$\begin{array}{r} 8x + 6y = \$105.00 \\ -(2x + 6y = \$\ 46.50) \\ \hline 6x = \$\ 58.50 \end{array}$$

Solving for x yields the solution.

$x = \$9.75$

Sample Test Questions and Rationale (cont.)

(Average)

2. A boat travels thirty miles upstream in three hours. It makes the return trip in one and a half hours. What is the speed of the boat in still water?

   A. 10 mph

   B. 15 mph

   C. 20 mph

   D. 30 mph

Answer: B. 15 mph

Let x = the speed of the boat in still water, and c = the speed of the current.

	Rate	Time	Distance
Upstream	$x - c$	3	30
Downstream	$x + c$	1.5	30

Solve the system:

$3x - 3c = 30$
$1.5x + 1.5c = 30$

COMPETENCY 7
INFORMAL GEOMETRY AND MEASUREMENT

SKILL 7.1 Understands properties of figures and relationships in two- and three-dimensional objects

We refer to three-dimensional figures in geometry as solids. A solid is the union of all points on a simple closed surface and all points in its interior. A polyhedron is a simple closed surface formed from planar polygonal regions. Each polygonal region is called a face of the polyhedron. The vertices and edges of the polygonal regions are called the vertices and edges of the polyhedron.

We may form a cube from three congruent squares. However, if we tried to put four squares around a single vertex, their interior angle measures would add up to 360° (i.e., four edge-to-edge squares with a common vertex lie in a common plane and therefore cannot form a corner figure of a regular polyhedron).

There are five ways to form corner figures with congruent regular polygons:

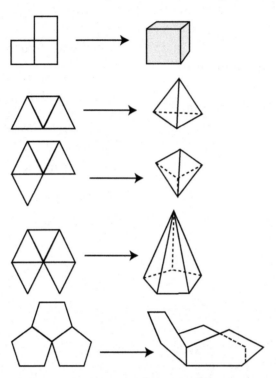

In order to represent three-dimensional figures, we need three coordinate axes (x, y, and z) that are perpendicular to each other. Since we cannot draw three mutually perpendicular axes on a two-dimensional surface, we use oblique representations.

Example: Represent a cube with sides of 2.
We draw three sides along the three axes to make things easier.

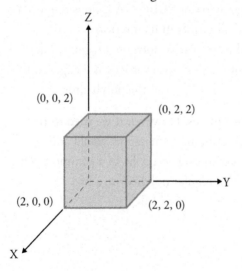

Each point has three coordinates (x, y, z).

Sample Test Question and Rationale

(Rigorous)

1. Three-dimensional figures in geometry are called:

    A. Solids

    B. Cubes

    C. Polygons

    D. Blocks

Answer: A. Solids

Three-dimensional figures are referred to as solids.

Understands transformations *(e.g., slides, flips, and turns),* **geometric models, and nets**

A transformation is a change in the position, shape, or size of a geometric figure. **TRANSFORMATIONAL GEOMETRY** is the study of manipulating objects by flipping, twisting, turning, and scaling them. Symmetry is exact similarity between two parts or halves, as if one were a mirror image of the other.

A **TRANSLATION** is a transformation that "slides" an object a fixed distance in a given direction. The original object and its translation have the same shape and size, and they face in the same direction.

An example of a translation in architecture is stadium seating. The seats are the same size and the same shape, and they face in the same direction.

A **ROTATION** is a transformation that turns a figure about a fixed point called the center of rotation. An object and its rotation are the same shape and size, but

> **TRANSFORMATIONAL GEOMETRY:** the study of manipulating objects by flipping, twisting, turning, and scaling them

> **TRANSLATION:** a transformation that "slides" an object a fixed distance in a given direction

> **ROTATION:** a transformation that turns a figure about a fixed point called the center of rotation

the figures may be turned in different directions. Rotations can occur in either a clockwise or a counterclockwise direction.

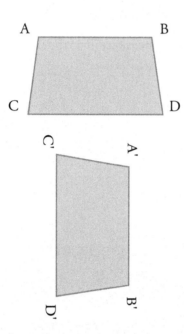

Rotations can be seen in wallpaper and art, and a Ferris wheel is an example of rotation.

An object and its **REFLECTION** have the same shape and size, but the figures face in opposite directions.

The line (where a mirror may be placed) is called the **LINE OF REFLECTION**. The distance from a point to the line of reflection is the same as the distance from the point's image to the line of reflection.

A **GLIDE REFLECTION** is a combination of a reflection and a translation.

REFLECTION: objects have the same shape and size, but the figures face in opposite directions

LINE OF REFLECTION: the line where a mirror may be placed; the distance from a point to this line is the same as the distance from the point's image to this line

GLIDE REFLECTION: a combination of a reflection and a translation

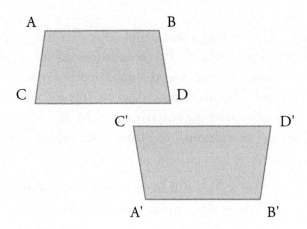

Another type of transformation is dilation. Dilation is a transformation that "shrinks" an object or makes it bigger.

Example: Use dilation to transform a diagram.
Starting with a triangle whose center of dilation is point P,

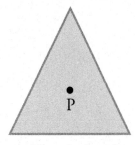

we dilate the lengths of the sides by the same factor to create a new triangle.

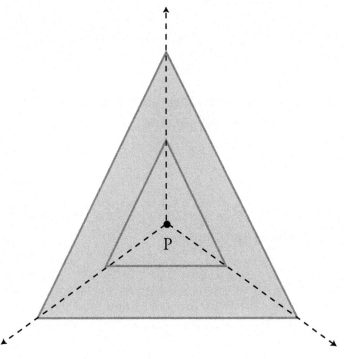

Geometric Models

A **TESSELLATION** is an arrangement of closed shapes that completely covers the plane without overlapping or leaving gaps. Unlike tilings, tessellations do not require the use of regular polygons. In art, the term is used to refer to pictures or tiles—mostly in the form of animals and other life forms—that cover the surface of a plane in a symmetrical way without overlapping or leaving gaps. M. C. Escher is known as the father of modern tessellations. Tessellations are used for tiling, mosaics, quilts, and art.

If you look at a completed tessellation, you will see that the original motif repeats in a pattern. There are seventeen possible ways that a pattern can be used to tile a flat surface. or "wallpaper."

The tessellation below is a combination of the four types of transformational symmetry we have discussed:

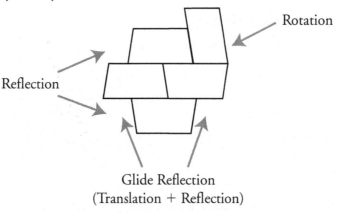

Rotation

Reflection

Glide Reflection
(Translation + Reflection)

When creating a three-dimensional figure, if we know any two values of the vertices, faces, and edges, we can find the remaining value by using Euler's formula: $V + F = E + 2$.

Example: We want to create a pentagonal pyramid, and we know it has six vertices and six faces. Using Euler's formula, we compute:

$$V + F = E + 2$$
$$6 + 6 = E + 2$$
$$12 = E + 2$$
$$10 = E$$

Thus, we know that our figure should have 10 edges.

Nets

The union of all points on a simple closed surface and all points in its interior form a space figure called a **SOLID**. The five regular solids, or **POLYHEDRA**, are the cube, tetrahedron, octahedron, icosahedron, and dodecahedron. A **NET** is a two-dimensional figure that can be cut out and folded up to make a three-dimensional solid. Below are models of the five regular solids with their corresponding face polygons and nets.

Cube   6 squares

Tetrahedron   4 equilateral triangles

Octahedron   8 equilateral triangles

Icosahedron   20 equilateral triangles

Dodecahedron   12 regular pentagons

Other examples of solids:

A **SPHERE** is a space figure having all its points the same distance from the center.

A **CONE** is a space figure having a circular base and a single vertex.

Sample Test Question and Rationale

(Average)

1. Which of the following polygons will not tessellate a plane?

    A. Obtuse triangle

    B. Parallelogram

    C. Regular hexagon

    D. Regular octagon

Answer: D. Regular octagon

The measures of the angles around a point must have a sum of 360 degrees. Each angle of a regular octagon measures 135 degrees. Since 135 is not a factor of 360, regular octagons cannot tessellate the plane. The sum of the angles of a triangle is 180 degrees, and of a parallelogram, 360 degrees. Each angle of a regular hexagon is 120 degrees. So, multiples of the angles of a triangle, a parallelogram, or a hexagon can form 360 degrees.

SKILL 7.3 Understands nonstandard, customary, and metric units of measurement *(e.g., length, time, temperature)*

> When you can measure what you are speaking about and express it in numbers, you know something about it; but when you cannot measure it, when you cannot express it in numbers, your knowledge is of a meager and unsatisfactory kind.
> —*Lord Kelvin*

Nonstandard units are sometimes used when standard instruments might not be available. For example, students might measure the length of a room by their arm-spans. An inch originated as the length of three barley grains placed end to end. Seeds or stones might be used for measuring weight. In fact, our current "carat," used for measuring precious gems, was derived from carob seeds. In ancient times, baskets, jars, and bowls were used to measure capacity.

To estimate measurement of familiar objects, it is first necessary to determine the units to be used.

Examples:

LENGTH	
The coastline of Florida	miles or kilometers
The width of a ribbon	inches or millimeters
The thickness of a book	inches or centimeters
The length of a football field	yards or meters
The depth of water in a pool	feet or meters

WEIGHT OR MASS	
A bag of sugar	pounds or grams
A school bus	tons or kilograms
A dime	ounces or grams

CAPACITY	
Paint to paint a bedroom	gallons or liters
Glass of milk	cups or liters
Bottle of soda	quarts or liters
Medicine for child	ounces or milliliters

It is necessary to be familiar with the metric and customary system in order to estimate measurements.

Some common equivalents include:

ITEM	APPROXIMATELY EQUAL TO	
	METRIC	CUSTOMARY
large paper clip	1 gram	0.1 ounce
capacity of sports bottle	1 liter	1 quart

Table continued on next page

average sized adult	75 kilograms	170 pounds
length of an office desk	1 meter	1 yard
math textbook	1 kilogram	2 pounds
length of dollar bill	15 centimeters	6 inches
thickness of a dime	1 millimeter	0.1 inches
area of football field		6,400 sq. yd
temperature of boiling water	100°C	212°F
temperature of ice	0°C	32°F
1 cup of liquid	240 mL	8 fl oz
1 teaspoon	5 ml	

Example: Estimate the measurement of the following items:

The length of an adult cow = ____3____ meters

The thickness of a compact disc = ____2____ millimeters

Your height = ____1.5____ meters

The length of your nose = ____4____ centimeters

The weight of your math textbook = ____1____ kilogram

The weight of an automobile = ____1,000____ kilogram

The weight of an aspirin = ____1____ gram

The units of length in the customary system are inches, feet, yards and miles.

12 inches (in.)	=	1 foot (ft.)
36 in.	=	1 yard (yd.)
3 ft.	=	1 yd.
5280 ft.	=	1 mile (mi.)
1760 yd.	=	1 mi.

To change from a **larger unit to a smaller unit, multiply**.

To change from a **smaller unit to a larger unit, divide**.

Example:

    4 mi. = _____ yd.

    Since 1760 yd. = 1 mile, multiply $4 \times 1760 = 7040$ yd.

Example:

    21 in. = _____ ft.

    $21 \div 12 = 1.75$ ft. (or 1 foot and 9 inches)

The units of weight are ounces, pounds, and tons.

16 ounces (oz.)	=	1 pound (lb.)
2000 lb.	=	1 ton (T.)

Example:

    2 T. = _____ lb.

    $2 \times 2000 = 4000$ lb.

The units of capacity are fluid ounces, cups, pints, quarts, and gallons.

8 fluid ounces (fl. oz.)	=	1 cup (c.)
2 c.	=	1 pint (pt.)
4 c.	=	1 quart (qt.)
2 pt.	=	1 qt.
4 qt.	=	1 gallon (gal.)

Example:

    3 gal. = _____ qt.

    $3 \times 4 = 12$ qt.

Example:

    1 cup = _____ oz.

    $1 \times 8 = 8$ oz.

Example:

    7 c. = _____ pt.

    $7 \div 2 = 3.5$ pt.

Square Units

Square units can be derived with knowledge of basic units of length by squaring the equivalent measurements.

1 square foot (sq. ft.)	=	144 sq. in.
1 sq. yd.	=	9 sq. ft.
1 sq. yd.	=	1296 sq. in.

Example:

14 sq. yd. = _____ sq. ft.

$14 \times 9 = 126$ sq. ft.

Metric Units

The metric system is based on multiples of ten. Conversions are made by simply moving the decimal point to the left or right.

METRIC PREFIXES AND THEIR MEANING		
kilo-	1000	thousands
hecto-	100	hundreds
deca-	10	tens
deci-	.1	tenths
centi-	.01	hundredths
milli-	.001	thousandths

The basic unit for length is the meter. One meter is approximately one yard.

The basic unit for weight or mass is the gram. A paper clip weighs about one gram.

The basic unit for volume is the liter. One liter is approximately a quart.

These are the most commonly used units.

1 m = 100 cm	1000 mL = 1 L
1 m = 1000 mm	1 kL = 1000 L
1 cm = 10 mm	1000 mg = 1 g
1000 m = 1 km	1 kg = 1000 g

The prefixes are commonly listed from left to right for ease in conversion.
K H D U D C M

Example:
    63 km = _____ m
Since there are 3 steps from **K**ilo to **U**nit, move the decimal point 3 places to the right.
    63 km = 63,000 m

Example:
    14 mL = _____ L
Since there are 3 steps from **M**illi to **U**nit, move the decimal point 3 places to the left.
    14 mL = 0.014 L

Example:
    56.4 cm = _____ mm
    56.4 cm = 564 mm

Example:
    9.1 m = _____ km
    9.1 m = 0.0091 km

Example:
    75 kg = _____ g
    75 kg = 75,000 g

Measuring Perimeter, Area, and Volume

The **PERIMETER** of any polygon is the sum of the lengths of the sides.

P = sum of sides

Since the opposite sides of a rectangle are congruent, the perimeter of a rectangle equals twice the sum of the length and width or

$$P_{rect} = 2l + 2w \text{ or } 2(l + w)$$

Similarly, since all the sides of a square have the same measure, the perimeter of a square equals four times the length of one side or

$$P_{square} = 4s$$

The **AREA** of a polygon is the number of square units covered by the figure.

$$A_{rect} = l \times w$$
$$A_{square} = s^2$$

Example: Find the perimeter and the area of this rectangle.

16 cm

9 cm

$$
\begin{aligned}
P_{rect} &= 2l + 2w \\
&= 2(16) + 2(9) \\
&= 32 + 18 = 50 \text{ cm}
\end{aligned}
\qquad
\begin{aligned}
A_{rect} &= l \times w \\
&= 16(9) \\
&= 144 \text{ cm}^2
\end{aligned}
$$

Example: Find the perimeter and area of this square.

3.6 in.

$$
\begin{aligned}
P_{square} &= 4s \\
&= 4(3.6) \\
&= 14.4 \text{ in.}
\end{aligned}
\qquad
\begin{aligned}
A_{square} &= s^2 \\
&= (3.6)(3.6) \\
&= 12.96 \text{ in}^2
\end{aligned}
$$

In the following formulas, b = the base and h = the height of an altitude drawn to the base.

$$A_{parallelogram} = bh \qquad A_{triangle} = \tfrac{1}{2}bh \qquad A_{trapezoid} = \tfrac{1}{2}h(b_1 + b_2)$$

Example: Find the area of a parallelogram whose base is 6.5 cm and the height of the altitude to that base is 3.7 cm.

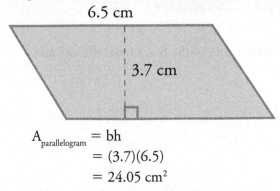

6.5 cm

3.7 cm

$$A_{parallelogram} = bh$$
$$= (3.7)(6.5)$$
$$= 24.05 \text{ cm}^2$$

Example: Find the area of this triangle.

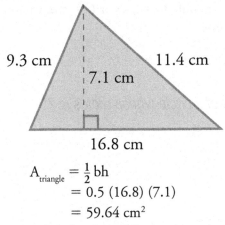

9.3 cm   11.4 cm

7.1 cm

16.8 cm

$$A_{triangle} = \tfrac{1}{2}bh$$
$$= 0.5\,(16.8)\,(7.1)$$
$$= 59.64 \text{ cm}^2$$

Note that the altitude is drawn to the base measuring 16.8 cm. The lengths of the other two sides are unnecessary information.

Example: Find the area of a right triangle whose sides measure 10 inches, 24 inches, and 26 inches.

Since the hypotenuse of a right triangle must be the longest side, then the two perpendicular sides must measure 10 and 24 inches.

$$A_{triangle} = \tfrac{1}{2}bh$$
$$= \tfrac{1}{2}(10)\,(24)$$
$$= 120 \text{ sq. in.}$$

Example: Find the area of this trapezoid.

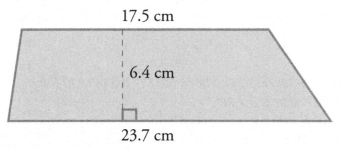

17.5 cm

6.4 cm

23.7 cm

The area of a trapezoid equals one-half the sum of the bases times the altitude.

$$A_{trapezoid} = \frac{1}{2} h (b_1 + b_2)$$
$$= 0.5 (6.4) (17.5 + 23.7)$$
$$= 131.84 \text{ cm}^2$$

Circles

The distance around a circle is the **CIRCUMFERENCE**. The ratio of the circumference to the diameter is represented by the Greek letter pi, $\pi \sim 3.14 \sim \frac{22}{7}$.

The circumference of a circle is found by the formula $C = 2\pi r$ or $C = \pi d$, where r is the radius of the circle and d is the diameter.

The area of a circle is found by the formula $A = \pi r^2$.

Example: Find the circumference and area of a circle whose radius is 7 meters.

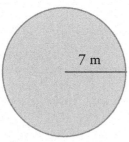

7 m

$$C = 2\pi r \qquad\qquad A = \pi r^2$$
$$= 2(3.14)(7) \qquad = 3.14(7)(7)$$
$$= 43.96 \text{ m} \qquad = 153.86 \text{ m}^2$$

You can also compute the area remaining when sections are cut out of a given figure composed of triangles, squares, rectangles, parallelograms, trapezoids, or circles. The strategy for solving problems of this nature should be to identify the given shapes and choose the correct formulas. Subtract the smaller cut out shape from the larger shape.

Example: Find the area of one side of the metal in the circular flat washer shown below:

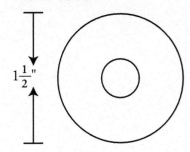

1. The shapes are both circles.

2. Use the formula $A = \pi r^2$ for both. (Inside diameter is $\frac{3}{8}$")

Area of larger circle
$A = \pi r^2$
$A = \pi(.75^2)$
$A = 1.77$ in²

Area of smaller circle
$A = \pi r^2$
$A = \pi(.1875^2)$
$A = .11$ in²

Area of metal washer = larger area − smaller area
= 1.77 in² − .11 in²
= 1.66 in²

The lateral area is the area of the faces excluding the bases.

The surface area is the total area of all the faces, including the bases.

The volume is the number of cubic units in a solid. This is the amount of space a figure holds.

Right Prism

Volume $V = Bh$ (where B = area of the base of the prism and h = the height of the prism)

Rectangular Right Prism

Surface area $S = 2(lw + hw + lh)$ (where l = length, w = width, and h = height)
Volume $V = lwh$

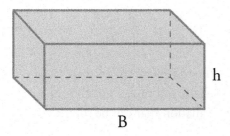

Example: Find the height of a box whose volume is 120 cubic meters and the area of the base is 30 square meters.

V = Bh

120 = 30h

h = 4 meters

Regular Pyramid

Volume $V = \frac{1}{3} Bh$

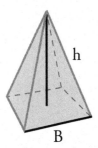

Right Circular Cylinder

Surface area $S = 2\pi r(r + h)$ (where r is the radius of the base)

Volume $V = \pi r^2 h$

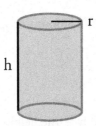

Right Circular Cone

Volume $V = \frac{1}{3} Bh$

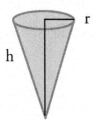

Rates

To solve word problems involving rates, first write the equation. To solve it, multiply each term by the LCD of all fractions. This will cancel out all of the denominators and give an equivalent algebraic equation that can be solved.

Example: Elly Mae can feed the animals in 15 minutes. Jethro can feed them in 10 minutes. How long will it take them to feed the animals if they work together?

If Elly Mae can feed the animals in 15 minutes, then she could feed $\frac{1}{15}$ of them in 1 minute, $\frac{2}{15}$ of them in 2 minutes, and $\frac{x}{15}$ of them in x minutes. In the same fashion, Jethro could feed $\frac{x}{10}$ of them in x minutes. Together they complete 1 job. The equation is:

$$\frac{x}{15} + \frac{x}{10} = 1$$

Multiply each term by the LCD (least common denominator) of 30:

$$2x + 3x = 30$$
$$x = 6 \text{ minutes}$$

Example: A salesman drove 480 miles from Pittsburgh to Hartford. The next day he returned the same distance to Pittsburgh in half an hour less time than his original trip took, because he increased his average speed by 4 mph. Find his original speed.

Since distance = rate × time, then time = $\frac{\text{distance}}{\text{rate}}$

original time − 1/2 hour = shorter return time

$$\frac{480}{x} - \frac{1}{2} = \frac{480}{x + 4}$$

Multiplying by the LCD of $2x(x + 4)$, the equation becomes:

$$480[2(x + 4)] - 1[x(x + 4)] = 480(2x)$$
$$960x + 3840 - x^2 - 4x = 960x$$
$$x^2 + 4x - 3840 = 0$$
$$(x + 64)(x - 60) = 0$$
$$x = 60$$

60 mph is the original speed, 64 mph is the faster return speed.

Measuring Angles

The classifying of angles refers to the angle measure. The naming of angles refers to the letters or numbers used to label the angle.

Example:

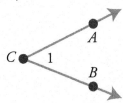

$\overrightarrow{CA}$ (read ray CA) and $\overrightarrow{CB}$ are the sides of the angle.
The angle can be called $\angle ACB$, $\angle BCA$, $\angle C$, or $\angle 1$.

Angles are classified according to their size as follows:

Acute: greater than 0 and less than 90 degrees

Right: exactly 90 degrees

Obtuse: greater than 90 and less than 180 degrees

Straight: exactly 180 degrees

Angles can be classified in a number of ways. Some of those classifications are outlined here.

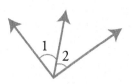

Adjacent angles have a common vertex and one common side but no interior points in common.

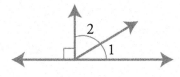

Complementary angles add up to 90 degrees.

Supplementary angles add up to 180 degrees.

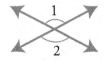

Vertical angles have sides that form two pairs of opposite rays.

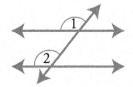

Corresponding angles are in the same corresponding position on two parallel lines cut by a transversal.

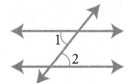

Alternate interior angles are diagonal angles on the inside of two parallel lines cut by a transversal.

Sample Test Questions and Rationale

(Average)

1. If a right triangle has legs with the measurements of 3 cm and 4 cm, what is the measure of the hypotenuse?

    A. 6 cm

    B. 1 cm

    C. 7 cm

    D. 5 cm

    Answer: D. 5 cm

    If you use the Pythagorean theorem, you will get 5 cm for the hypotenuse leg.

(Average)

2. What is the area of the shaded region below, where the circle has a radius r?

    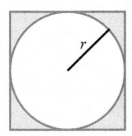

    A. r^2

    B. $(4 - \pi)r^2$

    C. $(2 - \pi)r^2$

    D. $4\pi r^2$

Answer: B. $(4 - \pi)r^2$

Notice that the figure is a circle of radius r inscribed in a quadrilateral—this quadrilateral must therefore be a square. Thus, the sides of the square each have a length twice that of the radius, as shown below.

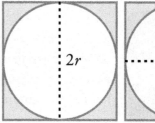
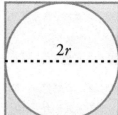

To find the area of the shaded region, subtract the area of the circle (πr^2) from the area of the square ($4r^2$).

$$A_{shaded} = 4r^2 - \pi r^2 = (4 - \pi)r^2$$

COMPETENCY 8
DATA ORGANIZATION AND INTERPRETATION

> **SKILL** **Understands visual displays of quantitative information** *(e.g., bar*
> **8.1** *graphs, pie charts, line graphs)*

BAR GRAPH: used to compare various quantities

PICTOGRAPHS: show comparison of quantities using symbols; each symbol represents a number of items

To make a **BAR GRAPH** or a **PICTOGRAPH**, determine the scale to be used for the graph. Then determine the length of each bar on the graph, or determine the number of pictures needed to represent each item of information. Be sure to include, in the legend, an explanation of the scale if the numbers on the axes do not represent the actual numbers.

Example: A class had the following grades: 4 As, 9 Bs, 8 Cs, 1 D, and 3 Fs. Graph these on a bar graph and a pictograph.

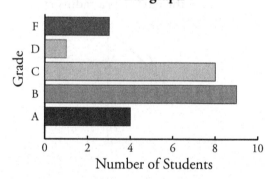

Pictograph

Grade	Number of Students
A	☺☺☺☺
B	☺☺☺☺☺☺☺☺☺
C	☺☺☺☺☺☺☺☺
D	☺
F	☺☺☺

Bar graph

To read a bar graph or a pictograph, read the explanation of the scale that was used in the legend (if there is a legend). Compare the length of each bar with the dimensions on the axes, and calculate the value each bar represents. On a pictograph, count the number of pictures used in the chart, and calculate the value of all the pictures.

LINE GRAPHS: show trends, often over a period of time

To make a **LINE GRAPH**, determine appropriate scales for both the vertical and horizontal axes (based on the information to be graphed). Describe what each axis represents, and mark the scale periodically on each axis. Graph the individual points of the graph, and connect the points on the graph from left to right.

Example: Graph the following information using a line graph.
The number of National Merit Scholarship finalists/school year.

	90–91	91–92	92–93	93–94	94–95	95–96
Central	3	5	1	4	6	8
Wilson	4	2	3	2	3	2

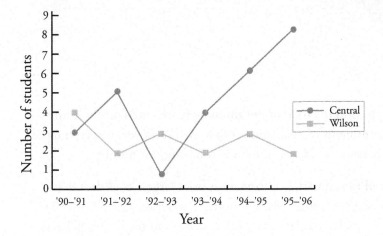

To make a **CIRCLE GRAPH**, total all the information that is to be included on the graph. Determine the central angle to be used for each sector of the graph using the following formula:

$$\frac{\text{information}}{\text{total information}} \times 360° = \text{degrees in central } \sphericalangle$$

Lay out the central angles to these sizes, label each section, and include each section's percent.

Example: Graph the following information about monthly expenses on a circle graph:

MONTHLY EXPENSES	
Rent	$400
Food	$150
Utilities	$75
Clothes	$75
Church	$100
Misc.	$200

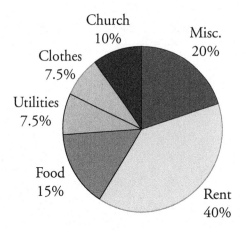

To read a circle graph, find the total of the amounts represented on the entire circle graph. To determine the actual amount that each sector of the graph represents, multiply the percent in a sector times the total amount number.

HISTOGRAMS:
summarize information from large sets of data that can be naturally grouped into intervals

HISTOGRAMS are used to summarize information from large sets of data that can be naturally grouped into intervals. The vertical axis indicates FREQUENCY (the number of times any particular data value occurs), and the horizontal axis indicates data values or ranges of data values. The number of data values in any interval is the FREQUENCY OF THE INTERVAL.

FREQUENCY: the number of times any particular data value occurs

FREQUENCY OF THE INTERVAL: the number of data values in any interval

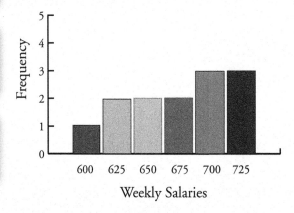

To read a chart, be sure to look at the row and column headings on the table. Use this information to evaluate the information given in the chart.

Sample Test Question and Rationale

(Average)

1. What conclusion can be drawn from the graph below?

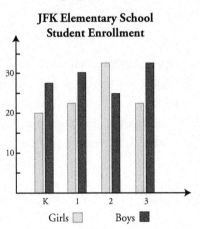

JFK Elementary School Student Enrollment

Girls ☐   Boys ■

A. The number of students in first grade exceeds the number in second grade

B. There are more boys than girls in the entire school

C. There are more girls than boys in first grade

D. Third grade has the greatest number of students

Answer: B. There are more boys than girls in the entire school

In Kindergarten, first grade, and third grade, there are more boys than girls. The number of extra girls in grade two is more than made up for by the extra boys in all the other grades put together.

Understands simple probability and intuitive concepts of chance *(e.g., flipping a coin, spinning a spinner, rolling a number cube)*

Dependent events occur when the probability of the second event depends on the outcome of the first event. For example, consider the two events: A) It is sunny on Saturday, and B) you go to the beach. If you intend to go to the beach on Saturday, rain or shine, then A and B may be independent. If, however, you plan to go to the beach only if it is sunny, then A and B may be dependent. In this situation, the probability of event B will change depending on the outcome of event A.

Suppose you have a pair of dice: one red and one green. If you roll a three on the red die and then roll a four on the green die, we can see that these events do not depend on the other. The total probability of the two independent events can be found by multiplying the separate probabilities.

$$P(A \text{ and } B) = P(A) \times P(B)$$
$$= \frac{1}{6} \times \frac{1}{6}$$
$$= \frac{1}{36}$$

Many times, however, events are not independent. Suppose a jar contains 12 red marbles and 8 blue marbles. If you randomly pick a red marble, replace it, and then randomly pick again, the probability of picking a red marble the second time remains the same. However, if you pick a red marble, and then pick again without replacing the first red marble, the second pick becomes dependent upon the first pick.

$$P(\text{red and red}) \text{ with replacement} = P(\text{red}) \times P(\text{red})$$
$$= \frac{12}{20} \times \frac{12}{20}$$
$$= \frac{9}{25}$$

$$P(\text{red and red}) \text{ without replacement} = P(\text{red}) \times P(\text{red})$$
$$= \frac{12}{20} \times \frac{11}{19}$$
$$= \frac{33}{95}$$

Odds are defined as the ratio of the number of favorable outcomes to the number of unfavorable outcomes. The sum of the favorable outcomes and the unfavorable outcomes should always equal the total number of possible outcomes.

For example, given a bag of 12 red and 7 green marbles, compute the odds of randomly selecting a red marble.

$$\text{Odds of getting red} = \frac{12}{19} : \frac{7}{19} \text{ or } 12{:}7$$
$$\text{Odds of not getting red} = \frac{7}{19} : \frac{12}{19} \text{ or } 7{:}12$$

In the case of flipping a coin, it is equally likely that a head or a tail will be tossed. The odds of tossing a head are 1:1. This is called "even odds."

Sample Spaces

SAMPLE SPACE: a list of all possible outcomes of an experiment

In probability, the **SAMPLE SPACE** is a list of all possible outcomes of an experiment. For example, the sample space of tossing two coins is the set {HH, HT, TT, TH}; the sample space of rolling a six-sided die is the set {1, 2, 3, 4, 5, 6}; and the sample space of measuring the height of students in a class is the set of all real numbers {R}.

When conducting experiments with a large number of possible outcomes, it is important to determine the size of the sample space. The size of the sample space can be determined by using the fundamental counting principle and the rules of combinations and permutations.

The fundamental counting principle states that if there are m possible outcomes for one task and n possible outcomes of another, there are $(m \times n)$ possible outcomes of the two tasks together.

A permutation is the number of possible arrangements of items, without repetition, where order of selection is important.

A combination is the number of possible arrangements, without repetition, where order of selection is not important.

Example: Find the size of the sample space of rolling two six-sided dice and flipping two coins.

List the possible outcomes of each event:

Each die: {1, 2, 3, 4, 5, 6}
Each coin: {Heads, Tails}

Apply the fundamental counting principle:

Size of sample space = $6 \times 6 \times 2 \times 2 = 144$

Sample Test Questions and Rationale

(Average)

1. Suppose you have a bag of marbles that contains two red marbles, five blue marbles, and three green marbles. If you replace the first marble chosen, what is the probability you will choose two green marbles in a row?

   A. $\frac{2}{5}$

   B. $\frac{9}{100}$

   C. $\frac{9}{10}$

   D. $\frac{3}{5}$

Answer: B. $\frac{9}{100}$

When solving a problem in which you replace the item, you multiply the first probability fraction by the second probability fraction and replace the item when finding the second probability. Since 3 of the 10 marbles are green, the probability of choosing two green marbles in a row $= \frac{3}{10} \times \frac{3}{10} = \frac{9}{100}$

Sample Test Questions and Rationale (cont.)

(Rigorous)

2. A bag contains four red marbles and six blue marbles. If three selections are made without replacement, what is the probability of choosing three red marbles?

   A. $\frac{3}{10}$

   B. $\frac{8}{125}$

   C. $\frac{1}{30}$

   D. $\frac{1}{60}$

Answer: C. $\frac{1}{30}$

Because the question tells us that this experiment is performed without replacement, we know that each time a marble is chosen, it is not returned to the bag. In the first selection, the probability of choosing a red marble is 4 out of 10, or $\frac{2}{5}$. In this case, a red marble is removed from the bag, leaving three red marbles and six blue marbles. The probability of then making another selection of a red marble is 3 out of 9, or $\frac{1}{3}$. This leaves two red marbles and six blue marbles. The probability of selecting a red marble in the final selection is then 2 out of 8, or $\frac{1}{4}$. To determine the probability of these three selections occurring consecutively, we multiply the probabilities from each step.

$$P(\text{three red}) = \frac{2}{5} \times \frac{1}{3} \times \frac{1}{4} = \frac{2}{60} = \frac{1}{30}$$

Thus, we have a $\frac{1}{30}$ chance of selecting (without replacement) three red marbles consecutively.

SKILL 8.3 Understands fundamental counting techniques *(e.g., permutations, combinations, tree diagrams)*

In the notation used below, $n(A)$ denotes the number of occurrences or sample space of event A. $n(AnB)$ denotes the intersection of the sample spaces of A and B.

Counting Principles

The addition principle of counting states:

   If A and B are events, $n(A \text{ or } B) = n(A) + n(B) - n(A \cap B)$

Example: In how many ways can you select a black card or a Jack from an ordinary deck of playing cards?

Let B denote the set of black cards, and let J denote the set of Jacks.
Then, $n(B) = 26$, $n(J) = 4$, $n(B \cap J) = 2$, and

   $n(B \text{ or } J) = n(B) + n(J) - n(B \cap A)$

   $= 26 + 4 - 2$

   $= 28.$

The addition principle of counting for mutually exclusive events:

If A and B are mutually exclusive events, $n(AorB) = n(A) + n(B)$.

Example: A travel agency offers 40 possible trips: 14 to Asia, 16 to Europe, and 10 to South America. In how many ways can you select a trip to Asia or Europe through this agency?

Let A denote trips to Asia, and let E denote trips to Europe. Then $A \cap E = \varnothing$, and $n(AorE) = 14 + 16 = 30$.

Therefore, the number of ways you can select a trip to Asia or Europe is 30.

The multiplication principle of counting for dependent events:

Let A be a set of outcomes of Stage 1, and B a set of outcomes of Stage 2. The number of ways, $\{n(AandB)\}$ that A and B can occur in a two-stage experiment is represented by:

$$n(AandB) = n(A)n(B|A)$$

where $n(B|A)$ denotes the number of ways B can occur, given that A has already occurred.

Example: How many ways from an ordinary deck of 52 cards can 2 Jacks be drawn in succession if the first card is drawn but not replaced in the deck, and then the second card is drawn?

This is a two-stage experiment where we must compute $n(AandB)$, where A is the set of outcomes for which a Jack is obtained on the first draw, and B is the set of outcomes for which a Jack is obtained on the second draw.

If the first card drawn is a Jack, then there are only 3 remaining Jacks left to choose from on the second draw. Thus, drawing two cards without replacement means that the events are dependent.

$$n(AandB) = n(A)n(B|A) = 4 \times 3 = 12$$

The multiplication principle of counting for independent events:

Let A be a set of outcomes of Stage 1, and B a set of outcomes of Stage 2. If A and B are independent events, then the number of ways, $n(AandB)$, that A and B can occur in a two-stage experiment is represented by:

$$n(AandB) = n(A)n(B).$$

Example: How many six-letter code "words" can be formed if repetition of letters is not allowed?

With code words, a word does not have to look like a word; for example, *abcdef* could be a code word. Since we must choose a first letter and a second letter and a third letter and a fourth letter and a fifth letter and a sixth letter, this experiment has six stages.

Since repetition is not allowed there are twenty-six choices for the first letter, twenty-five for the second, twenty-four for the third, twenty-three for the fourth, twenty-two for the fifth, and twenty-one for the sixth. Therefore, we have:

n (six-letter code words without repetition of letters)

$= 26 \times 25 \times 24 \times 23 \times 22 \times 21$

$= 165,765,600$

Tree Diagrams

Suppose you want to look at the possible sequence of events for having two children in a family. Since a child will be either a boy or a girl, the following tree diagram illustrates the possible outcomes:

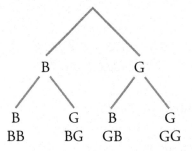

From the diagram, you see that there are four possible outcomes, two of which are the same.

Combinations

COMBINATIONS: an unordered collection of distinct elements

When we are dealing with the number of **COMBINATIONS**, the order in which elements are selected is not important. For instance,

2, 3, 4 and 4, 2, 3 are considered one combination.

The number of combinations represents the number of ways in which r elements can be selected from n elements (in no particular order).

Example: To determine how many different twelve-person juries can be chosen from a pool of twenty jurors, you would use the formula:

$$_nC_r = \frac{n!}{r!(n-r)!}$$

$$\frac{20!}{12!(20-12)!} = 125{,}970$$

The difference between permutations and combinations is that in permutations, all the possible ways of writing an arrangement of objects are given; in a combination, a given arrangement of objects is listed only once.

Permutations

A **PERMUTATION** is similar to a combination, but it has an ordered arrangement.

For example, suppose seven numbers are chosen for the lottery-winning number from a possible ten (0 to 9). The possible number of permutations would be determined as follows:

$$_nP_r = \frac{n!}{(n-r)!} = \frac{10!}{(10-7)!} = 604{,}800$$

Many problems involve finding both the combination and the permutation for a given set. In this way, the two concepts are inexorably linked.

> **PERMUTATION:** an ordering of a certain number of elements of a given set

Example: Given the set {1, 2, 3, 4}, list the arrangements of two numbers that can be written as a combination and as a permutation.

Combination	Permutation
12, 13, 14, 23, 24, 34	12, 21, 13, 31, 14, 41,
	23, 32, 24, 42, 34, 43,
Six ways	Twelve ways

Using the formulas given below, the same results can be found.

Permutation:

The notation $_nP_r$ is read "the number of permutations of n objects taken r at a time."

$$_nP_r = \frac{n!}{(n-r)!}$$

Substitute known values:

$$_4P_2 = \frac{4!}{(4-2)!}$$

Solve:

$$_4P_2 = 12$$

Combination:

The number of combinations when *r* objects are selected from *n* objects.

$$_nC_r = \frac{n!}{(n-r)!r!}$$

Substitute known values:

$$_4C_2 = \frac{4!}{(4-2)!2!}$$

Solve:

$$_4C_2 = 6$$

Sample Test Questions and Rationale

(Rigorous)

1. How many different five-letter words (not necessarily dictionary words) can be formed from the first ten letters of the alphabet, assuming no letter is repeated?

    A. 5

    B. 252

    C. 30,240

    D. 3,628,800

Answer: C. 30,240

Given the first ten letters of the alphabet, we want to find out how many five-letter words we can form. Examples would be

abcde
abcdf
abcdg
edcba

. . . and so on. To do this, we can use the formula for permutations. If you cannot recall the formula, however, simply note the following. Our first choice offers us ten possible letters; our second choice offers us nine; our third, eight; our fourth, seven; and our fifth, six. Thus, we need simply multiply these numbers to get the number of possible outcomes, *n*.

$$n = 10 \times 9 \times 8 \times 7 \times 6 = 30,240$$

The formula for permutations yields the same result: for ten objects taken five at a time,

$$_{10}P_5 = \frac{10!}{(10-5)!} = \frac{10!}{5!} =$$
$$\frac{10 \times 9 \times 8 \times 7 \times 6 \times 5 \times 4 \times 3 \times 2}{5 \times 4 \times 3 \times 2} =$$
$$10 \times 9 \times 8 \times 7 \times 6 = 30,240$$

Thus, there are 30,240 different words.

Sample Test Questions and Rationale (cont.)

(Average)

2. How many different three-card hands can be drawn from a standard deck of fifty-two playing cards?

A. 156

B. 2,704

C. 22,100

D. 140,608

Answer: C. 22,100

The number of ways 3 cards can be drawn from a deck of 52 = $_{52}C_3 = \frac{(52!)}{3!(52-3)!}$ = $(50 \times 51 \times 52)/6 = 22,100$.

Understands basic descriptive statistics *(e.g., mean, median, and mode)*

Mean, Median, and Mode

Descriptive statistics are numbers that describe characteristics of a group of data. Mean, median, and mode are three measures of central tendency. The MEAN is the average of the data items. The MEDIAN is found by putting the data items in order from smallest to largest and selecting the item in the middle (or the average of the two items in the middle). The MODE is the most frequently occurring item.

RANGE is a measure of variability. It is found by subtracting the smallest value from the largest value.

Example: Find the mean, median, mode, and range of these test scores:

85	77	65
92	90	54
88	85	70
75	80	69
85	88	60
72	74	95

MEAN: the sum of the numbers given, divided by the number of items being averaged

MEDIAN: the middle number of a set

MODE: the number that occurs with the greatest frequency in a set of numbers

RANGE: a measure of variability

Mean = sum of all scores ÷ number of scores = 78

Median = Put the numbers in order from smallest to largest. Pick the middle number.

54 60 65 69 70 72 74 75 | 77 80 | 85 85 85 88 88 90 92 95

both in middle

Therefore, the median is the average of two numbers in the middle, 78.5.

Mode = most frequent number
= 85

Range = the largest number minus the smallest number
= 95 − 54
= 41

Example: Different situations require different information. If we examine the circumstances under which an ice cream store owner may use statistics collected in the store, we find different uses for different information.
Over a seven-day period, the store owner collected data on the ice cream flavors sold. He found that the mean number of scoops sold was 174 per day. The best-selling flavor was vanilla. This information was useful in determining how much ice cream to order in all and how much of each flavor.

In this case, the median and range had little business value for the owner.

Example: Consider the set of test scores from a math class: 0, 16, 19, 65, 65, 65, 68, 69, 70, 72, 73, 73, 75, 78, 80, 85, 88, and 92.
The mean is 64.06 and the median is 71.

Since there are only three scores lower than the mean out of the eighteen scores, the median (71) would be a more descriptive score.

Using Definitions in Statistical Data

An understanding of the definitions is important in determining the validity and uses of statistical data. All definitions and applications in this section apply to ungrouped data.

Data item: each piece of data, represented by the letter X.

Mean: the average of all data, which is represented by the symbol $\overline{X}$.

Range: the difference between the highest and lowest values of data items.

Sum of the squares: the sum of the squares of the differences between each item and the mean.

$Sx^2 = $ Sum of $(X - \overline{X})^2$

Variance: the sum of the squares quantity divided by the number of items. The lowercase Greek letter sigma squared (σ^2) represents variance.

$\frac{Sx^2}{N} = \sigma^2$

The larger the value of the variance, the larger the spread.

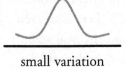

small variation

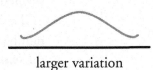

larger variation

Standard deviation: the square root of the variance. The lowercase Greek letter sigma (σ) is used to represent standard deviation.

$\sigma = \sqrt{\sigma^2}$

Most statistical calculators have standard deviation keys on them; you should use them when asked to calculate statistical functions. It is important to become familiar with the calculator and the location of the keys needed.

Example: Given the ungrouped data below, calculate the mean, range, standard deviation, and variance.

15	22	28	25	34	38
18	25	30	33	19	23

Mean ($\overline{X}$) = 25.8333333

Range: 38 − 15 = 23

Standard deviation (σ) = 6.6936952

Variance (σ^2) = 44.805556

Sample Test Question and Rationale

(*Rigorous*)

1. Given the following numbers, find the median:

    25, 18, 16, 45, 10, 27

    A. 21.5

    B. 25

    C. 18

    D. There is no median

Answer: A. 21.5

The median refers to the number that is in the middle. First, to find this number you must order the numbers from smallest to largest (or largest to smallest) and find the number in the middle. If there is an even number of numbers, you add the two numbers in the middle and divide by two.

DOMAIN III
SOCIAL STUDIES

PERSONALIZED STUDY PLAN

KNOWN MATERIAL/ SKIP IT

COMPETENCY 9
GEOGRAPHY, ANTHROPOLOGY, AND SOCIOLOGY

> SKILL **Knows world and regional geography** (e.g., spatial terms, places, and
> 9.1 regions)

SPATIAL ORGANIZATION is a description of how things are grouped in a given space. In geographical terms, this can describe people, places, and environments anywhere and everywhere on Earth.

The most basic form of spatial organization for people is where they live. The vast majority of people live near other people in villages, towns, cities, and settlements. People live near others in order to take advantage of the goods and services that naturally arise from cooperation. The villages, towns, cities, and settlements they live in are, to varying degrees, near bodies of water. Water is a staple of survival for every person on the planet; it is also a good source of energy for factories and industries, as well as a form of transportation for people and goods.

Another way to describe where people live is by the geography and topography around them. The vast majority of people on the planet live in areas that are very hospitable. Yes, people live in the Himalayas and in the Sahara, but the populations of those areas are very small when compared to those of the plains of China, India, Europe, and the United States. People naturally want to live where they do not have to work really hard just to survive, and world population patterns reflect this.

We can examine the spatial organization of the places where people live. For example, in a city, where are the factories and heavy industrial buildings? Are they near airports or train stations? Are they on the edge of town, near major roads? What about housing developments? Are they near these industries, or are they far away? Where are the other industrial buildings? Where are the schools and hospitals and parks? What about the police and fire stations? How close are people's homes to these various things?

Towns, and especially cities, are routinely organized into neighborhoods so that each house or home is near most things that its residents might need on a regular basis. This means that large cities have multiple schools, hospitals, grocery stores, fire stations, and so on.

SPATIAL ORGANIZATION: a description of how things are grouped in a given space; in geographical terms, this can describe people, places, and environments anywhere and everywhere on Earth

---

Settlement Patterns

The distances between cities, towns, villages, or settlements are also related to settlement patterns. In certain parts of the United States and in many European countries, population settlement patterns achieve megalopolis standards, with no clear boundaries from one town to the next. Other, more sparsely populated areas have towns that are few and far between with relatively few people in them. Some exceptions to this exist, of course, like oases in the deserts; for the most part, however, population centers tend to be relatively near one another or at least near smaller towns.

Most populated places in the world also tend to be close to agricultural lands. Food makes the world go round. Although some cities are more agriculturally inclined than others, it is rare to find a city that grows absolutely no crops. The kind of food grown is almost entirely dependent on the kind of available land and the climate of the area. Rice doesn't grow well in the desert, for instance, nor do bananas grow well in snowy lands. Certain crops are easier to transport than others, and the ones that aren't are usually grown near ports or other centers of exporting.

Five Themes of Geography

The five themes of geography are:

> **RELATIVE LOCATION:** refers to the surrounding geography (e.g., on the banks of the Mississippi River)

> **ABSOLUTE LOCATION:** refers to a specific point, such as latitude 41° north, longitude 90° west, or 123 Main Street

1. Location: This includes relative and absolute location. A **RELATIVE LOCATION** refers to the surrounding geography (e.g., on the banks of the Mississippi River). **ABSOLUTE LOCATION** refers to a specific point, such as latitude 41° north, longitude 90° west, or 123 Main Street.

2. Place: This is something that has both human and physical characteristics. Physical characteristics include features such as mountains, rivers, and deserts. Human characteristics are the features created by human interaction with the environment (such as canals and roads).

3. Human-environmental interaction: The theme of human-environmental interaction has three main concepts: humans adapt to the environment (wearing warm clothing in a cold climate); humans modify the environment (planting trees to block a prevailing wind); and humans depend on the environment (for food, water, and raw materials).

4. Movement: The theme of movement covers how humans interact with one another through trade, communications, emigration, and other forms of contact.

5. Regions: A region is an area that has some kind of unifying characteristic, such as a common language or a common government. There are three main types of regions: **FORMAL REGIONS** are areas defined by actual political boundaries, such as a city, county, or state. **FUNCTIONAL REGIONS** are defined by a common function, such as the area covered by a telephone service. **VERNACULAR REGIONS** are less formally defined areas that are formed by people's perception (e.g., "the Middle East" or "the South").

> **FORMAL REGIONS:** areas defined by actual political boundaries, such as a city, county, or state

> **FUNCTIONAL REGIONS:** are defined by a common function, such as the area covered by a telephone service

> **VERNACULAR REGIONS:** are less formally defined areas that are formed by people's perception (e.g., "the Middle East" or "the South")

LANDFORMS

A **LANDFORM** comprises a geomorphological unit. Landforms are categorized by characteristics such as elevation, slope, orientation, stratification, rock exposure, and soil type. By name, they include such features as berms, mounds, hills, cliffs, and valleys. Oceans and continents exemplify highest-order landforms; however, landform elements can be further broken down. The generic landform elements are pits, peaks, channels, ridges, passes, pools, and planes; these can often be extracted from a digital elevation model using automated or semiautomated techniques.

Elementary landforms (segments, facets, and relief units) are the smallest homogeneous divisions of the land surface at a given scale or resolution. A plateau or a hill can be observed at various scales, ranging from a few hundred meters to hundreds of kilometers. Hence, the spatial distribution of landforms is often fuzzy and scale-dependent, as is the case for soils and geological strata.

A number of factors, ranging from plate tectonics to erosion and deposition, can generate and affect landforms. Biological factors can also influence landforms—for example, consider the role of plants in the development of dune systems and salt marshes, and the work of corals and algae in the formation of coral reefs.

> **LANDFORM:** comprises a geomorphological unit, categorized by characteristics such as elevation, slope, orientation, stratification, rock exposure, and soil type

The Earth's surface is made up of 70 percent water and 30 percent land. Physical features of the land surface include mountains, hills, plateaus, valleys, and plains. Other minor landforms include deserts, deltas, canyons, mesas, basins, foothills, marshes, and swamps. Earth's water features include oceans, seas, lakes, rivers, and canals.

> *The Earth's surface is made up of 70 percent water and 30 percent land.*

EARTH'S PHYSICAL FEATURES	
Mountains	Landforms with rather steep slopes at least 2,000 feet or more above sea level. Mountains are found in groups called mountain chains or mountain ranges. At least one range can be found on six of the Earth's seven continents. North America has the Appalachian and Rocky Mountains; South America, the Andes; Asia, the Himalayas; Australia, the Great Dividing Range; Europe, the Alps; and Africa, the Atlas, Ahaggar, and Drakensburg Mountains. Mountains are commonly formed by volcanic activity, or when land is thrust upward where two tectonic plates collide.
Hills	Elevated landforms rising to an elevation of about five hundred to two thousand feet. Hills are found everywhere on Earth—including Antarctica, where they are covered by ice.
Plateaus	Elevated landforms that are usually level on top. Some plateaus are dry because they are surrounded by mountains that keep out any moisture. The plateau extending north from the Himalayas is extremely dry, while those in Antarctica and Greenland are covered with ice and snow. Plateaus can be formed by underground volcanic activity, erosion, or colliding tectonic plates.
Plains	Areas of flat or slightly rolling land, usually lower than the landforms next to them. Sometimes called *lowlands* (and often located along *seacoasts*), plains support the majority of the world's people. Many have been formed by large rivers, which provided extremely fertile soil for successful cultivation of crops and numerous large settlements of people. In North America, the vast plains areas extend from the Gulf of Mexico north to the Arctic Ocean and between the Appalachian and Rocky Mountains. In Europe, rich plains extend east from Great Britain into central Europe on into the Siberian region of Russia. Plains in river valleys are found in China (the Yangtze River valley), India (the Ganges River valley), and Southeast Asia (the Mekong River valley).
Valleys	Land areas that are found between hills and mountains. Some have gentle slopes containing trees and plants; others have very steep walls and are referred to as canyons. One famous example is Arizona's Grand Canyon of the Colorado River, which was formed by erosion.
Deserts	Large dry areas of land receiving ten inches or less of rainfall each year. Among the better known deserts are Africa's large Sahara desert, the Arabian desert on the Arabian Peninsula, and the desert outback covering roughly one-third of Australia. Deserts are found mainly in the tropical latitudes and are formed when surrounding features such as mountain ranges extract most of the moisture from the prevailing winds.
Deltas	Areas of lowlands formed by soil and sediment deposited at the mouths of rivers. The soil is generally very fertile; most fertile river deltas are important crop-growing areas. One well-known example is the delta of Egypt's Nile River, known for its production of cotton.
Mesas	The flat tops of hills or mountains, usually with steep sides. Mesas are similar to plateaus, but smaller.
Basins	Low areas drained by rivers or low spots in mountains.
Foothills	A low series of hills found between a plain and a mountain range.

Table continued on next page

Marshes and Swamps	Wet lowlands providing growth of such plants as rushes and reeds.
Oceans	The largest bodies of water on the planet. Five major oceans are usually recognized: the Pacific, Atlantic, Indian, Arctic, and Southern oceans; the last two listed are sometimes consolidated into the first three. The *Atlantic Ocean* is one-half the size of the Pacific and separates North and South America from Africa and Europe; the *Pacific Ocean* covers almost one-third of the entire surface of the Earth and separates North and South America from Asia and Australia; the *Indian Ocean* touches Africa, Asia, and Australia; the ice-filled *Arctic Ocean* extends from North America and Europe to the North Pole; and the *Southern Ocean* is made up of the southern portions of the Pacific, Atlantic, and Indian Oceans, which touch the shores of Antarctica.
Seas	Bodies of water smaller than oceans and surrounded by land. Some examples include the Mediterranean Sea found between Europe, Asia, and Africa and the Caribbean Sea, which touches the West Indies, South America, and Central America.
Lakes	Bodies of water surrounded by land. The Great Lakes in North America are a good example.
Rivers	Considered a nation's lifeblood, usually beginning as very small streams, formed by melting snow and rainfall. Rivers flow from higher to lower land, emptying into a larger body of water—usually a sea or an ocean. Examples of important rivers include the Nile, Niger, and Zaire rivers of Africa; the Rhine, Danube, and Thames rivers of Europe; the Yangtze, Ganges, Mekong, Hwang He, and Irrawaddy rivers of Asia; the Murray-Darling in Australia; and the Orinoco in South America. River systems are made up of large rivers as well as the numerous smaller rivers or tributaries flowing into them. Examples include the vast Amazon River system in South America and the Mississippi River system in the United States.
Canals	Man-made water passages constructed to connect two larger bodies of water. Famous examples include the *Panama Canal* across Panama's isthmus, which connects the Atlantic and Pacific oceans, and the *Suez Canal* in the Middle East between Africa and the Arabian Peninsula, connecting the Red and Mediterranean seas.

Weather and Climate

WEATHER is the condition of the air that affects the day-to-day atmospheric conditions. It includes factors such as temperature, air pressure, wind, and moisture or precipitation (which includes rain, snow, hail, or sleet).

CLIMATE is the term used to describe the average weather or daily weather conditions for a specific region over a long period of time. Studying the climate of an area includes information gathered on the area's monthly and yearly temperatures as well as its monthly and yearly amounts of precipitation. Another characteristic of an area's climate is the length of its growing season.

WEATHER: the condition of the air that affects the day-to-day atmospheric conditions

CLIMATE: the term used to describe the average weather or daily weather conditions for a specific region over a long period of time

Studying the climate of an area includes information gathered on the area's monthly and yearly temperatures as well as its monthly and yearly amounts of precipitation.

Humid continental climate

In northern and central United States, northern China, south central and southeastern Canada, and the western and southeastern parts of the former Soviet Union, there is a "climate of four seasons." This is also known as the humid continental climate, which includes spring, summer, fall, and winter. Cold winters, hot summers, and enough rainfall to grow a variety of crops are the major characteristics of this climate. In areas where the humid continental climate is found, there are some of the world's best farmlands as well as important activities such as trading and mining. Differences in temperatures throughout the year are typically determined by how far inland a place is, away from the coast.

Steppe or prairie climate

The steppe or prairie climate is located in the interiors of the large continents like Asia and North America. These dry flatlands are far from ocean breezes and are called prairies (or the Great Plains in Canada and the United States and steppes in Asia). Although the summers are hot and the winters are cold, the big difference is rainfall. In the steppe climate, rainfall is light and uncertain at ten to twenty inches per year. Where rain is more plentiful, grass grows; in areas of less rainfall, the steppes or prairies gradually become deserts. Examples of this are the Gobi desert of Asia, deserts in central and western Australia and the southwestern United States, and the smaller deserts found in Pakistan, Argentina, and Africa south of the equator.

Tundra and taiga

The two major climates found in the high latitudes are tundra and taiga. The word *tundra*, meaning marshy plain, is Russian; it aptly describes the climatic conditions in the northern areas of Russia, Europe, and Canada. Winters are extremely cold and very long. Most of the year the ground is frozen, but it becomes rather mushy during the very short summer months. Surprisingly, less snow falls in the area of the tundra than in the eastern part of the United States. However, due to the harshness of the extreme cold, very few people live there and almost no crops can be raised. Despite the small human population, many plants and animals are found there.

The taiga is the northern forest region located south of the tundra. The world's largest forestlands are found here, along with vast mineral wealth and fur-bearing animals. The climate is so extreme that very few people live here, as they are not able to raise crops due to the extremely short growing season. The winter temperatures are colder and the summer temperatures hotter than those in the tundra because the taiga climate region is farther from the waters of the Arctic Ocean. The taiga is found in the northern parts of Russia, Sweden, Norway, Finland, Canada, and Alaska, with most of their lands covered with marshes and swamps.

Subtropical climate

The humid subtropical climate is found north and south of the tropics. It is characterized by its high levels of moisture. The areas with this type of climate include the southeastern coasts of Japan, mainland China, Australia, Africa, South America, and the United States. One interesting feature of these locations is that warm ocean currents are found there. The winds that blow across these currents bring in warm moist air all year round. Long, warm summers; short, mild winters; and a long growing season allow for different crops to be grown several times a year. These conditions contribute to the productivity of this climate, which supports more people than any of the other climates.

Marine climate

The marine climate is found in Western Europe, the British Isles, the Pacific Northwest of the United States, the western coast of Canada, southern Chile, southern New Zealand, and southeastern Australia. A common characteristic of these lands is that they are either near water or surrounded by it. The ocean winds are wet and warm, bringing a mild rainy climate to these areas. In the summer, the daily temperatures average at or below 70° F. During the winter, because of the warming effect of the ocean waters, the temperatures rarely fall below freezing.

In certain areas of the Earth, there is a type of climate unique to areas with high mountains. This type of climate is called a vertical climate because the temperatures, crops, vegetation, and human activities change as one ascends through the different levels of elevation. At the foot of the mountain, a hot and rainy climate is found, with the cultivation of many lowland crops. As one climbs higher, the air becomes cooler, the climate changes sharply, and economic activities change to things such as grazing sheep and growing corn. At the top of many mountains, snow is found year round.

Sample Test Questions and Rationale

(Rigorous)

1. What are two factors that can generate and affect landforms?

   A. Observing a plateau at various scales

   B. Erosion and deposition

   C. The presence of oceans, lakes, seas, and canals

   D. The dry nature of some plateaus

   Answer: B. Erosion and deposition

   Observing plateaus at various scales, the presence of bodies of water, and the dry nature of some plateaus are important to geography, but are not considered to be factors that generate and affect landforms.

(Average)

2. Denver is called the "mile-high city" because it is:

   A. Located approximately one mile above the plains of eastern Colorado

   B. Located exactly one mile above the base of Cheyenne Mountain

   C. Located approximately one mile above sea level

   D. The city with the tallest buildings in Colorado

   Answer: C. Located approximately one mile above sea level

   Elevations of cities are calculated according to their height above sea level. That fact negates all answers except C.

SKILL 9.2 **Understands the interaction of physical and human systems** *(e.g., how humans change the environment, how the environment changes humans, importance of natural and human resources)*

Culture and Geography

CULTURE: the way of life of a group of people, including not only art, music, and literature, but also beliefs, customs, languages, traditions, and inventions

Social scientists use the term CULTURE to describe the way of life of a group of people. This term includes not only art, music, and literature but also beliefs, customs, languages, traditions, and inventions—in short, any way of life, whether complex or simple. Although the term GEOGRAPHY is defined as the study of the Earth's features, it also includes the study of living things as it pertains to their location, the relationships of these locations with each other, how they came to be there, and what impact these have on the world.

PHYSICAL GEOGRAPHY is concerned with the locations of such features as climate, water, and land as well as how these relate to and affect each other. It includes how they affect human activities and what forces shaped and changed them.

All three of these features of the Earth (climate, water, and land) affect the lives of all humans, ultimately having a direct influence on what is made and produced, where this production occurs, how it occurs, and what makes it possible. The combination of the different climatic conditions and types of landforms and other surface features work together all around the Earth to give the many varied cultures their unique characteristics and distinctions.

CULTURAL GEOGRAPHY studies the location, characteristics, and influence of the physical environment on different cultures around the Earth. Also included in these studies are comparisons and influences of the many varied cultures.

Physical locations of the Earth's surface features include the four major hemispheres and the parts of the Earth's continents in them. Political locations are the political divisions, if any, within each continent. Both physical and political locations are precisely determined in two ways:

1. Surveying is done to determine boundary lines and distance from other features.

2. Exact locations are precisely determined by imaginary lines of latitude (parallels) and longitude (meridians).

The intersection of these lines at right angles forms a grid, making it possible to pinpoint an exact location of any place using any two grid coordinates.

> **GEOGRAPHY:** the study of the Earth's features, including the study of living things as it pertains to their location, the relationships of these locations with each other, how they came to be there, and what impact these have on the world

> **PHYSICAL GEOGRAPHY:** concerned with the locations of such features as climate, water, and land as well as how these relate to and affect each other

> **CULTURAL GEOGRAPHY:** studies the location, characteristics, and influence of the physical environment on different cultures around the Earth

The Earth's Hemispheres

The Eastern Hemisphere is located between the North and South poles, between the prime meridian (0° longitude) east to the international date line (180° longitude). It consists of most of Europe, all of Australia, most of Africa, and all of Asia (except for a tiny piece of the easternmost part of Russia that extends east of 180° longitude).

The Western Hemisphere is located between the North and South poles, between the prime meridian (0° longitude) west to the international date line (180° longitude). It consists of all of North and South America, a tiny part of the easternmost part of Russia that extends east of 180° longitude, and a part of Europe that extends west of the prime meridian.

The Northern Hemisphere, located between the North Pole and the equator, contains all of the continents of Europe and North America and parts of South America, Africa, and most of Asia.

The Southern Hemisphere, located between the South Pole and the equator, contains all of Australia, a small part of Asia, about one-third of Africa, most of South America, and all of Antarctica.

The Seven Continents

Of the seven continents, Australia is the only one that contains just one country. It is also the only island continent. Its political divisions consist of six states and one territory: Western Australia, South Australia, Tasmania, Victoria, New South Wales, Queensland, and Northern Territory.

Africa is made up of fifty-four separate countries, including Egypt, Nigeria, South Africa, Zaire, Kenya, Algeria, Morocco, and the large island of Madagascar.

Asia consists of forty-nine separate countries, including China, Japan, India, Turkey, Israel, Iraq, Iran, Indonesia, Jordan, Vietnam, Thailand, and the Philippines.

Some of Europe's forty-three separate nations include France, Russia, Malta, Denmark, Hungary, Greece, and Bosnia.

North America consists of Canada, the United States of America, the island nations of the West Indies, and the "land bridge" of Middle America, including Cuba, Jamaica, Mexico, Panama, and other nations.

Thirteen separate nations together occupy the continent of South America; among them are the nations of Brazil, Paraguay, Ecuador, and Suriname.

The continent of Antarctica has no political boundaries or divisions but has a number of science and research stations managed by nations such as Russia, Japan, France, Australia, and India.

Sample Test Question and Rationale

(Easy)

1. _____ is the southernmost continent in the world.

   A. Australia

   B. New Zealand

   C. The Arctic

   D. Antarctica

Answer: D. Antarctica

Antarctica is the southernmost continent. It surrounds the South Pole. Australia is a continent in the southern hemisphere but it lies north of Antarctica. New Zealand is made up of two large islands but it is not a continent. The Arctic is a region that includes parts of several continents but it is not in and of itself a continent. In fact, much of the Arctic is ice-covered ocean.

Sample Test Questions and Rationale (cont.)

(Average)

2. **The Great Plains in the United States are an excellent place to grow corn and wheat for all of the following reasons EXCEPT:**

   A. Rainfall is abundant and the soil is rich

   B. The land is mostly flat and easy to cultivate

   C. The human population is modest in size, so there is plenty of space for large farms

   D. The climate is semitropical

Answer: D. The climate is semitropical

The climate on the Great Plains is not semitropical. It is temperate, with harsh winters. Rainfall and soil conditions are good. The land is flat. The human population is not overcrowded; there is room for large farms.

SKILL 9.3 **Knows the uses of geography** *(e.g., apply geography to interpret past, to interpret present, to plan for future)*

Studying the geographic features of the Earth is essential to understanding the history of the physical environment and the history of humanity. Only when a comprehensive worldview is obtained through extensive geographical research can we have a complete understanding of the Earth, its lands, and its peoples throughout time. In this way, geography is useful as a historical and evaluative tool.

At the same time, geography is also useful for looking toward the future. To understand the world we live in today and the world we will inhabit in the future, we have to be aware of the geographic concepts that drive world events. These include, but are not limited to, environmental concerns.

Geography is often studied within the context of anthropology and sociology, areas of social studies that encompass human development as it relates to place and society.

ANTHROPOLOGY is the scientific study of human culture and humanity: the relationship between humans and their cultures. Anthropologists study different groups, patterns of behavior, how they relate to one another, and their similarities and differences. Their research is twofold: it is cross-cultural and comparative. The major method of study is referred to as "participant observation." In this method, the anthropologist studies and learns about the culture's members by living among them and participating with them in their daily lives. Other methods may be used, but this is the most common. For example, in the 1920s, Margaret Mead

> *Studying the geographic features of the Earth is essential to understanding the history of the physical environment and the history of humanity.*

> **ANTHROPOLOGY:** the scientific study of human culture and humanity: the relationship between humans and their cultures

lived among the Samoans, observing their ways of life. Her study resulted in the book *Coming of Age in Samoa*. The Leakey family, consisting of Louis, his wife Mary, and their son Richard, were anthropologists who did much fieldwork to further the study of human origins.

Many aspects of anthropology and the study of human cultures intersect with the study of geography. Because the Earth's physical features contribute to the actions and livelihoods of all cultures around the globe, the two fields of study are inexorably linked. Therefore, it is not uncommon to find discussions of geography interspersed in cultural studies.

In general, geographical studies are divided into several categories:

- Regional: The elements and characteristics of a place or region
- Topical: An Earth feature or one human activity occurring throughout the entire world
- Physical: Earth's physical features; what creates and changes them; their relationships to each other; and their relationships to human activities
- Human: Human activity patterns and how they relate to the environment including political, cultural, historical, urban, and social geographical fields of study

Special research methods used by geographers include mapping, interviewing, field studies, mathematics, statistics, and scientific instruments.

Sample Test Question and Rationale

(Rigorous)

1. Human bones found during construction near an American Civil War battlefield would most likely be delivered to which of the following for study?

    A. The Department of Veterans Affairs

    B. A state medical examiner

    C. A homicide detective

    D. An anthropologist

Answer: D. An anthropologist

Anthropologists study bones that are found during construction excavations. The Department of Veterans Affairs might be the final recipient of Civil War bones, but the bones would initially go to an anthropologist for identification. A medical examiner and a homicide detective would not be interested because Civil War dead are not murder victims.

Knows how people of different cultural backgrounds interact with their environment, self, family, neighborhoods, and communities

Natural Resources

NATURAL RESOURCES are naturally occurring substances that are considered valuable in their natural form. A commodity is generally considered a natural resource when the primary activities associated with it are extraction and purification, as opposed to creation. Thus, mining, petroleum extraction, fishing, and forestry are generally considered natural resource industries while agriculture is not.

Natural resources are often classified into renewable and nonrenewable resources. **RENEWABLE RESOURCES** are generally living resources (fish, coffee, and forests, for example), which can restock (renew) themselves if they are not over-harvested. Renewable resources can restock themselves and be used indefinitely if they are sustained. Once renewable resources are consumed at a rate that exceeds their natural rate of replacement, the standing stock will diminish and eventually run out.

The rate of sustainable use of a renewable resource is determined by the replacement rate and amount of standing stock of that particular resource. Nonliving renewable natural resources include soil, water, wind, tides, and solar radiation. **NONRENEWABLE RESOURCES** are natural resources that cannot be remade or regenerated in the same proportion in which they are used. Examples of nonrenewable resources are fossil fuels such as coal, petroleum, and natural gas.

In recent years, the renewal of natural capital and attempts to move to sustainable development have been a major focus of development agencies. This is of particular concern in rainforest regions, which hold most of the Earth's natural biodiversity—irreplaceable genetic natural capital. Conservation of natural resources is the major focus of Natural Capitalism, environmentalism, the ecology movement, and Green parties. Some view this depletion as a major source of social unrest and conflicts in developing nations.

Environmental Policy

ENVIRONMENTAL POLICY is concerned with the sustainability of the Earth. The concern of environmental policy is the preservation of a region, habitat, or ecosystem. Because humans, both individually and within communities, rely upon the environment to sustain human life, social and environmental policies must be mutually supportable.

NATURAL RESOURCES: naturally occurring substances considered valuable in their natural form

The rate of sustainable use of a renewable resource is determined by the replacement rate and amount of standing stock of that particular resource.

RENEWABLE RESOURCES: living resources, which can restock themselves if they are not over-harvested

NONRENEWABLE RESOURCES: natural resources that cannot be regenerated in the same proportion in which they are used

ENVIRONMENTAL POLICY: concerned with the sustainability of the Earth and the preservation of a region, a habitat, or an ecosystem

---

If modern societies have no understanding of the limitations of natural resources or how their actions affect the environment, and they act without regard for the sustainability of the Earth, it will become impossible for the Earth to sustain human existence. For centuries, social, economic, and political policies have ignored the impact of human existence and human civilization upon the environment. Human civilization has disrupted the ecological balance, contributed to the extinction of animal and plant species, and destroyed ecosystems through uncontrolled harvesting.

In an age of global warming and unprecedented demand on natural resources, social and environmental policies must become increasingly interdependent if the planet is to continue to support life and human civilization.

Sample Test Question and Rationale

(Average)

1. **States that are near the Rocky Mountains, such as Montana, have exceptional trout fishing because of which of the following:**

   A. Lakes in mountain regions have warm water that trout enjoy

   B. Mountain regions are the only places that have large numbers of the aquatic insects trout like to eat

   C. There are fewer people in these areas, so the fishing pressure is light

   D. Trout thrive in the cold, clean rivers found in mountainous regions

Answer: D. Trout thrive in the cold, clean rivers found in mountainous regions

Trout cannot live in warm water. Aquatic insects eaten by trout are found in rivers all over the United States, not only in mountain regions. It is true that some mountain regions have low human populations, but the cold, clean water originating in mountain snowmelt is the best environment for trout.

COMPETENCY 10
WORLD HISTORY

SKILL 10.1 **Knows the major contributions of classical civilizations** *(e.g., Egypt, Greece, Rome)*

Mesopotamia

The ancient civilization of the Sumerians invented the wheel; developed irrigation through the use of canals, dikes, and devices for raising water; devised the system of cuneiform writing; learned to divide time; and built large boats for trade. The Babylonians devised the famous Code of Hammurabi, a code of laws.

Egypt

Egypt made numerous significant contributions, including construction of the great pyramids, development of hieroglyphic writing, preservation of bodies after death, creation of paper from papyrus, developments in arithmetic and geometry, invention of the method of counting in groups of 1-10 (the decimal system), completion of a solar calendar, and formation of the foundation for science and astronomy.

The earliest historical record of the Kush civilization is in Egyptian sources, which describe a region upstream from the first cataract of the Nile as "wretched." This civilization was characterized by a settled way of life in fortified mud-brick villages. The people subsisted on hunting and fishing, herding cattle, and gathering grain. Skeletal remains suggest that they were a blend of Negroid and Mediterranean peoples. This civilization appears to be the second oldest in Africa (after Egypt).

During the period of Egypt's Old Kingdom (ca. 2700–2180 BCE), this civilization was essentially a diffused version of Egyptian culture and religion. When Egypt came under the domination of the Hyksos, Kush reached its greatest power and cultural energy (1700–1500 BCE). When the Hyksos were eventually expelled from Egypt, the New Kingdom brought Kush back under Egyptian colonial control.

China

China is considered by some historians to be the oldest uninterrupted civilization in the world; it was in existence at about the same time as the ancient civilizations found in Egypt, Mesopotamia, and the Indus Valley. The Chinese studied nature and weather; stressed the importance of education, family, and a strong central government; followed the religions of Buddhism, Confucianism, and Taoism; and invented such things as gunpowder, paper, printing, and the magnetic compass. China began building the Great Wall, practiced crop rotation and terrace farming, increased the importance of the silk industry, and developed caravan routes across Central Asia for extensive trade. The Chinese also increased proficiency in rice cultivation and developed a written language based on drawings or pictographs.

Persia

The ancient Persians developed an alphabet; contributed the religions and philosophies of Zoroastrianism, Mithraism, and gnosticism; and allowed conquered peoples to retain their own customs, laws, and religions.

Greece

The classical civilization of Greece reached the highest levels of human achievement based on the foundations already laid by such ancient groups as the Egyptians, Phoenicians, Minoans, and Mycenaeans.

Among the more important contributions of Greece was the Greek alphabet derived from the Phoenician letters, which formed the basis for the Roman alphabet and our present-day alphabet. Extensive trading and colonization resulted in the spread of Greek civilization. The love of sports, with emphasis on a physically sound body, led to the tradition of the Olympic Games. Greece was responsible for the rise of independent, strong city-states. Other important areas that the Greeks are credited with influencing include drama, epic and lyric poetry, fables, myths centered on their many gods and goddesses, science, astronomy, medicine, mathematics, philosophy, art, architecture, and the recording of historical events.

The conquests of Alexander the Great spread Greek ideas to the lands he conquered and brought many ideas from Asia to the Greek world. The desire to learn as much about the world as possible was a major objective of his conquests.

Ancient Greece is often called the cradle of western civilization because of the enormous influence it had, not only on the time in which it flourished, but on western culture ever since.

Early Greek institutions have survived for thousands of years and have influenced the entire world. The Athenian form of democracy, with all citizens having an equal vote in their own government, is a philosophy upon which all modern democracies are based. In the United States, the Greek tradition of democracy was honored in the choice of Greek architectural styles for the nation's government buildings. The modern Olympic Games are a revival of an ancient Greek tradition, and many of the events are re-creations of original contests.

The works of the Greek epic poet Homer, author of the *Iliad* and the *Odyssey*, are considered the earliest in western literature, and are still read and taught today. The tradition of the theater was born in Greece, with the plays of Aristophanes and others. In philosophy, Aristotle developed an approach to learning that emphasized observation and thought, and Socrates and Plato contemplated the nature of being and the origins and ideals of government and political relations. Greek mythology has been the source of inspiration for literature into the present day.

In the field of mathematics, Pythagoras and Euclid laid the foundations of geometry and Archimedes calculated the value of *pi*. Herodotus and Thucydides were the first to apply research and interpretation to written history.

In the arts, Greek sensibilities were held as perfect forms which others might strive for. In sculpture, the Greeks achieved an idealistic aesthetic that had not been perfected before that time.

The Greek civilization served as an inspiration to the Roman Republic, which followed in its tradition of democracy and was directly influenced by its achievements in art and science. Later, during the Renaissance, European scholars and artists would rediscover ancient Greece's love for dedicated inquiry and artistic expression, leading to a surge in scientific discoveries and advancements in the arts.

Rome

The ancient civilization of Rome owed much to the Greeks. Romans admired Greek architecture and arts, and built upon these traditions to create a distinct tradition of their own that would influence the western world for centuries.

The ancient civilization of Rome lasted approximately a thousand years (including the periods of the Roman Republic and the Roman Empire), although its influence on Europe and its history was felt for a much longer period. There was a sharp contrast between the curious, imaginative, inquisitive Greeks and the

The ancient civilization of Rome lasted approximately a thousand years.

practical, simple, down-to-earth Romans, who spread and preserved the ideas of ancient Greece and other cultural groups. The accomplishments of the Romans are numerous, but their greatest contributions included language, engineering, building, law, government, roads, trade, and the Pax Romana. The Pax Romana was the long period of peace allowing free travel and trade, spreading people, cultures, goods, and ideas all over a vast area of the known world.

In government, the Romans took the Athenian concept of democracy and built it into a complex system of a representative government that included executive, legislative, and judicial functions. In the arts, Romans created a realistic approach to portraiture, in contrast to the more idealized form of the Greeks. In architecture, Rome borrowed directly from the Greek tradition, but also developed the dome and the arch, allowing for larger and more dramatic forms. The Romans continued the Greek tradition of learning, often employing Greeks to educate their children.

The Roman Republic flourished in the centuries leading up to the advent of the Christian era. An organized bureaucracy and active political population provided elite Roman citizens with the means to ascend to positions of considerable authority. During the first century BCE, Gaius Julius Caesar ambitiously began to gather support among the ruling authorities of the Republic, eventually being named one of the two consuls who were elected annually. Caesar was ultimately named dictator for life, and was the transitional leader between the Roman Republic and what would become the Roman Empire.

Like the Republic, the Roman Empire also looked to the east, to Greece, for inspiration. The Macedonian conqueror Alexander, who had unified Greece and introduced the culture throughout the eastern world, provided many Roman emperors with a role model.

The Roman Empire extended through much of Europe, and Roman culture extended with it. Everywhere the Romans went, they built roads, established cities, and left their mark on the local population. The Roman language, Latin, spread as well and was transformed into the Romance languages of French and Spanish. The Roman alphabet, which was based on the Greek transformation of Phoenician letters, was adopted throughout the empire and is still used today.

The empire itself has served as a model for modern government, especially in federal systems such as that found in the United States. The eventual decline and fall of the empire has been a subject that has occupied historians for centuries.

Sample Test Questions and Rationale

(Average)

1. **Our present-day alphabet comes from which of the following:**

   A. Cuneiform

   B. The Greek alphabet

   C. Hieroglyphic writing

   D. Hebrew Scriptures

   Answer: B. The Greek alphabet

   Cuneiform was introduced by the Sumerians. Hieroglyphics were created by the Egyptians. Hebrew Scriptures were introduced by the Hebrew people.

(Rigorous)

2. **What is the "Pax Romana"?**

   A. Long period of peace allowing free travel and trade, spreading people, cultures, goods, and ideas all over the world

   B. A period of war where the Romans expanded their empire

   C. The Roman government

   D. A time where the government was over-ruled

   Answer: A. Long period of peace allowing free travel and trade, spreading people, cultures, goods, and ideas all over the world

   The "Pax Romana" was a time when the Romans were peaceful and wanted to spread their culture all over the world.

SKILL 10.2 Understands twentieth-century developments and transformations in World history

During the twentieth century, the world witnessed unprecedented strides in communications, a major expansion of international trade, and significant international diplomatic and military activity, including two world wars.

The rise of nationalism in Europe at the end of the nineteenth century led to a series of alliances and agreements among European nations. These agreements eventually led to the First World War, as nations called on their military allies to provide assistance and defense.

A new model of international relations was proposed following the devastation of World War I, one based on the mission to preserve peace. The League of Nations was formed to promote this peace, but it ultimately failed, having no way to enforce its resolutions. When Germany, led by Adolph Hitler, rebelled against the restrictions placed on it following World War I and began a campaign of military expansion through Europe, the Second World War ensued. Great

> *During the twentieth century, the world witnessed unprecedented strides in communications, a major expansion of international trade, and significant international diplomatic and military activity, including two world wars.*

Britain, the United States, and other allied nations combined forces to defeat Germany and the Axis powers.

Taking a lesson from the failure of the League of Nations, the world's nations organized the United Nations, an international assembly given the authority to arrange and enforce international resolutions.

World War II left Europe in ruins. As a result, the United States and the Soviet Union emerged as the two major world powers. Although allies in the war, tension arose between the two powers as the United States engaged in a policy of halting the spread of communism sponsored by the Soviets and China. The United States and the Soviet Union never engaged in direct military conflict during this cold war, but they were both involved in protracted conflicts in Korea and Vietnam. The threat of nuclear war increased as each power produced more and more weapons in an extended arms race. The threat of the spread of nuclear weapons largely diminished after the fall of the Soviet Union in the early 1990s, which ended the cold war.

In Asia, new economies matured and the formerly tightly-controlled Chinese market became more open to foreign investment, increasing China's influence as a major economic power. In Europe, the European Union made a bold move to a common currency, the euro, in a successful effort to consolidate the region's economic strength. In South America, countries such as Brazil and Venezuela showed growth despite political unrest, as Argentina suffered a near complete collapse of its economy. As the technology sector expanded, so did the economy of India, where high-tech companies found a highly educated workforce.

Conflict between the Muslim world and the United States increased during the last decade of the twentieth century, culminating in a terrorist attack on New York City and Washington, D.C., in 2001. These attacks, sponsored by the radical group Al Qaeda, prompted a military invasion by the United States of Afghanistan, where the group is based. Shortly afterwards, the United States, England, and several smaller countries addressed further instability in the region by ousting Iraqi dictator Saddam Hussein in a military campaign. In the eastern Mediterranean, tension between Israelis and Palestinians continued to build, regularly erupting into violence.

Sample Test Question and Rationale

(Rigorous)

1. **The Cold War involved which two countries that both emerged as world powers?**

   A. China and Japan

   B. The United States and the Soviet Union

   C. England and Brazil

   D. Afghanistan and the United States

Answer: B. The United States and the Soviet Union

After World War II, the United States and the Soviet Union constantly competed in space exploration and the race to develop nuclear weapons.

SKILL 10.3 **Understands the role of cross-cultural comparisons in World history instruction**

Maintaining an awareness of the variations among cultures is crucial to understanding world history. Each country or group has its own perspective on key events. Some cultures developed in isolation, while others developed in direct relation to others. Understanding these differences and similarities allows for a fuller understanding of historical events.

CULTURAL IDENTITY is the identification of individuals or groups as they are influenced by their belonging to a particular group or culture. This refers to the sense of who one is, what values are important, and what racial or ethnic characteristics are important in one's self-understanding and manner of interacting with the world and with others. In a nation such as the United States, with a well-deserved reputation as a "melting pot," the attachment to cultural identities can become a divisive factor in communities and societies. Cosmopolitanism, its alternative, tends to blur those cultural differences in the creation of a shared new culture.

> **CULTURAL IDENTITY:** the identification of individuals or groups as they are influenced by their belonging to a particular group or culture

Throughout history, groups have defined themselves and/or assimilated into the larger population to varying degrees. In order for a society to function as a cohesive and unifying force, there must be some degree of enculturation of all groups. The alternative is a competing, and often conflicting, collection of subgroups that are not able to cohere into a society. The failure to assimilate often results in culture wars as values and lifestyles come into conflict.

> *In order for a society to function as a cohesive and unifying force, there must be some degree of enculturation of all groups.*

Cross-cultural exchanges, however, can enrich every involved group of persons with the discovery of shared values and needs, as well as an appreciation for the unique cultural characteristics of each. Historically, as the main civilizations grew and came into contact with each other, cultural exchanges took place at an increasing rate. Nevertheless, distinct religions, governments, and technological differences existed among the major civilizations during the first millennium CE. Such patterns of exchange and difference are woven throughout history and continue into the twenty-first century.

Sample Test Question and Rationale

(Rigorous)

1. **Cultural diffusion is:**

   A. The process that individuals and societies go through in changing their behavior and organization to cope with social, economic, and environmental pressures

   B. The complete disappearance of a culture

   C. The exchange or adoption of cultural features when two cultures come into regular direct contact

   D. The movement of cultural ideas or materials between populations independent of the movement of those populations

Answer: D. The movement of cultural ideas or materials between populations independent of the movement of those populations

By definition, cultural diffusion is the movement of cultural ideas or materials between populations independent of the movement of those populations.

COMPETENCY 11
UNITED STATES HISTORY

> **SKILL 11.1** Knows European exploration and colonization in United States history and growth and expansion of the United States

Colonists from England, France, Holland, Sweden, and Spain all settled in North America on lands once frequented by Native Americans. Spanish colonies were mainly in the south, French colonies were mainly in the extreme north and in the middle of the continent, and the rest of the European colonies were in the northeast and along the Atlantic coast. These colonists got along with their new neighbors with varying degrees of success.

The French colonists seemed the most willing to work with the Native Americans. Even though their pursuit of animals to fill the growing demand for the fur trade was overpowering, they managed to find a way to maintain a relative peace with their new neighbors; the French and Native Americans even fought on the same side of the war against England. The Dutch and Swedish colonists were interested mostly in surviving in their new homes. However, they didn't last long in their struggles against England.

The English and Spanish colonists had the worst relations with the Native Americans, mainly because the Europeans made a habit of taking land, signing and then breaking treaties, massacring, and otherwise abusing their new neighbors. The Native Americans were only too happy to share their agriculture and jewelry-making secrets with the Europeans; what they got in return was grief and deceit. The term Manifest Destiny meant nothing to the Native Americans, who believed that they lived on land loaned to them by the gods above.

The colonies were generally divided into three regions: New England, Middle Atlantic, and Southern. The culture of each region was distinct and affected attitudes, ideas about politics, religion, and economic activities. The geography of each region also contributed to the colonies' unique characteristics.

The New England Colonies

The NEW ENGLAND COLONIES consisted of Massachusetts, Rhode Island, Connecticut, and New Hampshire. Life in these colonies was centered on the towns. Each family farmed its own plot of land, but a short summer growing season and limited amount of good soil gave rise to other economic activities such as manufacturing, fishing, shipbuilding, and trade. The vast majority of the settlers had similar origins, most having arrived from England and Scotland. Towns were carefully planned and laid out in similar fashion. The form of government was the town meeting where all adult males met to make the laws. The legislative body, the General Court, consisted of an upper and a lower house.

> **NEW ENGLAND COLONIES:** consisted of Massachusetts, Rhode Island, Connecticut, and New Hampshire

The Middle Atlantic Colonies

The MIDDLE or MIDDLE ATLANTIC COLONIES included New York, New Jersey, Pennsylvania, Delaware, and Maryland. New York and New Jersey were at one time the Dutch colony of New Netherland, and Delaware was at one time New Sweden. These five colonies, from their beginnings, were considered "melting

> **MIDDLE OR MIDDLE ATLANTIC COLONIES:** included New York, New Jersey, Pennsylvania, Delaware, and Maryland

pots," with settlers from many different nations and backgrounds. The main economic activity was farming; the settlers were scattered over the countryside cultivating rather large farms. The Native Americans were not as much of a threat as they were in New England so the colonists did not have to settle in small farming villages. The soil was very fertile, the land was gently rolling, and a milder climate provided a longer growing season. These farms produced a large surplus of food, not only for the colonists themselves but also for sale. This colonial region became known as the "breadbasket" of the New World, and the New York and Philadelphia seaports were constantly filled with ships being loaded with meat, flour, and other foodstuffs for the West Indies and England.

Other economic activities in these colonies included shipbuilding, iron mining, and the production of paper, glass, and textiles in factories. The legislative body in Pennsylvania was unicameral (consisting of one house). In the other four colonies, the legislative body had two houses. Units of local government were found in counties and towns.

The Southern Colonies

SOUTHERN COLONIES:
Virginia, North and South Carolina, and Georgia

Virginia was the first permanent successful English colony and Georgia was the last.

The **SOUTHERN COLONIES** were Virginia, North and South Carolina, and Georgia. Virginia was the first permanent successful English colony and Georgia was the last. The year 1619 was a very important year in the history of Virginia as well as the United States, with the occurrence of three significant events:

- Sixty women were sent to Virginia to marry and establish families

- Twenty Africans, the first of thousands, arrived

- The Virginia colonists were granted the right to self-government

The granting of the right to self-government was the most important event. The colonists immediately elected their own representatives to the House of Burgesses—their own legislative body.

The major economic activity in this region was farming. Here too the soil was very fertile, and the climate was mild, with an even longer growing season than farther north. The large plantations, eventually requiring large numbers of slaves, were found in the coastal or tidewater areas. Although the wealthy slave-owning planters set the pattern of life in this region, most of the people lived inland, away from coastal areas. They were small farmers and few, if any, owned slaves.

The settlers in these four colonies came from diverse backgrounds and cultures. Virginia was colonized mostly by people from England, while Georgia was started as a haven for debtors from English prisons. Pioneers from Virginia settled in North Carolina, while South Carolina welcomed people from England and

Scotland, French Protestants, Germans, and emigrants from islands in the West Indies.

Products from farms and plantations included rice, tobacco, indigo, cotton, some corn, and wheat. Other economic activities in the southern colonies included lumber and naval stores (tar, pitch, rosin, and turpentine) from the pine forests and fur trade on the frontier. Cities such as Savannah and Charleston were important seaports and trading centers.

Sample Test Questions and Rationale

(Rigorous)

1. The economic activities of the Middle Atlantic colonies included:

    A. Manufacturing

    B. Fishing

    C. Iron mining

    D. Melting pots

    Answer: C. Iron mining

    Iron mining is mentioned as an economic activity of the Middle Atlantic colonies. Manufacturing and fishing occurred in New England. "Melting pot" is an expression used to describe the wide variety of settlers in the Middle Atlantic colonies, not an expression denoting an economic activity.

(Average)

2. English and Spanish colonists took what from Native Americans?

    A. Land

    B. Water rights

    C. Money

    D. Religious beliefs

    Answer: A. Land

    The settlers took a lot of land from Native Americans. Water rights, money, and religious beliefs were not areas of contention between the European settlers and the Native Americans.

SKILL 11.2 **Knows about the American Revolution and the founding of the nation in United States History**

Causes of the War of Independence

With the end of the French and Indian War (the Seven Years' War), England decided to reassert control over the colonies in America. The government particularly needed the revenue from the control of trade to pay for the recent war and to defend the new territory obtained as a result of the war.

English leaders decided to impose a tax that would pay for the military defense of the American lands. The colonists rejected this idea for two reasons: 1) They were undergoing an economic recession, and 2) They believed it unjust to be taxed unless they had representation in Parliament.

England passed a series of laws that provoked fierce opposition:

- The Proclamation Act prohibited English settlement beyond the Appalachian Mountains to appease the Native Americans

- The Sugar Act imposed a tax on foreign molasses, sugar, and other goods imported into the colonies

- The Currency Act prohibited colonial governments from issuing paper money

Opposition arose in Massachusetts. Leaders denounced "taxation without representation" and a boycott was organized against imported English goods. The movement rapidly spread to other colonies.

The Stamp Act

The Stamp Act placed a tax on newspapers, legal documents, licenses, almanacs, and playing cards. This was the first instance of an "internal" tax on the colonies. In response, the colonists formed secret groups called the "Sons of Liberty" and staged riots against the agents who collected the taxes and marked items with a special stamp.

In October of 1765, representatives of nine colonies met in the Stamp Act Congress. They drafted resolutions stating their reasons for opposing the act and sent them to England. Merchants throughout the colonies applied pressure with a large boycott of imported English goods. The Stamp Act was repealed three months later.

The Townshend Acts

England then had a dual concern: to generate revenue and to regain control of the colonists. They passed the Townshend Acts in 1767. These acts placed taxes on lead, glass, paint, paper, and tea.

This led to another very successful boycott of English goods. England responded by limiting the tax to tea. This ended the boycotts of everything except tea.

The situation between colonists and British troops was becoming increasingly strained. Despite a skirmish in New York and the Boston Massacre in 1770, tensions abated over the next few years.

The Boston Tea Party

The Tea Act of 1773 gave the British East India Company a monopoly on sales of tea. The colonists responded with the Boston Tea Party. England responded with the Coercive Acts (called the Intolerable Acts by the colonists) in 1774. This closed the port of Boston, changed the charter of the Massachusetts colony, and suppressed town meetings.

Continental Congress

Eleven colonies sent delegates to the First Continental Congress in 1774. The group issued the Declaration of Rights and Grievances, which vowed allegiance to the king but protested the right of Parliament to tax the colonies. The boycotts resumed at the same time.

Massachusetts mobilized its colonial militia in anticipation of difficulties with England. The British troops attempted to seize their weapons and ammunition. The result was two clashes with minutemen at Lexington and Concord. The Second Continental Congress met a month later. Many of the delegates recommended a declaration of independence from Britain. The group established an army and commissioned George Washington as its commander.

British forces attacked patriot strongholds at Breed's Hill and Bunker Hill. Although the colonists withdrew, the the British lost nearly half of their army. The next month King George III declared the American colonies to be in a state of rebellion. The war quickly began in earnest. On July 3, 1776, British General Howe arrived in New York harbor with 10,000 troops to prepare for an attack on the city. The following day, the Second Continental Congress accepted the final draft of the Declaration of Independence by unanimous vote.

Colonial Army versus British Army

Although the colonial army was quite small compared to the British army, and lacked formal military training, the colonists had learned a new method of warfare from the Native Americans. To be sure, many battles were fought in the traditional style of two lines of soldiers facing off and firing weapons, but the advantage the patriots had was the understanding of guerilla warfare—fighting from behind trees and other defenses.

Founding of the Nation

When the war began, the colonies began to establish state governments. To a significant extent, the government that was defined for the new nation was intentionally weak. The colonies/states feared centralized government; however, the lack of continuity between the individual governments was confusing and economically damaging.

Sample Test Question and Rationale

(Average)

1. **All of the following were causes of the American Revolution EXCEPT:**

   A. The Tea Act of 1773

   B. The Stamp Act

   C. The colonists were forced to house English troops

   D. The colonists wanted more schools

Answer: D. The colonists wanted more schools

The colonists were not concerned about the number of schools they had, and this was not a factor in the American Revolution.

SKILL 11.3 **Knows the major events and developments in United States history from founding to present** *(e.g., westward expansion, industrialization, Great Depression)*

The Constitutional Convention of 1787 devised an entirely new form of government and outlined it in the Constitution of the United States. The Constitution was ratified quickly and took effect in 1789. Concerns that had been raised in or by the states regarding civil liberties and states' rights led to the immediate adoption of twelve amendments to the Constitution; the first ten are known as the Bill of Rights.

The American Political System

It is important to realize that political parties are never mentioned in the U.S. Constitution.

It is important to realize that political parties are never mentioned in the U.S. Constitution. In fact, George Washington himself warned against the creation of "factions" in American politics that cause "jealousies and false alarms" as well as the damage they could cause to the body politic. Thomas Jefferson echoed this warning, yet he would come to lead a party himself.

Americans had good reason to fear the emergence of political parties. They had witnessed how parties worked in Great Britain. Parties, called "factions" in Britain, were made up of a few people who schemed to win favors from the government, and who were more interested in their own personal profits and advantages than in the public good. Thus, the new American leaders were interested in keeping factions from forming. It was, ironically, disagreements between two of Washington's chief advisors, Thomas Jefferson and Alexander Hamilton, which spurred the formation of the first political parties in the newly formed United States of America.

Formation of the two-party system

The two parties that developed in the early 1790s were led by Jefferson as the secretary of state and Hamilton as the secretary of the treasury. Jefferson and Hamilton were different in many ways, including their views on what should be the proper form of government of the United States. This difference helped to shape the parties that formed around them.

Hamilton wanted the federal government to be stronger than the state governments. Jefferson believed that the state governments should be stronger. Hamilton supported the creation of the first bank of the United States; Jefferson opposed it because he felt that it gave too much power to wealthy investors who would help to run it. Jefferson interpreted the Constitution strictly; he argued that nowhere did the Constitution give the federal government the power to create a national bank.

Hamilton interpreted the Constitution much more loosely. He pointed out that the Constitution gave Congress the power to make all laws "necessary and proper" to carry out its duties. He reasoned that since Congress had the right to collect taxes, then Congress had the right to create the bank.

Hamilton also wanted the government to encourage economic growth. He favored the growth of trade, manufacturing, and the rise of cities as necessary parts of economic growth. He favored business leaders and mistrusted the common people. Jefferson believed that the common people, especially farmers, were the backbone of the nation. He thought that the rise of big cities and manufacturing would corrupt American life.

Before long, leaders in other states began to organize support for either Jefferson or Hamilton. Jefferson's supporters called themselves Democratic-Republicans (often this was shortened to just Republicans, though in actuality this was the forerunner of today's Democratic Party). Hamilton and his supporters were known as Federalists, because they favored a strong federal government. The Federalists had the support of the merchants and shipowners in the Northeast and some planters in the South. Small farmers, craftspeople, and some of the wealthier landowners supported Jefferson and the Democratic-Republicans.

By the time Washington retired from office in 1796, the new political parties would come to play an important role in choosing his successor. Each party would put up its own candidates for office. The election of 1796 was the first one in which political parties played a role. By the beginning of the 1800s, the Federalist Party, torn by internal divisions, began suffering a decline. This was exacerbated in 1800 when Thomas Jefferson was elected president. After the leader of the Federalist Party, Alexander Hamilton, was killed in 1804 in a duel with Aaron Burr, the Federalist Party began to collapse. By 1816, after losing a string of important elections (Jefferson was reelected in 1804, and James Madison, a Democratic-Republican was elected in 1808), the Federalist Party ceased to be an effective political force, and soon passed off the national stage.

By the late 1820s, new political parties had grown up. The Democratic-Republican Party, or simply the Republican Party, had been the major party for many years, but differences within the party about the direction the country was headed caused a split after 1824. Those who favored strong national growth took the name Whigs after a similar party in Great Britain and united around then-President John Quincy Adams. Many businesspeople in the Northeast as well as some wealthy planters in the South supported it.

Those who favored slower growth and were more worker- and small farmer-oriented went on to form the new Democratic Party, with Andrew Jackson acting as its first leader (he also became its first president). This was the forerunner of today's party of the same name.

In the mid-1850s, the slavery issue was beginning to heat up; in 1854, those opposed to slavery, the Whigs, along with some Northern Democrats, united to form the Republican Party. Before the Civil War, the Democratic Party was more heavily represented in the South and was thus primarily pro-slavery.

> By the time of the Civil War, the present configuration of the major political parties had been formed.

Therefore, by the time of the Civil War, the present configuration of the major political parties had been formed. Though there would sometimes be drastic changes in ideology and platforms over the years, no other political parties would manage to gain enough strength to seriously challenge the "Big Two" parties.

In fact, they have shown themselves adaptable to changing times. In many instances, they have managed to shut out other parties by simply adapting their platforms, such as in the 1930s during the Great Depression and in the years immediately preceding. The Democratic Party adapted much of the Socialist Party platform and, under Franklin Roosevelt, put much of it into effect, thus managing to eliminate the Socialist Party as a serious threat.

Since the Civil War, no other political party has managed to gain enough support to either elect a substantial number of members of Congress or to elect a president. Some have come closer than others, but barring unforeseen circumstances, the absolute monopoly on national political debate seems secure in the hands of the Republican and Democratic parties.

Westward Movement

In the United States, territorial expansion occurred in the expansion westward under the banner of Manifest Destiny. In addition, the United States was involved in the War with Mexico, the Spanish-American War, and the support of the Latin American colonies of Spain in their revolt for independence. In Latin America, the Spanish colonies were successful in their fight for independence and self-government.

After the United States purchased the Louisiana Territory, Jefferson appointed Captains Meriwether Lewis and William Clark to explore it, to find out exactly what had been bought. The expedition, called the Corps of Discovery, eventually included a slave named York, a dog, forty young men, a female Shoshone Indian named Sacagawea, and her infant son. They went all the way to the Pacific Ocean, returning two years later with maps, journals, and artifacts. This led the way for future explorers to discover more about the territory; it also resulted in the westward movement and the later belief in the doctrine of Manifest Destiny.

Initially, the United States and Britain shared the Oregon country. By the 1840s, with the increase in the free and slave populations and the demand of the settlers for control and government by the United States, the conflict had to be resolved. In a treaty signed in 1846 by both nations, a peaceful resolution occurred, with Britain giving up its claims south of the 49th parallel.

In the American Southwest, the results were exactly the opposite. Spain had claimed this area since the 1540s, had spread northward from Mexico City, and, in the 1700s, had established missions, forts, villages, towns, and very large ranches. After the purchase of the Louisiana Territory in 1803, Americans began moving into Spanish territory. A few hundred American families in what is now Texas were allowed to live there but had to agree to become loyal subjects of Spain.

In 1821, Mexico successfully revolted against Spanish rule, won independence, and chose to be more tolerant of American settlers and traders. The Mexican government encouraged and allowed extensive trade and settlement, especially in Texas. Many of the new settlers were southerners who brought their slaves with them. Slavery was outlawed in Mexico and technically illegal in Texas, although the Mexican government often looked the other way.

Friction increased between land-hungry Americans swarming into western lands and the Mexican government that controlled these lands. The clash was not only political but also cultural and economic. The Spanish influence permeated all parts of southwestern life: law, language, architecture, and customs. By this time, the doctrine of Manifest Destiny was in the hearts and on the lips of those seeking new areas of settlement and a new life. Americans were demanding U.S. control of not only the Mexican Territory but also of Oregon. Although peaceful negotiations with Great Britain secured Oregon, it took two years of war to gain control of the southwestern United States.

To make tensions worse, the Mexican government owed debts to U.S. citizens whose property had been damaged or destroyed during its struggle for independence from Spain. By the time war broke out in 1845, Mexico had not paid its war debts. The government was weak, corrupt, irresponsible, torn by revolutions, and in poor financial condition. Mexico was also bitter over American expansion into Texas and the 1836 revolution, which resulted in Texas's independence. In the 1844 presidential election, the Democrats pushed for the annexation of Texas and Oregon and after winning, they started the procedure to admit Texas to the Union.

When statehood was granted, diplomatic relations between the United States and Mexico were ended. President Polk wanted U.S. control of the entire Southwest, from Texas to the Pacific Ocean. He sent a diplomatic mission with an offer to purchase New Mexico and upper California, but the Mexican government refused to even receive the diplomats. Consequently, in 1846, each nation claimed aggression on the part of the other and war was declared. The treaty signed in 1848 and a subsequent treaty in 1853 completed the southwestern boundary of the United States, reaching to the Pacific Ocean, as President Polk wished.

The impact of the entire westward movement resulted in the completion of the borders of the present-day contiguous United States. Overall, the major contributing factors included the bloody War with Mexico; the ever-growing controversy over slave versus free states, which affected the balance of power in the U.S. Congress, especially the Senate; and the Civil War.

Civil War

The Civil War began through a series of events that spanned decades. Tensions between the southern states and the northern states were increasing; in 1833, Congress lowered tariffs, this time to a level acceptable to South Carolina, which had been growing increasingly dissatisfied with the federal government. Although President Jackson believed in states' rights, he also firmly believed in and was determined to preserve the Union. Through Jackson's efforts, a constitutional crisis had been averted, but sectional divisions were getting deeper and more pronounced. The abolition movement was also growing rapidly, becoming an important issue in the North. The slavery issue was at the root of every problem, crisis, event, decision, and struggle from then on.

The next crisis involved the issue concerning Texas. By 1836, Texas was an independent republic with its own constitution. During its fight for independence, Americans were sympathetic to and supportive of the Texans, and some individuals recruited volunteers who crossed into Texas to help the struggle. Problems arose when the state petitioned Congress for statehood. Texas wanted to allow slavery, but Northerners in Congress opposed admission to the Union because it would disrupt the balance between free and slave states and give Southerners in Congress increased influence.

A few years later, Congress took up consideration of new territories between Missouri and present-day Idaho. Again, heated debate over permitting slavery in these areas flared up. Those opposed to slavery used the Missouri Compromise to prove their point showing that the land being considered for territories was part of the area the Compromise had designated as banned for slavery.

On May 25, 1854, Congress passed the infamous Kansas-Nebraska Act, which nullified the provision creating the territories of Kansas and Nebraska. This allowed the people of these two territories to decide for themselves whether or not to permit slavery there. Feelings were so deep and divided that any further attempts to compromise met with little success. Political and social turmoil swirled everywhere. Kansas was called "Bleeding Kansas" because of the extreme violence and bloodshed throughout the territory due to the two governments that existed there: one pro-slavery and the other anti-slavery.

Dred Scott decision

In 1857, the Supreme Court handed down a decision guaranteed to cause explosions throughout the country. Dred Scott was a slave whose owner had taken him from slave state Missouri, then to free state Illinois, into Minnesota Territory (free under the provisions of the Missouri Compromise), and finally back to slave state Missouri. Abolitionists pursued the issue by presenting a court case, stating that since Scott had lived in a free state and free territory, he was in actuality a free man.

Two lower courts ruled before the Supreme Court became involved: one ruling in favor and one against. The Supreme Court decided that residing in a free state and free territory did not make Scott a free man because Scott (like all other slaves) was not a U.S. citizen or a state citizen of Missouri. Therefore, he did not have the right to sue in state or federal courts. The Court went a step further and ruled that the old Missouri Compromise was now unconstitutional because Congress did not have the power to prohibit slavery in the Territories.

Lincoln-Douglas debates

In 1858, Abraham Lincoln and Stephen A. Douglas were running for the office of U.S. Senator from Illinois; they participated in a series of debates that directly affected the outcome of the 1860 presidential election. Douglas, a Democrat, was up for reelection and knew that if he won that race, he had a good chance of becoming president in 1860. Lincoln, a Republican, was not an abolitionist but he believed that slavery was morally wrong. He firmly believed in and supported the Republican Party principle that slavery must not be allowed to extend any further. The final straw came with the election of Lincoln to the presidency the next year. Due to a split in the Democratic Party, there were four candidates from four political parties. With Lincoln receiving a minority of the popular vote and a majority of electoral votes, the southern states, one by one, voted to secede from the Union, as they had promised they would if Lincoln and the Republicans were victorious. The die was cast.

North versus South

Both sides quickly prepared for war. The North had more in its favor: a larger population; superiority in finances and transportation facilities; and manufacturing, agricultural, and natural resources. The North possessed most of the nation's gold, had about 92 percent of all industries, and had almost all the known supplies of copper, coal, iron, and various other minerals. Most of the nation's railroads were in the North and Midwest; men and supplies could be moved wherever needed and food could be transported from the farms of the Midwest to workers in the East as well as to soldiers on the battlefields. Trade with nations overseas could go on as usual due to control of the navy and the merchant fleet.

The Northern states numbered twenty-four and included Western (California and Oregon) and border (Maryland, Delaware, Kentucky, Missouri, and West Virginia) states. The Southern states numbered eleven and included South Carolina, Georgia, Florida, Alabama, Mississippi, Louisiana, Texas, Virginia, North Carolina, Tennessee, and Arkansas, making up the Confederacy.

Although outnumbered in population, the South was completely confident of victory. They knew that all they had to do was fight a defensive war and protect their own territory. The North had to invade and defeat an area almost the size of Western Europe. Another advantage of the South was that a number of its best officers had graduated from the U.S. Military Academy at West Point and had long years of army experience. Many had exercised varying degrees of command in the Indian Wars and the War with Mexico. Men from the South were conditioned to living outdoors and were more familiar with horses and firearms than men from northeastern cities. Since cotton was such an important crop, Southerners felt that British and French textile mills were so dependent on raw cotton that they would be forced to help the Confederacy in the war.

The South was winning the war until the Battle of Gettysburg, July 1–3, 1863. Until Gettysburg, Lincoln's commanders, McDowell and McClellan, were less than desirable; Burnside and Hooker, not what was needed. Lee, on the other hand, had many able officers; he depended heavily on Jackson and Stuart. Jackson died at Chancellorsville and was replaced by Longstreet. Lee decided to invade the North and depended on J. E. B. Stuart and his cavalry to keep him informed of the location of Union troops and their strengths.

The day after Gettysburg, on July 4, Vicksburg, Mississippi surrendered to Union General Ulysses Grant, thus severing the western Confederacy from the eastern part. In September 1863, the Confederacy won its last important victory at Chickamauga. In November, the Union victory at Chattanooga made it possible for Union troops to go into Alabama and Georgia, splitting the eastern Confederacy in two. Lincoln gave Grant command of all Northern armies in March of 1864. Grant led his armies into battles in Virginia while General Philip Sheridan and his cavalry did as much damage as possible. In a skirmish at a place called Yellow Tavern, Virginia, Sheridan's and Stuart's forces met, with Stuart being fatally wounded.

The Civil War took more American lives than any other American war in history, the South losing one-third of its soldiers in battle compared to about one-sixth for the North. More than half of the total deaths were caused by disease and the horrendous conditions of field hospitals. Destruction was pervasive in towns, farms, trade, and industry. After the war, the South had no voice in the political, social, and cultural affairs of the nation, lessening to a great degree the influence of the more traditional Southern ideals. The Northern Yankee Protestant ideals of hard work, education, and economic freedom became the standard of the United States and helped influence the development of the nation into a modern, industrial power.

> *The Civil War took more American lives than any other American war in history.*

Effects of the Civil War

The effects of the Civil War were tremendous. It changed the methods of waging war and has been called the first modern war. It introduced weapons and tactics which, when improved later, were used extensively in wars of the late 1800s and 1900s. Civil War soldiers were the first to fight in trenches, the first to fight under a unified command, and the first to wage a defense called "major cordon defense" (a strategy of advancing on all fronts). They were also the first to use repeating and breech-loading weapons. Observation balloons were first used during the war along with submarines, ironclad ships, and mines. Telegraphy and railroads were also first put to use during this time.

By executive proclamation and constitutional amendment, slavery was officially ended, although there remained deep prejudice and racism (still apparent today). The Union was preserved and the states were finally truly united. Sectionalism, especially in the area of politics, remained strong for another hundred years but not to the degree and with the violence that existed before 1861.

It has been noted that the Civil War may have been American democracy's greatest failure, as calm reason, which is basic to democracy, fell victim to human passion. Yet democracy did survive. The victory of the North established that no state has the right to end or leave the Union. Because of this unity, the United States became a major global power. It is important to remember that Lincoln never proposed to punish the South. He was most concerned with restoring the South to the Union in a program that was flexible and practical rather than rigid and unbending. In fact, he never really felt that the states had succeeded in leaving the Union, but rather that they had left the "family circle" for a short time.

The conclusion of the Civil War opened the floodgates for westward migration and the settlement of new land. The availability of cheap land and the expectation of great opportunities prompted thousands to travel across the Mississippi River and settle the Great Plains and California. The primary activities of the new western economy were farming, mining, and ranching. Both migration and the economy were facilitated by the expansion of the railroad and the completion of the transcontinental railroad in 1869.

> The conclusion of the Civil War opened the floodgates for westward migration and the settlement of new land.

Migration and settlement were not easy. As the settlers moved west, they encountered Native American tribes who believed they had a natural right to the lands upon which their ancestors had lived for generations. Resentment of the encroachment of new settlers was particularly strong among the tribes that had been ordered to relocate to "Indian Country" prior to 1860. Conflict was intense and frequent until 1867, when the government established two large tracts of land called "reservations" in Oklahoma and the Dakotas, to which all tribes would be confined.

With the war over, troops were sent west to enforce the relocation and reservation containment policies. There were frequent wars, particularly as white settlers attempted to move onto Native American lands and the tribes resisted their confinement.

Continuing conflict led to the passage of the Dawes Act of 1887. This was a recognition that confinement in reservations was not working. The law was intended to break up the Native American communities and bring about assimilation into white culture by deeding portions of the reservation lands to individual Native Americans who were expected to farm their land. The policy continued until 1934.

Armed resistance essentially came to an end by 1890. The surrender of Geronimo and the massacre at Wounded Knee led to a change of strategy by the Indians. Thereafter, the resistance strategy was to preserve their culture and traditions.

Industrialization

There was a marked degree of industrialization before and during the Civil War, but at war's end, there was not much industry in the United States. After the war, dramatic changes took place: machines replaced hand labor; extensive nation-wide railroad service facilitated the wider distribution of goods; new products were made available in large quantities; and large amounts of money from bankers and investors were available for the expansion of business operations.

American life was significantly affected by this phenomenal industrial growth. Cities became the centers of this new business activity, resulting in mass popula-tion movements and tremendous growth. This new boom in business resulted in huge fortunes for some Americans and extreme poverty for many others. The discontent this caused resulted in a number of new reform movements from which came measures controlling the power and size of big business and helping the poor.

The use of machines in industry enabled workers to produce a large quantity of goods much faster than they could by hand. With the increase in business, hundreds of workers were hired and assigned to perform specific jobs in the pro-duction process. This was a method of organization called the "division of labor"; because of its ability to increase the rate of production, businesses lowered prices for their products, making the products affordable for more people. As a result, sales and businesses were increasingly successful and profitable.

A great variety of new products and inventions became available, including the typewriter, the telephone, barbed wire, the electric light, the phonograph, and the gasoline-powered automobile. From this list, the one that had the greatest effect on America's economy was the automobile.

The increase in business and industry was greatly affected by the many rich natu-ral resources that were found throughout the nation. The industrial machines were powered by an abundant water supply. The construction industry as well as products made from wood depended heavily on lumber from the forests. Coal and iron ore in abundance were needed for the steel industry, which profited and increased from the use of steel in such things as skyscrapers, automobiles, bridges, railroad tracks, and machines. Other minerals such as silver, copper, and petro-leum played a large role in industrial growth (especially petroleum, from which gasoline was refined as fuel for the increasingly popular automobile).

The developments in communication, such as the telephone and telegraph, increased the efficiency and prosperity of big business. Steam-power generation, sophisticated manufacturing equipment, the ability to move about the country quickly by railroad, and the invention of the steam-powered tractor resulted in a

During the last forty years of the nineteenth century, inventors registered almost seven hundred thousand new patents.

phenomenal growth in industrial output. The new steel and oil industries provided a significant impetus to industrial growth and added thousands of new jobs. The inventive spirit of the time was a major force propelling the industrial revolution forward. This spirit led to an improvement in products, the development of new production processes and equipment, and even to the creation of entirely new industries. During the last forty years of the nineteenth century, inventors registered almost seven hundred thousand new patents.

One result of industrialization was the growth of the Labor Movement. There were numerous boycotts and strikes that often became violent when the police or the militias were called in. Labor and farmer organizations were created and became a political force. Industrialization also brought an influx of immigrants from Asia (particularly from China and Japan) and from Europe (particularly European Jews, the Irish, and Russians). High rates of immigration led to the creation of cultural communities within various cities, such as "little Russia" or "little Italy."

Industrialization also led to the overwhelming growth of cities as workers moved closer to their places of work. The economy was booming, but it was based on basic needs and luxury goods, for which there was to be only limited demand, especially during times of economic recession or depression.

The Great Depression and Its Aftermath

In September 1929, stock prices began to slip somewhat, yet people remained optimistic. On Monday, October 21, prices began to fall quickly. The volume traded was so high that the tickers were unable to keep up. Investors were frightened, and they started selling very quickly. This caused further collapse. For the next two days prices stabilized somewhat. On Black Thursday, October 24, 1929, prices plummeted again. By this time investors had lost confidence. On Friday and Saturday an attempt to stop the crash was made by some leading bankers. But on Monday the 28th, prices began to fall again, declining by 13% in one day. The next day, Black Tuesday, October 29, saw 16.4 million shares traded. Stock prices fell so far that at many times no one was willing to buy at any price.

Unemployment quickly reached 25 percent nationwide. People thrown out of their homes created makeshift domiciles of cardboard, scraps of wood, and tents. With unmasked reference to President Hoover, who was quite obviously overwhelmed by the situation and incompetent to deal with it, these communities were called Hoovervilles. Families stood in bread lines, rural workers left the dust bowl of the plains to search for work in California, and banks failed. More than one hundred thousand businesses failed between 1929 and 1932. The despair that swept the nation left an indelible scar on all who endured the Depression.

When the stock market crashed, businesses collapsed. Without demand for products, other businesses and industries collapsed. This set in motion a domino effect, bringing down the businesses and industries that provided raw materials or components to these industries. Hundreds of thousands became jobless. Then the jobless often became homeless. Desperation prevailed. Little had been done to assess the toll hunger, inadequate nutrition, or starvation took on the health of those who were children during this time. While food was cheap, relatively speaking, there was little money to buy it.

Everyone who lived through the Great Depression was permanently affected in some way. Many never trusted banks again. Many people of this generation later hoarded cash so they would not risk losing everything again. Some permanently rejected the use of credit.

In the immediate aftermath of the stock market crash, many urged President Herbert Hoover to provide government relief. Hoover responded by urging the nation to be patient. By the time he signed relief bills in 1932, it was too late.

Hoover's bid for reelection in 1932 failed. The new president, Franklin D. Roosevelt, won the White House on his promise to the American people of a "new deal." Upon assuming office, Roosevelt and his advisers immediately launched a massive program of innovation and experimentation to try to bring the Depression to an end and get the nation back on track. Congress gave the president unprecedented power to act to save the nation. During the next eight years, the most extensive and broad-based legislation in the nation's history was enacted. The legislation was intended to accomplish three goals: relief, recovery, and reform.

The New Deal

The first step in the New Deal was to relieve suffering. This was accomplished through a number of job-creation projects. The second step, the recovery aspect, was to stimulate the economy. The third step was to create social and economic change through innovative legislation.

The National Recovery Administration attempted to accomplish a number of goals:

- Restore employment
- Increase general purchasing power
- Provide character-building activity for unemployed youth

- Encourage decentralization of industry and thus divert population from crowded cities to rural or semirural communities

- Develop river resources in the interest of navigation and inexpensive power and light

- Complete flood control on a permanent basis

- Enlarge the national program of forest protection and develop forest resources

- Control farm production and improve farm prices

- Assist home builders and homeowners

- Restore public faith in banking and trust operations

- Recapture the value of physical assets, whether in real property, securities, or other investments

These objectives and their accomplishment implied a restoration of public confidence and courage.

Among the "alphabet organizations" set up to work out the details of the recovery plan, the most prominent were:

- Agricultural Adjustment Administration (AAA): Designed to readjust agricultural production and prices, thereby boosting farm income

- Civilian Conservation Corps (CCC): Designed to give wholesome, useful activity in the forestry service to unemployed young men

- Civil Works Administration (CWA) and the Public Works Administration (PWA): Designed to give employment in the construction and repair of public buildings, parks, and highways

- Works Progress Administration (WPA): Designed to move individuals from relief rolls to work projects or private employment

The Tennessee Valley Authority (TVA) was of a more permanent nature, designed to improve the navigability of the Tennessee River and increase productivity of the timber and farm lands in its valley. This program built sixteen dams that provided water control and hydroelectric generation.

The Public Works Administration employed Americans on over thirty-four thousand public works projects at a cost of more than $4 billion. Among these projects was the construction of a highway that linked the Florida Keys and Miami, the Boulder Dam (now the Hoover Dam), and numerous highway projects.

To provide economic stability and prevent another crash, Congress passed the Glass-Steagall Act, which separated banking and investing. The Securities and Exchange Commission was created to regulate dangerous speculative practices on Wall Street. The Wagner Act guaranteed a number of rights to workers and unions in an effort to improve worker-employer relations.

The Social Security Act of 1935 established pensions for the aged and infirm as well as a system of unemployment insurance.

Much of the recovery program was designed to respond to an emergency, but certain permanent national policies emerged. The intention of the public was to employ their government in supervising and, to an extent, regulating business operations—from corporate activities to labor problems. This included protecting bank depositors and the credit system of the country, employing gold resources and currency adjustments to aid permanent restoration of normal living, and, if possible, establishing a line of subsistence below which no useful citizen would be permitted to sink.

Many of the steps taken by the Roosevelt administration have had far-reaching effects. They alleviated the economic disaster of the Great Depression, enacted controls that would mitigate the risk of another stock market crash, and provided greater security for workers. The nation's economy, however, did not fully recover until the United States entered World War II.

U.S. Policy after World War II

In the aftermath of the Second World War, with the Soviet Union having emerged as the second strongest power in the world, the United States embarked on a policy known as containment of the Communist menace. This involved what came to be known as the Marshall Plan and the Truman Doctrine. The MARSHALL PLAN involved the economic aid that was sent to Europe in the aftermath of the Second World War aimed at preventing the spread of communism. To that end, the U.S. has devoted a larger and larger share of its foreign policy, diplomacy, and both economic and military might to combating it.

The TRUMAN DOCTRINE offered military aid to those countries that were in danger of communist upheaval. This led to the era known as the cold war, in which the United States took the lead along with the Western European nations against the Soviet Union and the Eastern Bloc countries. It was also at this time that the United States finally gave up on George Washington's advice against "European entanglements" and joined the NORTH ATLANTIC TREATY ORGANIZATION (NATO). This was formed in 1949 and comprised the United States and several Western European nations for the purposes of opposing communist aggression.

The United Nations was also formed at this time (1945) to replace the defunct League of Nations for the purposes of ensuring world peace. Even with American

MARSHALL PLAN: aimed at preventing the spread of communism, involved the economic aid that was sent to Europe in the aftermath of the Second World War

TRUMAN DOCTRINE: offered military aid to countries in danger of communist upheaval

NORTH ATLANTIC TREATY ORGANIZATION (NATO): formed in 1949 for the purposes of opposing communist aggression

involvement, the UN would prove largely ineffective in maintaining world peace.

In the 1950s, the United States embarked on what was called the Eisenhower Doctrine, after then-President Eisenhower. This aimed at trying to maintain peace in a troubled area of the world, the Middle East. However, unlike the Truman Doctrine in Europe, it would have little success.

The United States also became involved in a number of world conflicts in the ensuing years. Each had at the core the struggle against communist expansion. Among these were the Korean Conflict (1950–1953), the Vietnam War (1965–1975), and various continuing entanglements in Central and South America and the Middle East. By the early 1970s under the leadership of then-Secretary of State Henry Kissinger, the United States and its allies embarked on the policy that came to be known as détente. This was aimed at the easing of tensions between the United States and its allies and the Soviet Union and its allies.

By the 1980s, the United States embarked on what some saw as a renewal of the cold war. This owed to the fact that the United States was becoming more involved in trying to prevent communist insurgency in Central America. A massive expansion of its armed forces and the development of space-based weapons systems were undertaken at this time. As this occurred, the Soviet Union, with a failing economic system and a foolhardy adventure in Afghanistan, found itself unable to compete. By 1989, events had come to a head. This ended with the breakdown of the Communist Bloc, the virtual end of the monolithic Soviet Union, and the collapse of the communist system by the early 1990s.

Sample Test Questions and Rationale

(Easy)

1. **The belief that the United States should control all of North America was called:**

    A. Westward Expansion

    B. Pan Americanism

    C. Manifest Destiny

    D. Nationalism

Answer: C. Manifest Destiny

The belief that the United States should control all of North America was called Manifest Destiny. This idea fueled much of the violence and aggression toward those already occupying the lands such as the Native Americans. Manifest Destiny was certainly driven by sentiments of nationalism and gave rise to westward expansion.

Sample Test Questions and Rationale (cont.)

(Rigorous)

2. **How did manufacturing change in the early 1800s?**

    A. The electronics industry was born

    B. Production moved from small shops or homes into factories

    C. Industry benefited from the Federal Reserve Act

    D. The timber industry was hurt when Theodore Roosevelt set aside 238 million acres of federal lands to be protected from development

    Answer: B. Production moved from small shops or homes into factories

    Factories had modern machinery in them that could produce goods efficiently. The electronics industry did not exist in the early 1800s. The Federal Reserve Act came much later, in the twentieth century. Theodore Roosevelt's protection of federal lands from development also took place in the twentieth century.

(Rigorous)

3. **The post World-War II years in the United States saw the emergence of the largest consumer culture in the world. What was not a benefit of this culture?**

    A. Improved working conditions in third world countries

    B. Improved American economy

    C. Improved global economy

    D. Improved standard of living in the United States

    Answer: A. Improved working conditions in third world countries

    The war industry fueled another period of economic prosperity that lasted through the postwar years. The 1950s saw the emergence of a large consumer culture in the United States, which has not only bolstered the American economy ever since, but has been an important development for other countries that produce goods for the U.S. market.

SKILL 11.4 **Knows about twentieth-century developments and transformations in the United States** *(e.g., assembly line, space age)*

Social and Economic changes

The United States underwent significant social and economic changes during the twentieth century, and it became a dominant world power internationally. Economically, the United States saw great prosperity as well as severe depression emerging as primary economic forces.

The industrialization that had started following the end of the Civil War in the mid-nineteenth century continued into the early decades of the twentieth century. A huge wave of immigration at the turn of the century provided industry with a

A huge wave of immigration at the turn of the century provided industry with a large labor pool and established millions of immigrants and their families in the working class.

large labor pool and established millions of immigrants and their families in the working class.

POPULISM is a philosophy concerned with the common-sense needs of average people. Populism often finds expression as a reaction against perceived oppression of the average people by the wealthy elite in society. The prevalent claim of populist movements is that they will put the people first. Populist movements claim to represent the majority of the people and call them to stand up to institutions or practices that seem detrimental to their well-being.

Populism flourished in the late nineteenth and early twentieth centuries in the United States. Several political parties were formed out of this philosophy, including the Greenback Party, the Populist Party, the Farmer-Labor Party, the Single Tax movement of Henry George, the Share Our Wealth movement of Huey Long, the Progressive Party, and the Union Party.

The tremendous changes caused by the Industrial Revolution led to a demand for reform that would control the power wielded by big corporations. The gap between the industrial moguls and the working people was growing; this disparity resulted in a public outcry for reform at the same time there was an outcry for governmental reform that would end the political corruption and elitism of the day.

The reforms initiated by leaders and the spirit of Progressivism were far-reaching. Politically, many states enacted initiatives and referendums for progressive movements. The adoption of the recall occurred in many states, and several states enacted legislation that would undermine the power of political machines. On a national level, the two most significant political changes were:

- The ratification of the Seventeenth Amendment, which required that all U.S. Senators be chosen by popular election

- The ratification of the Nineteenth Amendment, which granted women the right to vote

Major economic reforms of the period included the aggressive enforcement of the Sherman Antitrust Act and the passage of the Elkins Act and the Hepburn Act, which gave the Interstate Commerce Commission greater power to regulate the railroads. The Pure Food and Drug Act prohibited the use of harmful chemicals in food; the Meat Inspection Act regulated the meat industry to protect the public against tainted meat; over two-thirds of the states passed laws prohibiting child labor; workmen's compensation was mandated; and the Department of Commerce and Labor was created.

Responding to concern over the environmental effects of the timber, ranching, and mining industries, Roosevelt set aside 238 million acres of federal lands to be protected from development. Wildlife preserves were established, the national park system was expanded, and the National Conservation Commission was created. The Newlands Reclamation Act also provided federal funding for the construction of irrigation projects and dams in semi-arid areas of the country.

The Wilson Administration carried out additional reforms. The Federal Reserve Act created a national banking system, providing a more stable money supply. The Sherman Act and the Clayton Antitrust Act defined unfair competition, made corporate officers liable for the illegal actions of employees, and exempted labor unions from antitrust lawsuits. The Federal Trade Commission was established to enforce these measures. Finally, the Sixteenth Amendment was ratified, establishing an income tax. This measure was designed to relieve the poor of a disproportionate burden in funding the federal government and to make the wealthy pay a greater share of the nation's tax burden.

Before 1800, most manufacturing took place in small shops or in homes. However, starting in the early 1800s, factories with modern machines were built, making it easier to produce goods faster. The eastern part of the country became a major industrial area, although some industry also developed in the west. At about the same time, improvements began to be made in building roads, railroads, canals, and steamboats.

The increased ease of travel facilitated westward movement and boosted the economy with faster and cheaper shipment of goods and products, covering larger and larger areas. Some of the innovations arising from these changes included the Erie Canal, which connects the interior and Great Lakes with the Hudson River and the coastal port of New York. Many other natural waterways were connected by canals during this time.

Robert Fulton's Clermont, the first commercially successful steamboat, led the pack as the fastest way to ship goods, making it the most important means to do so. Later, steam-powered railroads became the biggest rival of the steamboat as a means of shipping, eventually becoming the most important transportation method opening the west.

With expansion into the interior of the country, the United States became the leading agricultural nation in the world. The hardy pioneer farmers produced a vast surplus, and emphasis went to producing products with a high sale value. Implements such as the cotton gin and the reaper aided in higher production. Travel and shipping were greatly assisted in areas not yet reached by railroad; they were also facilitated by improved and new roads, such as the National Road in the east and the Oregon and Santa Fe trails in the west.

> With expansion into the interior of the country, the United States became the leading agricultural nation in the world.

As travel and communication became faster, people became more exposed to works of literature, art, newspapers, drama, live entertainment, and political rallies. More information was desired about previously unknown areas of the country, especially the West, and the discovery of gold and other mineral wealth resulted in a literal surge of settlers.

Public schools were established in many states, and more and more children were able to get an education. With higher literacy and more participation in literature and the arts, the young nation was developing its own unique culture, and becoming less and less influenced by and dependent on European culture.

At the same time, more industries and factories required more labor. Women, children, and, at times, entire families worked dangerously long hours until the 1830s. By that time, factories were getting even larger and employers began hiring immigrants who were coming to America in huge numbers. Before then, efforts were made to organize a labor movement to improve working conditions and increase wages. These efforts never really caught on until after the Civil War.

World War I and World War II

The prosperity of industrial and economic changes was interrupted by America's entry into the First World War in 1917. While reluctant to enter the hostilities, the United States played a decisive role in ending the war and in the creation of the League of Nations that followed, establishing its central position in international relations that would increase in importance through the century.

The World War I effort required a massive production of weapons, ammunition, radios, and other equipment of war. During wartime, work hours were shortened, wages were increased, and working conditions improved. When the war ended, and business and industrial owners attempted to return to prewar conditions, the workers revolted. These conditions contributed to the establishment of new labor laws.

The United States resumed its prosperous industrial growth in the years after World War I, but even as industrial profits and stock market investments skyrocketed, farm prices and wages fell, creating an unbalanced situation that caused an economic collapse in 1929, when the stock market crashed. The United States plummeted into economic depression with high unemployment. This period is known as the Great Depression.

President Franklin Roosevelt proposed that the federal government assist in rebuilding the economy, something his predecessor, President Hoover, thought the government should not do. Roosevelt's New Deal policies were adopted to wide success, and marked an important shift in the role that the U.S. government plays in economic matters and social welfare.

The nation's recovery was underway when, in late 1941, it entered the Second World War to fight against Japan and Germany and their allied Axis powers. Fifty-nine nations became embroiled in World War II, which began September 1, 1939 and ended September 2, 1945. These dates include both the European and Pacific theaters of war. The horribly tragic results of this second global conflagration were more deaths and more destruction than those of any other armed conflict. Millions of people were uprooted and displaced. The end of the war brought renewed power struggles, especially in Europe and China; many Eastern European nations as well as China came under the control and domination of the communists, supported and backed by the Soviet Union.

With the development of atomic bombs and their deployment against two Japanese cities, the world found itself in the nuclear age. The peace settlement established by the United Nations after the war still operates today.

The years between World War I and World War II produced significant advancements in aircraft technology, and the pace of aircraft development and production dramatically increased during World War II. Major developments included flight-based weapon delivery systems, the long-range bomber, the first jet fighter, the first cruise missile, and the first ballistic missile. Although they were invented, cruise and ballistic missiles were not widely used during the war. Glider planes were heavily used in World War II because they were silent upon approach. Another significant development was the broad use of paratrooper units. Hospital planes also came into use to extract the seriously wounded from the front and to transport them to hospitals for treatment.

Weapons and technology in other areas also improved rapidly during this time. These advances were critical in determining the outcome of the war. Radar, electronic computers, nuclear weapons, and new tank designs were used for the first time. More new inventions were registered for patents than ever before; most of these new ideas were aimed either to kill or to prevent people from being killed.

The war began with essentially the same weaponry that had been used in World War I. However, as the war progressed, so did technology. The aircraft carrier joined the battleship; the Higgins boat, the primary landing craft, was invented; light tanks were developed to meet the needs of a changing battlefield; and other armored vehicles were developed. Submarines were also perfected during this period.

Numerous other weapons were also developed or invented to meet the needs of battle during World War II: the bazooka, the rocket-propelled grenade, anti-tank weapons, assault rifles, the tank destroyer, mine-clearing Flail tanks, Flame tanks, submersible tanks, cruise missiles, rocket artillery and air-launched rockets, guided weapons, torpedoes, self-guiding weapons, and napalm. The atomic bomb was also developed and used for the first time during World War II.

The 1950s saw the emergence of a large consumer culture in the United States.

The war industry fueled another period of economic prosperity that lasted through the postwar years. The 1950s saw the emergence of a large consumer culture in the United States, which has not only bolstered the American economy ever since, but has been an important development for other countries that produce goods for the U.S. market.

The United States first established itself as an important world military leader at the turn of the twentieth century during the Spanish American War; it cemented this position during the two world wars. Following World War II, with Europe struggling to recover from the fighting, the United States and the Soviet Union emerged as the two dominant world powers. This remained the situation for three decades while the two super powers engaged in a cold war between the ideals of communism and capitalism. In the 1980s, the Soviet Union underwent a series of reforms that resulted in the collapse of the country and the end of the cold war, leaving the United States as the true world power. Thus, the United States changed from a reluctant participant in international affairs into a central leader.

Technological Developments Post-World War II

Major technological developments in the post–World War–II era include:

- Discovery of penicillin (1945)
- Detonation of the first atomic bombs (1945)
- Xerography process invented (1946)
- Exploration of the South Pole
- Studies of X-ray radiation
- U.S. airplane first flies at supersonic speed (1947)
- Invention of the transistor (1947)
- Long-playing record invented (1948)
- Studies begin in the science of chemo-genetics (1948)
- Mount Palomar reflecting telescope created (1948)
- Idlewild Airport (now known as JFK International Airport) opens in New York City
- Cortisone discovered (1949)
- USSR tests first atomic bomb (1949)
- U.S. guided missile launched and travels 250 miles (1949)

- Plutonium separated (1950)

- Tranquilizer meprobamate comes into wide use (1950)

- Antihistamines become popular in treating colds and allergies (1950)

- Electric power produced from atomic energy (1951)

- First heart-lung machine devised (1951)

- First solo flight over the North Pole (1951)

- Yellow fever vaccine developed (1951)

- Isotopes used in medicine and industry (1952)

- Contraceptive pill produced (1952)

- First hydrogen bomb exploded (1952)

- Nobel Prize in medicine awarded for discovery of streptomycin (1952)

- Cave Cougnac discovered with prehistoric paintings (1953)

- USSR explodes hydrogen bomb (1953)

- Hillary and Tenzing reach the summit of Mount Everest (1953)

- Lung cancer connected to cigarette smoking (1953)

- First U.S. submarine converted to nuclear power (1954)

- Polio vaccine invented (1954)

- Discovery of Vitamin B12 (1955)

- Discovery of the molecular structure of insulin (1955)

- First artificial manufacture of diamonds (1955)

- Beginning of development of "visual telephone" (1956)

- Beginning of transatlantic cable telephone service (1956)

- USSR launches first Earth satellites (Sputnik I and II) (1957)

- Mackinac Straits Bridge in Michigan opens as the longest suspension bridge (1957)

- Stereo recordings introduced (1958)

- NASA created (1958)

- USSR launches rocket with two monkeys aboard (1959)

- Nobel Prize in Medicine for synthesis of RNA and DNA (1959)

Sample Test Question and Rationale

(Average)

1. **What happened to weapons and technology during World War II?**

   A. They remained about the same as in World War I

   B. They saw dramatic changes in terms of new equipment and new technology

   C. These areas suffered because radar had not yet been invented

   D. Weapons, like submarines, remained very primitive

Answer: B. They saw dramatic changes in terms of new equipment and new technology

Weapons in World War II advanced far beyond those of World War I. Radar did exist at the outset of World War II. Submarines and other weapons became very advanced in World War II; they did not remain primitive.

SKILL 11.5 Understands connections between causes and effects of events

See Skills 11.1, 11.2, 11.3, and 11.4

Sample Test Question and Rationale

(Rigorous)

1. **After a string of Republican Presidents, the American public elected Franklin D. Roosevelt on a promise to do what?**

   A. Provide relief to citizens

   B. Focus on recovering the economy

   C. Reforming the economic system

   D. All of the above

Answer: D All of the above.

Hoover's bid for reelection in 1932 failed. The new president, Franklin D. Roosevelt, won the White House on his promise to the American people of a "new deal." Upon assuming office, Roosevelt and his advisers immediately launched a massive program of innovation and experimentation to try to bring the Depression to an end and get the nation back on track. Congress gave the president unprecedented power to act to save the nation. During the next eight years, the most extensive and broad-based legislation in the nation's history was enacted. The legislation was intended to accomplish three goals: relief, recovery, and reform.

COMPETENCY 12
GOVERNMENT, CITIZENSHIP, AND DEMOCRACY

The Nature and Purpose of Government

Historically, the functions of government (or people's concepts of government and its purpose and function) have varied considerably. In the theory of political science, the function of government is to secure the common welfare of the members of the given society over which it exercises control. In different historical eras, governments have attempted to achieve the common welfare in accordance with the traditions and ideologies of the given society.

Among primitive peoples, systems of control were rudimentary at best. They arose directly from the ideas of right and wrong that had been established in the group and that were common in that particular society. Control was exercised most often by means of group pressure, typically in the form of taboos and superstitions—and in many cases by ostracism, or banishment from the group. Thus, in most cases, because of the extreme tribal nature of society in those early times, this led to very unpleasant circumstances for the individual so treated. Without the protection of the group, a lone individual did not survive long.

Among civilized peoples, governments began to assume more institutional forms. They rested on a well-defined legal system. They imposed penalties on violators of the social order. They used force, which was supported and sanctioned by their people. The government was charged with establishing the social order and was supposed to do so in order to discharge its functions.

Eventually, the ideas of government, such as who should govern and how, came to be considered by various thinkers and philosophers. The most influential of these were the ancient Greek philosophers Plato and Aristotle.

Aristotle's conception of government was based on a simple idea. The function of government was to provide for the general welfare of its people. A good government, and one that should be supported, was one that did so in the best way possible, with the least pressure on the people. Bad governments were those that subordinated the general welfare to that of the individuals who ruled. At no time should any function of any government be that of personal interest of any one

> *The function of government is to secure the common welfare of the members of the given society over which it exercises control.*

individual, no matter who that individual is. This does not mean that Aristotle had no sympathy for the individual or individual happiness (accusations that have sometimes been made against Plato). Rather, Aristotle believed that a society is greater than the sum of its parts, or that "the good of the many outweighs the good of the few and also of the one."

Yet, a good government, and one that carries out its functions well, will always weigh the relative merits of what is good for a given individual in society and what is good for the society as a whole. This basic concept has continued to our own time and has found its fullest expression in the idea of representative democracy and political and personal freedom. In addition, the most ideal government is one that maintains social order while allowing the greatest possible autonomy for individuals.

FORMS OF GOVERNMENT	
Anarchism	A political movement believing in the elimination of all government and its replacement by a cooperative community of individuals. Anarchism has sometimes involved political violence, such as assassinations of important political or governmental figures. The historical banner of this movement is a black flag.
Communism	A belief as well as a political system characterized by a classless, stateless social organization. Communism calls for the common ownership of national goods. This ideology is the same as Marxism. The historical banner of the movement is a red flag and variation of stars, hammer, and sickle, representing the various types of workers.
Dictatorship	Also called an oligarchy, rule by an individual or small group of individuals; a dictatorship centralizes all political control in itself and enforces its will with a strong police force.
Fascism	A belief as well as a political system opposed ideologically to Communism, though similar in basic structure, with a one-party state and centralized political control. Unlike Communism, fascism tolerates private ownership of the means of production, although it maintains tight overall control. Central to its belief is the idolization of the leader, a "cult of personality," and most often an expansionist ideology. Examples have been German Nazism and Italian Fascism.
Monarchy	The rule of a nation by a monarch (a nonelected, usually hereditary leader), most often a king or queen. This form of government may or may not be accompanied by some measure of democratically open institutions and elections at various levels. A modern example is Great Britain, which is called a constitutional monarchy.

Table continued on next page

Parliamentary System	A system of government with a legislature, usually involving a multiplicity of political parties and often coalition politics. There is division between the head of state and head of government. The head of government is usually known as a prime minister, who is also usually the head of the largest party. The head of government and cabinet usually both sit and vote in the parliament. The head of state is most often an elected president (though in the case of a constitutional monarchy, like Great Britain, the sovereign may take the place of a president as head of state). A government may fall when a majority in parliament votes "no confidence" in the government.
Presidential System	A system of government with a legislature, involving few or many political parties, with no division between head of state and head of government: The president serves in both capacities. The president is elected either by direct or indirect election. A president and cabinet usually do not sit or vote in the legislature, and the president may or may not be the head of the largest political party. A president can thus rule even without a majority in the legislature. He or she can only be removed from office for major infractions of the law.
Socialism	A political belief and system in which the state takes a guiding role in the national economy and provides extensive social services to its population. The state may or may not own outright the means of production, but even where it does not, it exercises tight control. It usually promotes democracy (Democratic-Socialism), though the heavy state involvement produces excessive bureaucracy and usually inefficiency. Taken to an extreme, it may lead to Communism as government control increases and democratic practice decreases. Ideologically, the two movements are very similar in belief and practice, as Socialists also preach the superiority of their system to all others and that it will become the eventual natural order. For that reason it is also considered a variant of Marxism. Socialism has also used a red flag as a symbol.

U.S. Government System

The various governments of the United States and of Native American tribes have many similarities and a few notable differences. They are more similar than not; all in all, they reflect the tendency of their people to prefer a representative government that has checks and balances and that looks out for the people as a whole.

The United States government has three distinct branches: the executive, the legislative, and the judicial. Each has its own function and its own "check" on the other two.

> The United States government has three distinct branches: the executive, the legislative, and the judicial.

Legislative branch

The legislative branch consists primarily of the House of Representatives and the Senate. Each house has a set number of members, the House with 435 apportioned according to national population trends and the Senate with one hundred (two from each state). House members serve two-year terms; senators serve six-year terms. Each house can initiate a bill, but that bill must be passed by a majority of both houses in order to become a law. The House is primarily responsible for initiating spending bills; the Senate is responsible for ratifying treaties that the president might sign with other countries.

Executive branch

The executive branch has the president and vice-president as its two main figures. The president is the commander-in-chief of the armed forces and the person who can approve or veto all bills from Congress. (Vetoed bills can become law anyway if two-thirds of each house of Congress votes to pass them over the president's objections.) The president is elected to a four-year term by the electoral college, which usually mirrors the popular will of the people. The president can serve a total of two terms. The executive branch also has several departments consisting of advisors to the president. These departments include State, Defense, Education, Treasury, and Commerce, among others. Members of these departments are appointed by the president and approved by Congress.

Judicial branch

The judicial branch consists of a series of courts and related entities, with the top body being the Supreme Court. The Court decides whether laws of the land are constitutional; any law invalidated by the Supreme Court is no longer in effect. The Court also regulates the enforcement and constitutionality of the amendments to the Constitution. The Supreme Court is the highest court in the land. Cases make their way to it from federal appeals courts, which hear appeals of decisions made by federal district courts. These lower two levels of courts are found in regions around the country. Supreme Court justices are appointed by the president and confirmed by the Senate. They serve for life. Lower-court judges are elected in popular votes in their states.

State and local government

State governments are mirror images of the federal government, with a few important exceptions:

- Governors are not technically commanders-in-chief of armed forces

- State supreme court decisions can be appealed to federal courts

- Terms of state representatives and senators vary

- Judges, even of the state supreme courts, are elected by popular vote

- Governors and legislators have term limits that vary by state

Local governments vary widely across the country, although none of them has a judicial branch per se. Some local governments consist of a city council, of which the mayor is a member who has limited powers; in other cities, the mayor is the head of the government and the city council members are the chief lawmakers. Local governments also have fewer strict requirements for people running for office than do the state and federal governments.

The form of government of the various Native American tribes varies as well. Most tribes have governments along the lines of the U.S. federal or state governments. An example is the Cherokee Nation, which has a fifteen-member tribal council as the head of the legislative branch; a principal chief and deputy chief who head the executive branch and carry out the laws passed by the tribal council; and a judicial branch made up of the judicial appeals tribunal and the Cherokee Nation district court. Members of the tribunal are appointed by the principal chief. Members of the other two branches are elected by popular vote of the Cherokee Nation.

Sample Test Questions and Rationale

(Average)

1. **A communist government is:**

   A. A government that is ruled by one individual or a small group of individuals

   B. A government with a legislature, usually involving a multiplicity of political parties and often coalition politics

   C. A political system characterized by the ideology of class conflict and revolution and that the product of all the people is shared by each and every person

   D. A political system that values conflict and revolution with central political control that allows for private ownership of the means of production

   Answer: C. A political system characterized by the ideology of class conflict and revolution and that the product of all the people is shared by each and every person

   C is the correct definition of a communist government. Choices C and D are different because D states that the citizens are allowed to have private ownership, whereas in choice C, the citizens are not allowed private ownership.

(Average)

2. **The U.S. House of Representatives has:**

   A. One hundred members

   B. 435 members

   C. Three branches

   D. A president and a vice-president

   Answer: B. 435 members

   The U.S. Senate has one hundred members. The U.S. government as a whole has three branches. The executive branch of the U.S. government has a president and a vice-president.

SKILL
12.2 **Knows key documents and speeches in the history of the United States** *(e.g., United States Constitution, Declaration of Independence, Gettysburg Address)*

Declaration of Independence

DECLARATION OF INDEPENDENCE:
written in 1776 by Thomas Jefferson, it was a call to the colonies to unite against the king, articulating the philosophical framework upon which the United States is founded

The **DECLARATION OF INDEPENDENCE** was written in 1776 by Thomas Jefferson. It was a call to the colonies to unite against the king, detailing the grievances of the colonies and articulating the philosophical framework upon which the United States is founded.

The Declaration of Independence is an outgrowth of both ancient Greek ideas of democracy and individual rights and the ideas of the European Enlightenment and the Renaissance, especially the ideology of the political thinker John Locke. Thomas Jefferson (1743–1826), the principle author of the Declaration, borrowed much from Locke's theories and writings.

The Declaration of Independence is an outgrowth of both ancient Greek ideas of democracy and individual rights and the ideas of the European Enlightenment and the Renaissance, especially the ideology of the political thinker John Locke.

John Locke was one of the most influential political writers of the seventeenth century, who put great emphasis on human rights and put forth the belief that when governments violate those rights people should rebel. In 1690, he wrote the book *Two Treatises of Government*, which had tremendous influence on political thought in the American colonies and helped shape the U.S. Constitution and Declaration of Independence.

The Declaration of Independence was the founding document of the United States of America. The Articles of Confederation were the first attempt of the newly independent states to reach a new understanding among themselves. The Declaration was intended to demonstrate the reasons that the colonies were seeking separation from Great Britain. Conceived by and written for the most part by Thomas Jefferson, it is not only important for what it says, but also for how it says it. The Declaration is in many respects a poetic document. Instead of a simple recitation of the colonists' grievances, it set out clearly the reasons the colonists were seeking their freedom from Great Britain. They had tried all means to resolve the dispute peacefully. It was the right of a people, when all other methods of addressing their grievances have been tried and have failed, to separate themselves from that power that was keeping them from fully expressing their rights to "life, liberty, and the pursuit of happiness."

For more information about this important document, go to:

http://www.archives.gov/exhibits/charters/declaration.html

U.S. Constitution

U.S. CONSTITUTION:
the written document that describes and defines the system and structure of the U.S. government

The **U.S. CONSTITUTION** is the written document that describes and defines the system and structure of the U.S. government. Ratification of the Constitution by the required number of states (nine of the original thirteen), was completed on June 21, 1788, and thus the Constitution officially became the law of the land.

In 1786, an effort to regulate interstate commerce ended in what is known as the **Annapolis Convention**. Because only five states were represented, this convention was not able to accomplish definitive results. The debates, however, made it clear that foreign and interstate commerce could not be regulated by a government with as little authority as the government established by the Confederation. Congress was therefore asked to call a convention to provide a constitution that would address the emerging needs of the new nation.

The convention met under the presidency of George Washington, with fifty-five of the sixty-five appointed members present. A constitution was written in four months. The Constitution of the United States is the fundamental law of the republic. It is a precise, formal, written document of the extraordinary, or supreme, type of constitution. The founders of the Union established it as the highest governmental authority. There is no national power superior to it. The foundations were so broadly laid as to provide for the expansion of national life and to make it an instrument that would last for all time.

To maintain the stability of the Constitution, its framers created a difficult process for making any changes to it. No amendment can become valid until it is ratified by three-fourths of all of the states.

The British system of government was part of the basis of the final document. However, significant changes were necessary to meet the needs of a partnership of states that were tied together as a single federation yet sovereign in their own local affairs. This constitution established a system of government that was unique and advanced far beyond other systems of its day.

There were, to be sure, differences of opinion. The compromises that resolved these conflicts are reflected in the final document. The first point of disagreement and compromise was related to the presidency. Some wanted a strong, centralized, individual authority. Others feared autocracy or the growth of monarchy. The compromise was to give the president broad powers but to limit the amount of time, through term of office, that any individual could exercise that power. The power to make appointments and to conclude treaties was controlled by the requirement of the consent of the Senate.

The second conflict was between large and small states. The large states wanted power proportionate to their voting strength; the small states opposed this plan. The compromise was that all states should have equal voting power in the Senate, but to have membership in the House of Representatives be determined in proportion to population.

The third conflict was about slavery. The compromise was:

- Fugitive slaves should be returned by states to which they might flee for refuge

- No law would be passed for twenty years prohibiting the importation of slaves

The fourth major area of conflict was how the president would be chosen. One side argued for election by direct vote of the people. The other side thought that the president should be chosen by Congress. One group feared the ignorance of the people; the other feared the power of a small group of people. The compromise was the electoral college.

The Constitution binds the states in a governmental unity in everything that affects the welfare of all. At the same time, it recognizes the rights of the people of each state to independence of action in matters that relate only to them. Since the federal Constitution is the law of the land, all other laws must conform to it.

The debates conducted during the Continental Congress represent the issues and the arguments that led to the compromises in the final document. The debates also reflect the concerns of the founding fathers that the rights of the people be protected from abrogation by the government itself as well as the determination that no branch of government should have enough power to override the others. There is, therefore, a system of checks and balances.

Federalist Papers

The **FEDERALIST PAPERS** were written to win popular support for the new proposed Constitution. In these publications, the debates of the Congress and the concerns of the founding fathers were made available to the people of the nation. In addition to providing an explanation of the underlying philosophies and concerns of the Constitution and the compromises that were made, the Federalist Papers conducted what has frequently been called the most effective marketing and public relations campaign in human history.

Constitutional Amendments

An **AMENDMENT** is a change or addition to the U.S. Constitution. To date, only twenty-seven amendments to the Constitution have passed. An amendment may be used to cancel out a previous one (e.g., the Eighteenth Amendment of 1919, known as Prohibition, was canceled by the Twenty-First Amendment in 1933). Amending the Constitution is an extremely difficult thing to do.

An amendment must start in Congress. One or more lawmakers propose it, and then each house votes on it in turn. The amendment must have the support of two-thirds of each house separately in order to progress on its path into law. (It should be noted here that this two-thirds need be only two-thirds of a quorum,

FEDERALIST PAPERS: the debates of the Congress and the concerns of the founding fathers were made available to the people of the nation in order to win popular support for the new proposed Constitution

The Federalist Papers conducted what has frequently been called the most effective marketing and public relations campaign in human history.

AMENDMENT: a change or addition to the U.S. Constitution

which is just a simple majority. Thus, it is theoretically possible for an amendment to be passed and to become legal even though it has been approved by less than half of one or both houses.)

The final and most difficult step for an amendment is the ratification of the state legislatures. A total of three-fourths of those must approve the amendment. Approvals there need be only a simple majority, but the number of states that must approve the amendment is thirty-eight. Hundreds of amendments have been proposed through the years.

A key element in some of those failures has been the time limit that Congress has the option to put on amendment proposals. A famous example of an amendment that got close but didn't reach the threshold before the deadline expired was the Equal Rights Amendment, which was proposed in 1972 but couldn't muster enough support for passage, even though its deadline was extended from seven to ten years.

The first ten amendments are called **THE BILL OF RIGHTS**; they were approved at the same time, shortly after the Constitution was ratified. The Eleventh and Twelfth amendments were ratified around the turn of the nineteenth century and, respectively, voided foreign suits against states and revised the method of presidential election. The Thirteenth, Fourteenth, and Fifteenth amendments were passed in succession after the end of the Civil War. Slavery was outlawed by the Thirteenth Amendment. The Fourteenth and Fifteenth amendments provided for equal protection and for voting rights, respectively, without consideration of skin color.

THE BILL OF RIGHTS: the first ten amendments of the Constitution, approved at the same time, shortly after the Constitution was ratified

The first amendment of the twentieth century was the Sixteenth Amendment, which provided for a federal income tax. Providing for direct election to the Senate was the Seventeenth Amendment. (Before this, senators were appointed by state leaders, not elected by the public at large.)

The Eighteenth Amendment prohibited the use or sale of alcohol across the country. The long battle for voting rights for women ended in success with the passage of the Nineteenth Amendment. The date for the beginning of terms for the president and the Congress was changed from March to January by the Twentieth Amendment. With the Twenty-first Amendment came the only instance in which an amendment was repealed. In this case, it was the Eighteenth Amendment and its prohibition of alcohol consumption or sale.

The long battle for voting rights for women ended in success with the passage of the Nineteenth Amendment.

The Twenty-second Amendment limited the number of terms that a president could serve to two. Presidents since George Washington had followed Washington's practice of not running for a third term; this changed when Franklin D. Roosevelt ran for reelection a second time, in 1940. He was reelected that time and a third time, too, four years later. He didn't live out his fourth term, but he did convince Congress and most of the state legislature that some sort of term limit should be in place.

The little-known Twenty-third Amendment provided for representation of Washington, D.C., in the electoral college. The Twenty-fourth Amendment prohibited poll taxes, which people had had to pay in order to vote.

Presidential succession is the focus of the Twenty-fifth Amendment, which provides a blueprint of what to do if the president is incapacitated or killed. The Twenty-sixth Amendment lowered the legal voting age for Americans from twenty-one to eighteen. The final amendment, the Twenty-seventh, prohibits members of Congress from substantially raising their own salaries. This amendment was one of twelve originally proposed in the late eighteenth century. Ten of those twelve became the Bill of Rights, and one has yet to become law.

A host of potential amendments have made news headlines in recent years. A total of six amendments have been proposed by Congress and passed muster in both houses but have not been ratified by enough state legislatures. The aforementioned Equal Rights Amendment is one. Another one, which would grant the District of Columbia full voting rights equivalent to states' rights, has not passed; like the Equal Rights Amendment, its deadline has expired. A handful of others remain on the books without expiration dates, including an amendment to regulate child labor.

Gettysburg Address

The **GETTYSBURG ADDRESS** was given by President Abraham Lincoln when he visited Gettysburg several months after the Battle of Gettysburg in 1863 at the dedication of the national cemetery in Gettysburg. In this short speech, Lincoln gave voice to a spirit that inspired many by referring to this time as a "new birth of freedom." His eloquence is remembered by many and often quoted.

For detailed information and images of the Constitution and the Bill of Rights, go to:

http://www.archives.gov/exhibits/charters/constitution.html

GETTYSBURG ADDRESS: given by President Abraham Lincoln in 1863 at the dedication of the national cemetery in Gettysburg

For the complete text and more information about the Gettysburg Address, go to:

http://www.ourdocuments.gov/doc.php?flash=true&doc=36

Sample Test Question and Rationale

(Average)

1. **The Constitution of the United States:**

   A. Is an unwritten constitution

   B. Is a precise, formal, written document

   C. Does not allow states to be sovereign in their own affairs

   D. Can be amended on the vote of two-thirds of the states

Answer: B. Is a precise, formal, written document

The U.S. Constitution is not an unwritten constitution. It is not true that the U.S. Constitution fails to allow states to be sovereign in their own affairs. It requires three-fourths of the states, not two-thirds, to amend the Constitution.

Knows the rights and responsibilities of citizenship in a democracy

Bill of Rights

The first ten amendments to the U.S. Constitution address civil liberties and civil rights. They were written mostly by James Madison. Here they are in brief:

1. Freedom of religion

2. Right to bear arms

3. Security from the quartering of troops in homes

4. Right against unreasonable search and seizure

5. Right against self-incrimination

6. Right to trial by jury, right to legal council

7. Right to jury trial for civil actions

8. No cruel or unusual punishment allowed

9. These rights shall not deny other rights the people enjoy

10. Powers not mentioned in the Constitution shall be retained by the states or the people

It is presumed that all citizens of the United States will recognize their responsibilities to the country and that the surest way of protecting their rights is by exercising those rights, which also entail a responsibility. Some examples include the *right* to vote and the *responsibility* to be well-informed on various issues, the *right* to a trial by jury and the *responsibility* to ensure the proper working of the justice system by performing jury duty (rather than avoiding it). In the end, it is only by the mutual recognition of the fact that an individual has both rights and responsibilities in society that enables the society to function in order to protect those very rights.

Sample Test Question and Rationale

(Rigorous)

1. All of the following are rights that are granted by the Bill of Rights EXCEPT:

   A. Freedom of religion

   B. No cruel or unusual punishment allowed

   C. Right to a free education

   D. Security from the quartering of troops in homes

Answer: C. Right to a free education

The right to a free education is not included in the Bill of Rights.

COMPETENCY 13
ECONOMICS

SKILL 13.1 Knows key terms and basic concepts of economics *(e.g., supply and demand, scarcity and choice, money and resources)*

MARKET: the mechanism that brings buyers and sellers in contact with each other so that they can buy and sell

INPUT MARKET: the market in which factors of production, or resources, are bought and sold

A **MARKET** is defined as the mechanism that brings buyers and sellers in contact with each other so that they can buy and sell. Buyers and sellers do not have to meet face to face; for example, when the consumer buys a good from a catalog or through the Internet, the buyer never comes face to face with the seller, yet both buyer and seller are part of a bona fide market.

Markets exist in both the input and output sides of the economy. The **INPUT MARKET** is the market in which factors of production, or resources, are bought and sold. Factors of production, or inputs, fall into four broad categories:

- Land

- Labor

- Capital

- Entrepreneurship

Each of these four inputs is used in the production of every good and service. **OUTPUT MARKETS** refer to the market in which goods and services are sold. When the consumer goes to the local shoe store to buy a pair of shoes, the shoes are the output, and the consumer is taking part in the output market. However, the shoe store is a participant in both the input and output market. The sales clerk and workers are hiring out their resource of labor in return for a wage rate. Therefore they are participating in the input market.

In a market-oriented economy, all of these markets function on the basis of supply and demand. The **EQUILIBRIUM PRICE** is determined as the overlap of the buying decisions of buyers with the selling decision of sellers. This is true whether the market is an input market, with a market rate of wage, or an output market, with a market price of the output. A market-oriented economy results in the most efficient allocation of resources.

The best place to see supply and demand and markets in action is at a stock exchange or a commodity futures exchange. Buyers and sellers come face to face in the trading pit and accomplish trades by open outcry. Sellers who want to sell stocks or futures contracts call out the prices at which they will sell. Buyers who want to buy stocks or futures contracts call out the prices at which they will buy. When the two sides agree on price, a trade is made. This process goes on throughout trading hours. It is easiest to see how markets and supply and demand function in this kind of setting because it is open and obvious.

The same kinds of forces are at work at your local shopping mall or grocery store, even though the price appears as a given to you, the consumer. The price you see was arrived at through the operation of supply and demand. In this way, the equilibrium price is the price that clears the markets. The phrase "clears the market" means that there are no shortages or surpluses. If the price is too high, consumers won't buy the product and the store will have a surplus of the good. The stores then have to lower prices to eliminate the surplus merchandise. If the price is too low, consumers will buy so much that there will be a shortage. The shortage is then alleviated as the price goes up, rationing the good to those who are willing and able to pay the higher price for it.

In cases where government imposes legally mandated prices, the result can either be a shortage—with a price imposed that is above the market price—or a surplus, with a price imposed below the market price. The existence of price supports in agriculture is the reason for the surplus in agricultural products.

OUTPUT MARKETS: the market in which goods and services are sold

EQUILIBRIUM PRICE: the overlap of the buying decisions of buyers with the selling decision of sellers

Sample Test Questions and Rationale

(Rigorous)

1. **What is a market?**

   A. A place where people buy groceries

   B. The mechanism that brings buyers and sellers in contact with each other

   C. A stock exchange or a commodity futures exchange

   D. The process of supply and demand

   Answer: B. The mechanism that brings buyers and sellers in contact with each other

   People do buy groceries in markets but that is not the kind of market that is being discussed here. A stock exchange and a commodity futures exchange are features of a market but do not make up a market by themselves. The process of supply and demand is intimately related to market activity, but it is not a market.

(Easy)

2. **Which of the following terms best describes the international nature of commerce today?**

   A. Industrialization

   B. Laissez-faire

   C. Globalization

   D. Autarky

   Answer: C. Globalization

   Industrialization is an "older" term in that it describes the transformation of the economies of mostly western nations from an agricultural base to an industrial production base. Laissez-faire means allowing the markets to operate in an unimpeded fashion without excessive rules and regulations. Autarky was the effort by some nations, such as Germany during the Nazi period to become economically self-sufficient. Autarky is often seen as an economic preparation for war.

SKILL 13.2 **Understands how economics effects population, resources, and technology**

The scarcity of resources is the basis for the existence of economics. Economics is defined as a study of how scarce resources are allocated to satisfy unlimited wants. In this sense, resources refer to these four factors of production:

- **Labor:** Anyone who sells his or her ability to produce goods and services.

- **Capital:** Anything that is manufactured to be used in the production process.

- **Land:** The land itself and everything occurring naturally on it (such as oil, minerals, and lumber).

- **Entrepreneurship:** The ability of an individual to combine the three inputs with his or her own talents to produce a viable good or service. The entrepreneur takes the risk and experiences the losses or profits.

The fact that the supply of these resources is finite means that society cannot have as much of everything that it wants. There is a constraint on production and consumption as well as on the kinds of goods and services that can be produced and consumed.

Scarcity means that choices have to be made. If society decides to produce more of one good, this means that fewer resources are available for the production of other goods. For example, assume that a society can produce two goods: good x and good y. The society uses resources in the production of each good. If producing one unit of good x requires the same amount of resources used to produce three units of good y, then producing one more unit of good x results in a decrease in three units of good y. In effect, one unit of good x "costs" three units of good y. This cost is referred to as opportunity cost.

Opportunity cost is essentially the value of the sacrificed alternative: the value of what had to be given up in order to have the output of good x. Opportunity cost does not just refer to production. Your opportunity cost of studying with this guide is the value of what you are not doing because you are studying, whether it is watching TV, spending time with family, or working. Every choice has an opportunity cost.

If wants were limited and/or if resources were unlimited, the concepts of choice and opportunity cost would not exist, and neither would the field of economics. There would be enough resources to satisfy the wants of consumers, businesses, and governments. The allocation of resources wouldn't be a problem. Society could have more of both good x and good y without having to give up anything. There would be no opportunity cost. However, this isn't the situation that societies are faced with.

Because resources are scarce, society doesn't want to waste them. Society wants to obtain the most satisfaction it can from the consumption of the goods and services produced with its scarce resources. The members of society don't want their scarce resources wasted through inefficiency. This means that producers must choose an efficient production process, which is the lowest-cost means of production. High costs mean wasted resources.

Consumers also don't want society's resources to be wasted by producing goods that they don't want. Producers reduce this kind of inefficiency by determining which goods their consumers want. They do this by watching how consumers spend their money, essentially "voting" with their dollar spending. A desirable good, one that consumers want, earns profits. A good that incurs losses is a good that society doesn't want its resources wasted on. This signals the producer that society, as a whole, wants its resources used in another way.

Sample Test Question and Rationale

(Rigorous)

1. The following are factors of production EXCEPT:

   A. Labor

   B. Entrepreneurship

   C. Land

   D. Income

Answer: D. Income

Income is not a factor of production. However, it would be a possible factor of demand.

SKILL 13.3 **Understands the government's role in economics and impact of economics on government**

The Role of Government

Government is required to provide the framework for the functioning of the economy.

Even in a capitalist economy, there is a role for government. Government is required to provide the framework for the functioning of the economy. This requires a legal system, a monetary system, and a "watchdog" authority to protect consumers from bad or dangerous products and practices. Society needs a government to correct for the misallocation of resources when the market doesn't function properly, as in the case of externalities, like pollution. Another function of the government is to correct for the unequal distribution of income that results from a market-oriented system. Government functions to provide public goods, like national defense, and to correct for macro-instability like inflation and unemployment through the use of monetary and fiscal policies. Although there are countless more ways in which the government acts on the economy, these are the more important ways.

In the same way, economics has an impact on government. First, the government has to respond to economic situations. Inflation and unemployment call on the government to implement various economic policies. The business cycle and the policies implemented to counter the business cycle affect the level of tax revenues that the government receives. This affects the budget and the amount of dollars that government has to spend on various programs.

A government that has lower tax revenues due to economic conditions has to postpone certain discretionary spending programs until the economy improves. Unlike individuals, government can spend more tax dollars than it receives and operate in a debt condition financed by selling bonds. These are dollars that have to be repaid at some future date. Different economic conditions and situations call on the government to respond with different policies; the government has to figure out what to do and how much to do in each situation.

Types of Economic Systems

Economic systems refer to the arrangements a society has devised to answer what are known as the "three questions":

1. What goods to produce

2. How to produce the goods

3. For whom the goods are being produced (or how the allocation of the output is determined)

Different economic systems answer these questions in different ways.

A **MARKET ECONOMY** answers these questions in terms of demand and supply and the use of markets. Consumers vote for the products they want with their dollar spending. Goods acquiring enough dollar votes are profitable, signaling to the producers that society wants its scarce resources used in this way. This is how the *what* question is answered. The producer then hires inputs in accordance with the goods consumers want, looking for the most efficient or lowest-cost method of production. The lower a firm's costs for any given level of revenue, the higher the firm's profits. This is the way the *how* question is answered in a market economy. The for *whom* question is answered in the marketplace by the determination of the equilibrium price. Price serves to ration the goods to those who can and will transact at the market price or better. Those who can't or won't are excluded from the market. The United States has a market economy.

The opposite of the market economy is called the **CENTRALLY PLANNED ECONOMY**. This used to be called Communism, even though the term is not correct in a strict Marxian sense. In a planned economy, the means of production are publicly owned, with little, if any private ownership. Instead of the "three questions" being solved by markets, there is a planning authority that makes the decisions. The

> **MARKET ECONOMY:** an economy that operates by voluntary exchange in a free market and is not planned or controlled by a central authority

> *The United States has a market economy.*

> **CENTRALLY PLANNED ECONOMY:** the opposite of the market economy, the means of production are publicly owned, with little, if any private ownership

planning authority decides what will be produced and how. Since most planned economies direct resources into the production of capital and military goods, there is little remaining for consumer goods; the result is often chronic shortages. Price functions as an accounting measure and does not reflect scarcity. The former Soviet Union and most of the Eastern Bloc countries were planned economies of this sort.

> **MARKET SOCIALISM:** a mixed economic system that uses both markets and planning

In between the two extremes is **MARKET SOCIALISM**. This is a mixed economic system that uses both markets and planning. Planning is usually used to direct resources at the upper levels of the economy, with markets used to determine the prices of consumer goods and wages. This kind of economic system answers the "three questions" with planning and markets. The former Yugoslavia was a market socialist economy.

You can put each nation of the world on a continuum in terms of these characteristics and rank them from most capitalistic to most planned. The United States would probably rank as the most capitalistic and North Korea would probably rank as the most planned, but this doesn't mean that the United States doesn't engage in planning or that economies like mainland China don't use markets.

Sample Test Question and Rationale

(Average)

1. **The United States has which type of economy?**

    A. A market economy

    B. A centrally planned economy

    C. A market socialist economy

    D. None of the above

Answer: A. A market economy

A market economy is one that is dependent on forces in the marketplace to determine what goods are manufactured and how they are distributed.

COMPETENCY 14

SOCIAL STUDIES AS INQUIRY AND SOCIAL STUDIES PROCESSES

> **SKILL 14.1** **Understands social studies as inquiry** *(e.g., questioning, gathering data, drawing reasonable conclusions)*

Research in social studies can take many forms in order to test hypotheses. Qualitative studies are more common in social sciences than the scientific method described below. Descriptive, phenomenological studies may be utilized. The type of research is not as important as the willingness to be open to what the data say. This includes exploring unusual ideas and sources, gathering data according to stringent standards, and safeguarding against bias.

Qualitative studies are more common in social sciences than the scientific method.

The Scientific Method

The scientific method is the process by which social science (and other) researchers over time endeavor to construct an accurate (that is, reliable, consistent and nonarbitrary) representation of the world. Recognizing that personal and cultural beliefs influence both our perceptions and our interpretations of natural phenomena, standard procedures and criteria minimize those influences when developing a theory.

The scientific method has four steps:

1. Observation and description of a phenomenon or group of phenomena

2. Formulation of a hypothesis to explain the phenomena

3. Use of the hypothesis to predict the existence of other phenomena or to predict quantitatively the results of new observations

4. Performance of experimental tests of the predictions by several independent experimenters and properly performed experiments

While the researcher may bring certain biases to the study, it's important that bias not be permitted to enter into the interpretation. It's also important that data that do not fit the hypothesis not be ruled out. This is unlikely to happen if the researcher is open to the possibility that the hypothesis might turn out to be null.

Another important caution is to be certain that the methods for analyzing and interpreting are flawless. Abiding by these mandates is important if the discovery is to make a contribution to human understanding.

The phenomena that interest social scientists are usually complex. Capturing that complexity more fully requires the assessment of simultaneous covariations along the following dimensions: the units of observation, their characteristics, and time. This is how behavior occurs. For example, obtaining a richer and more accurate picture of the progress of schoolchildren means measuring changes in their knowledge attainment over time together with changes in the school over time. This acknowledges that changes in one area of behavior are usually contingent on changes in other areas. Models used for research in the past were inadequate to handle the complexities suggested by multiple covariations. However, the evolution of computerized data processing has taken away that constraint.

While descriptions of the research project and presentation of outcomes along with analysis must be a part of every report, graphs, charts, and sometimes maps are necessary to make the results clearly understandable.

Maps and Graphs

> Maps are a quick way to convey information that otherwise might take hundreds of words to explain.

Maps are a quick way to convey information that otherwise might take hundreds of words to explain. Maps reflect the great variety of knowledge covered by social sciences. To show such a variety of information, maps are made in many different ways. Because of this variety, maps must be understood in order to make the best sense of them. Once they are understood, maps provide a solid foundation for social science studies.

To apply information obtained from graphs, one must understand the two major reasons graphs are used:

1. To present a *model* or *theory* visually in order to show how two or more variables interrelate

2. To present *real-world* data visually in order to show how two or more variables interrelate

Teaching students to organize information

Giving students an outline of the purpose of a project or research presentation is extremely useful. Such an outline often includes:

- Purpose: Identify the reason for the research.
- Objective: Have students define a clear thesis for a project to allow them opportunities to be specific on Internet searches.

- **Preparation:** When using resources or collecting data, instruct students to create folders for sorting through the information. Providing labels for the folders will create a system of organization that will make construction of the final project or presentation easier and less time-consuming.

- **Procedure:** Instruct students to organize folders and create a procedural list of what the project or presentation needs to include.

- **Visuals or artifacts:** Have students choose data or visuals that are specific to the subject content or presentation. Make sure that poster boards or PowerPoint presentations can be seen from all areas of the classroom. Teachers can provide laptop computers for PowerPoint presentations.

Sample Test Questions and Rationale

(Average)

1. The literature that exists in a particular field of historical study is often called:

   A. The historiography

   B. The bibliography

   C. The histology

   D. The faculty

   Answer: A. The historiography

   A bibliography is a list of sources at the end of a book. Histology is a medical term that has nothing to do with the study of history. Faculty are the members of the teaching staff at a school or university.

(Rigorous)

2. What is a major drawback to using maps in social studies?

   A. They provide a solid foundation for social science studies

   B. They quickly convey complex information

   C. They reflect a great variety of knowledge

   D. They must be understood to be of value

   Answer: D. They must be understood to be of value

   Maps are a quick way to convey information that, otherwise, might take hundreds of words to explain. Maps reflect the great variety of knowledge covered by social sciences. To show such a variety of information, maps are made in many different ways. Because of this variety, maps must be understood in order to make the best sense of them. Once they are understood, maps provide a solid foundation for social science studies.

SKILL 14.2 **Understands how to use resource and research material in social studies**

Historical data can come from a wide range of sources, beginning with libraries. Records and guides are almost universally digitally organized and available for instant searching by era, topic, event, personality, or area. The Internet offers possibilities for finding even the most obscure information. However, even with all these resources available, nothing is more valuable than a visit to the site being researched, including a visit to historical societies, local libraries, sometimes even local schools.

A historian was searching for an answer to the question as to why her great-great-grandfather had enlisted in the Union army even though he lived in the Deep South, so she went to the site where he grew up and found the answer in the historical records stored in the local schoolhouse for lack of a formal historical society. The residents of the little town were also able to answer her question. She would never have found that historical information if she hadn't visited the site.

The same things could be said about geographical data. It's possible to find a map of almost any area online; however, the best maps are available locally as is knowledge and information about the development of the area. For example, a courthouse had been moved from one small town to another in a county in Tennessee for no apparent reason. However, the local oldtimers can tell you. The railroad wanted to come through town, and the farmers in the area surrounding the old courthouse didn't want to raise the $100,000 it would take; they were also concerned that the trains would scare their cows. This type of information is not in a history book, yet it would be very important to a study of the geography of the area.

Having noted the value of direct information, reference sources also can be of great value, and teaching students how to access these will give them skills that will help them access more in-depth databases and sources of information.

REFERENCE MATERIALS	
Encyclopedias	Reference materials that appear in book or electronic form and can be considered general or specific. General encyclopedias peripherally cover most fields of knowledge; specific encyclopedias cover a smaller amount of material in greater depth. Encyclopedias are good first sources of information for students. While their scope is limited, they can provide a quick introduction to topics so that students can get familiar with the topics before exploring them in greater depth.

Table continued on next page

Almanacs	References that provide statistical information on various topics. Typically, these references are rather specific. They often cover a specific period of time. One famous example is the Farmer's Almanac. This annual publication summarizes weather conditions for the previous year, among many other things.
Bibliographies	Usually organized topically, bibliographies contain references for further research. They point people to the in-depth resources they will need for a complete review of a topic.
Databases	Collections of material, typically electronic, on specific topics. For example, teachers can go online and find many databases of science articles for students on a variety of topics. The Internet and other research resources provide a wealth of information on thousands of interesting topics for students preparing presentations or projects. Using search engines like Google and Yahoo!, students can search multiple Internet resources or databases in one subject search.
Atlases	Collections of maps usually bound into a book that contain geographic features, political boundaries, and perhaps social, religious, and economic statistics. Atlases can be found at most libraries but they are widely available on the Internet. The U.S. Library of Congress holds more than 53,000 atlases, most likely the largest and most comprehensive collection in the world.
Periodical Guides	References that categorize articles and special editions of journals and magazines to help archive and organize the vast amount of material that is put in periodicals each year.
Statistical Surveys	Surveys used in the social sciences to collect information on a sample of the population. With any kind of information, care must be taken to accurately record information so the results are not skewed or distorted.
Opinion Polls	Records of the opinions of a population obtained by asking a number of people a series of questions about a product, place, person, or event and then using the results to apply the answers to a larger group or population. Polls, like surveys, are subject to errors in the process. Errors can occur based on who is asked the question, where they are asked, the time of day, or the biases one may hold related to the poll being taken.

Primary and Secondary Sources

The resources used in the study of history and social studies can be divided into two major groups: primary sources and secondary sources.

PRIMARY SOURCES are works that were created during the period being studied or immediately after it. **SECONDARY SOURCES** are works written significantly after the period being studied and based upon primary sources.

Primary sources include documents that reflect the immediate and everyday concerns of people. Guidelines for the use of primary sources:

1. Understand them in the context in which they were produced

PRIMARY SOURCES:
works created during the period being studied or immediately after it

SECONDARY SOURCES:
works written significantly after the period being studied and based upon primary sources

2. Do not read history blindly; be certain that you understand both explicit and implicit references in the material

3. Read the entire text you are reviewing; do not simply extract a few sentences to read

4. Although anthologies of materials may help you identify primary source materials, consult the full original text

Secondary sources include the following kinds of materials:

1. Books written on the basis of primary materials about the period of time

2. Books written on the basis of primary materials about persons who played a major role in the events under consideration

3. Books and articles written on the basis of primary materials about the culture, the social norms, the language, and the values of the period

4. Quotations from primary sources

5. Statistical data on the period

6. The conclusions and inferences of other historians

7. Multiple interpretations of the ethos of the time

Guidelines for the use of secondary sources:

1. Do not rely upon only a single secondary source

2. Check facts and interpretations against primary sources whenever possible

3. Do not accept the conclusions of other historians uncritically

4. Place greatest reliance on secondary sources created by the best and most respected scholars

5. Do not use the inferences of other scholars as if they were facts

6. Ensure that you recognize any bias the writer brings to his or her interpretation of history

7. Understand the primary point of the book as a basis for evaluating the value of the material presented in it to your questions

Sample Test Questions and Rationale

(Average)

1. Which of the following is a primary source document?

   A. A book recounting the events surrounding the 1932 kidnapping of aviator Charles Lindbergh's son

   B. A newspaper story about the Wall Street crash of 1987

   C. The text of Franklin D. Roosevelt's address to Congress of December 8, 1941, requesting a declaration of war against Japan

   D. A movie dramatizing the life of a fictional family living in Poland during the German invasion of 1939

   Answer: C. The text of Franklin D. Roosevelt's address to Congress of December 8, 1941, requesting a declaration of war against Japan

   A book or a newspaper story describing a historical event are secondary sources. A movie can only be a primary source if it presents primary source materials—such as a documentary that presents archival photographs and interviews with actual survivors of a historical event.

(Average)

2. An example of something that is not a primary source is:

   A. The published correspondence between Winston Churchill and Franklin D. Roosevelt during World War II

   B. Martin Gilbert's biography of Winston Churchill

   C. The diary of Field Marshal Sir Alan Brooke, the head of the British Army during World War II

   D. Franklin D. Roosevelt's handwritten notes from the World War II era

   Answer: B. Martin Gilbert's biography of Winston Churchill

   Martin Gilbert's biography of Winston Churchill is a secondary source because it was not written by Churchill himself. The Churchill-Roosevelt correspondence, Brooke's diary, and FDR's handwritten notes are all primary source documents written by actual historical figures.

Sample Test Questions and Rationale (cont.)

(Rigorous)

3. Which of the following is NOT an effective way to compile research sources?

A. Analyze the applicability and validity of the massive amounts of information in cyberspace

B. Discern authentic sources of information from the mass collections of Web sites and information databases available

C. Bookmark Web sites of interest and cut and paste relevant information onto word documents for citation and reference

D. Avoid using large search engines like Google and Yahoo to minimize the amount of irrelevant, unauthentic sources and save a lot of research time

Answer: D. Avoid using large search engines like Google and Yahoo to minimize the amount of irrelevant, unauthentic sources and save a lot of research time.

The world of electronic research opens up a global library, and large search engines like Google, combined with effective keywords and constructive search strategies, will help a writer find valid sources. It is important to analyze each source for both validity and authenticity to avoid nonsense sources, and it is acceptable to bookmark and copy/paste relevant information into a word document as long as it is for citation and reference and not plagiarism.

SKILL 14.3 **Understands process skills in social studies** *(e.g., interpreting different types of information; evaluating relationships; drawing conclusions using tools of the field)*

Interpreting Information

Making a decision based on a set of given information requires a careful interpretation of the information to decide the strength of the evidence supplied and what it means.

For example, a chart showing that the number of people of foreign birth living in the United States has increased annually over the last ten years might allow one to make conclusions about population growth and changes in the relative sizes of ethnic groups in the United States. The chart would not give information about the reason the number of foreign-born citizens increased, or address matters of immigration status. Conclusions in these areas would be invalid based on this information.

Analyzing an event or issue from multiple perspectives involves seeking out sources that advocate or express those perspectives, and comparing them with one another. Listening to the speeches of Martin Luther King, Jr. provides insight into the perspective of one group of people concerning the issue of civil rights in the U.S. in the 1950s and 1960s. The public statements of George Wallace, an American governor opposed to desegregation, provides another perspective from the same time period. Looking at the legislation that was proposed at the time and how it came into effect offers a window into the thinking of the day.

Comparing these perspectives on the matter of civil rights provides information on the key issues that each group was concerned about, and gives a fuller picture of the societal changes that were occurring at that time. Analysis of any social event, issue, problem, or phenomenon requires that various perspectives be taken into account in this way.

One way to analyze historical events, patterns, and relationships is to focus on historical themes. There are many themes that run throughout human history, and they can be used to make comparisons between different historical times as well as between nations and peoples. While new themes are always being explored, a few of the widely recognized historical themes are:

- Politics and political institutions can provide information about the prevailing opinions and beliefs of a group of people and how they change over time. Historically, Texas, for example, has produced several important political figures and was a traditional supporter of the Democratic Party for nearly a century. This has changed in recent years, with the Republican Party gaining more influence and control of Texas politics. Looking at the political history of the state can reveal the popular social ideals that have developed in Texas, and how they have changed over time.

- Race is a term used most generally to describe a population of people from a common geographic area that share certain common physical traits. Skin color and facial features have traditionally been used to categorize individuals by race. The term has generated some controversy among sociologists, anthropologists, and biologists in terms of what, if anything, is meant by race and racial variation. Biologically speaking, a race consists of people who share a common genetic lineage. Socially, race can be more complicated to define, with many people identifying themselves as part of a racial group that others might not. This self-perception of race, and the perception of race by others, is perhaps more crucial than any genetic variation when trying to understand the social implications of variations in race.

- An ethnic group is a group of people who identify themselves as having a common social background and set of behaviors, and who perpetuate their culture by traditions of marriage within their own group. Ethnic groups often share a common language and ancestral background, and frequently exist within larger populations with which they interact. Ethnicity and race are sometimes interlinked, but differ in that many ethnic groups can exist within a population of people thought to be of the same race. Ethnicity is based more on common cultural behaviors and institutions than common physical traits.

- The study of gender issues is a theme that focuses on the relative places men and women hold in a society, and is connected to many other themes such as politics and economics. In the United States, for many years women were not allowed to vote, for example. In economic matters, married women were expected not to hold jobs. For women who did work, a limited number of types of work were available. Investigating the historical theme of gender can reveal changes in public attitudes, economic changes, and shifting political attitudes, among other things.

- Economic factors drive many social activities, such as where people live and work and the relative wealth of nations. As a historical theme, economic history can connect events to their economic causes and explore the results. Mexican immigration is a national political issue currently. Economic imbalances between the United States and Mexico are driving many Mexicans to look for work in the United States. As a border state with historic ties to Mexico, Texas receives a large number of these immigrants and has the second largest Hispanic population in the country, which plays a crucial role in Texas's current economy. The subject of immigration in Texas is an example of how the historical themes of politics, economics, and race can intersect, each providing a line of historic interpretation into Texas's past.

- Historical concepts are movements, belief systems, or other phenomena that can be identified and examined individually or as part of a historical theme. Capitalism, communism, democracy, racism, and globalization are all examples of historical concepts. Historical concepts can be interpreted as part of larger historical themes and provide insight into historical events by placing them in a larger historical context. The historical concept of colonialism, for example, is that a nation should seek to control areas outside of its borders for economic and political gain by establishing settlements and controlling the native inhabitants. Beginning in the seventeenth century, France and Spain were both actively colonizing North America, with the French establishing a colony at the mouth of the Mississippi River. Spain moved into the area to contain the French and keep them away from their settlements in present-day Mexico.

Sample Test Question and Rationale

(Rigorous)

1. Which of the following is an example of a historical concept?

    A. Capitalism

    B. Racism

    C. Globalization

    D. All of the above

Answer: D. All of the above

Historical concepts are movements, belief systems, or other phenomena that can be identified and examined individually or as part of a historical theme. Capitalism, communism, democracy, racism, and globalization are all examples of historical concepts. Historical concepts can be interpreted as part of larger historical themes and provide insight into historical events by placing them in a larger historical context.

DOMAIN IV
SCIENCE

PERSONALIZED STUDY PLAN

KNOWN MATERIAL/ SKIP IT

COMPETENCY 15
EARTH SCIENCE

> SKILL **Understands the structure of the Earth system** *(e.g., structure and*
> 15.1 *properties of the solid Earth, the hydrosphere, the atmosphere)*

Earth's Plates

Data obtained from many sources led scientists to develop the theory of **PLATE TECTONICS**. This theory is the most current model that explains not only the movement of the continents but also the changes in the Earth's crust caused by internal forces.

PLATES are rigid blocks of the Earth's crust and upper mantle. These rigid solid blocks make up the lithosphere. The Earth's lithosphere is broken into nine large sections and several small ones. These moving slabs are called plates. The major plates are named after the continents they are "transporting." The plates float on and move with a layer of hot, plastic-like rock in the upper mantle. Geologists believe that the heat currents circulating within the mantle cause this plastic zone of rock to slowly flow, carrying along the overlying crustal plates.

Movement of these crustal plates creates areas where the plates diverge as well as areas where the plates converge. A major area of divergence is located in the Mid-Atlantic. Currents of hot mantle rock rise and separate at this point of divergence, creating new oceanic crust at the rate of two to ten centimeters per year. Convergence is when the oceanic crust collides with either another oceanic plate or a continental plate. The oceanic crust sinks, forming an enormous trench and generating volcanic activity. Convergence also includes continent-to-continent plate collisions. When two plates slide past one another, a transform fault is created.

These movements produce many major features of the Earth's surface, such as mountain ranges, volcanoes, and earthquake zones. Most of these features are located at plate boundaries, where the plates interact by spreading apart, pressing together, or sliding past each other. These movements are very slow, averaging only a few centimeters a year.

Boundaries form between spreading plates where the crust is forced apart in a process called rifting. Rifting generally occurs at mid-ocean ridges. Rifting can

PLATE TECTONICS: theory that explains not only the movement of the continents but also the changes in the Earth's crust caused by internal forces

PLATES: rigid blocks of the Earth's crust and upper mantle

also take place within a continent, splitting the continent into smaller landmasses that drift away from each other, thereby forming an ocean basin between them. The Red Sea is a product of rifting. As the seafloor spreading takes place, new material is added to the inner edges of the separating plates. In this way the plates grow larger, and the ocean basin widens. This is the process that broke up the supercontinent Pangaea and created the Atlantic Ocean.

Boundaries between plates that are colliding are zones of intense crustal activity. When a plate of ocean crust collides with a plate of continental crust, the more dense oceanic plate slides under the lighter continental plate and plunges into the mantle. This process is called subduction, and the site where it takes place is called a subduction zone. A subduction zone is usually seen on the sea floor as a deep depression called a trench.

The crustal movement identified by plates sliding sideways past each other produces a plate boundary characterized by major faults that are capable of unleashing powerful earthquakes. The San Andreas fault forms such a boundary between the Pacific plate and the North American plate.

Atmosphere

Dry air has three basic components: dry gas, water vapor, and solid particles (dust from soil, etc.).

The most abundant dry gases in the atmosphere are:

(N_2) Nitrogen 78.09 %	(Ar) Argon 0.93 %
(O_2) Oxygen 20.95 %	(CO_2) Carbon Dioxide 0.03 %

The atmosphere is divided into four main layers based on temperature:

- Troposphere: This layer is the closest to the Earth's surface. All weather phenomena occur here because it is the layer with the most water vapor and dust. Air temperature decreases with increasing altitude. The average thickness of the troposphere is seven miles (eleven kilometers).

- Stratosphere: This layer contains very little water. Clouds within this layer are extremely rare. The ozone layer is located in the upper portions of the stratosphere. Air temperature is fairly constant but does increase somewhat with height due to the absorption of solar energy and ultraviolet rays from the ozone layer.

- Mesosphere: Air temperature again decreases with height in this layer. This is the coldest layer, with temperatures in the range of -1000C at the top.

• Thermosphere: This layer extends upward into space. Oxygen molecules in this layer absorb energy from the Sun, causing temperatures to increase with height. The lower part of the thermosphere is called the ionosphere. Here, charged particles (ions) and free electrons can be found. When gases in the ionosphere are excited by solar radiation, the gases give off light and glow in the sky. These glowing lights are called the aurora borealis in the Northern Hemisphere and aurora australis in the Southern Hemisphere. The upper portion of the thermosphere is called the exosphere. Gas molecules are very far apart in this layer. Layers of exosphere are also known as the Van Allen belts and are held together by the Earth's magnetic field.

Sample Test Question and Rationale

(Easy)

1. **Which of the following layers comprises the Earth's plates?**

   A. Mesosphere

   B. Troposphere

   C. Asthenosphere

   D. Lithosphere

Answer: D. Lithosphere

The lithosphere is made up of the crust and the upper mantle. The lithosphere "floats" on the asthenosphere, causing the plates to move across the Earth's surface.

SKILL 15.2 **Understands the processes of the Earth system** *(e.g., earth processes of the solid Earth, the hydrosphere, the atmosphere)*

Mountains

OROGENY is the term given to natural mountain building. A mountain is terrain that has been raised high above the surrounding landscape by volcanic action, or some form of tectonic plate collisions. The plate collisions could either be intercontinental collisions or ocean floor collisions with a continental crust (subduction).

The physical composition of mountains includes igneous, metamorphic, and sedimentary rocks; some may have rock layers that are tilted or distorted by plate collision forces.

OROGENY: natural mountain building

The physical composition of mountains includes igneous, metamorphic, and sedimentary rocks

There are many different types of mountains. The physical attributes of a mountain range depend upon the angle at which plate movement thrusts layers of rock to the surface. Many mountains (the Adirondacks, the Southern Rockies) were formed along high-angle faults.

Folded mountains (the Alps, the Himalayas) are produced by the folding of rock layers during their formation. The Himalayas are the highest mountains in the world; they contain Mount Everest, which rises almost nine kilometers above sea level. The Himalayas were formed when India collided with Asia. The movement that created this collision is still in process at the rate of a few centimeters per year.

Fault-block mountains (in Utah, Arizona, and New Mexico) are created when plate movement produces tension forces instead of compression forces. The area under tension produces normal faults, and rock along these faults is displaced upward.

Dome mountains are formed as magma tries to push up through the crust but fails to break the surface. Dome mountains resemble a huge blister on the Earth's surface.

Upwarped mountains (the Black Hills of South Dakota) are created in association with a broad arching of the crust. They can also be formed by rock thrust upward along high angle faults.

The Formation of Mountains

Mountains are produced by different types of processes. Most major mountain ranges are formed by the processes of folding and faulting.

In folding, mountains are produced by the folding of rock layers. Crustal movements may press horizontal layers of sedimentary rock together from the sides, squeezing them into wavelike folds. Up-folded sections of rock are called anticlines; down-folded sections of rock are called synclines. The Appalachian Mountains are an example of folded mountains, with long ridges and valleys in a series of anticlines, and synclines formed by folded rock layers.

The Appalachian Mountains are an example of folded mountains.

Faults are fractures in the Earth's crust that have been created by either tension or compression forces transmitted through the crust. These forces are produced by the movement of separate blocks of crust. Faultings are categorized on the basis of the relative movement between the blocks on both sides of the fault plane. The movement can be horizontal, vertical, or oblique.

A dip-slip fault occurs when the movement of the plates is vertical and opposite. The displacement is in the direction of the inclination, or dip, of the fault. Dip-slip faults are classified as normal faults when the rock above the fault plane moves down relative to the rock below.

Reverse faults are created when the rock above the fault plane moves up relative to the rock below. Reverse faults with a very low angle to the horizontal are also referred to as thrust faults.

Faults in which the dominant displacement is horizontal movement along the trend or strike (length) of the fault are called strike-slip faults. When a large strike-slip fault is associated with plate boundaries it is called a transform fault. The San Andreas fault in California is a well-known transform fault.

Faults that have both vertical and horizontal movement are called oblique-slip faults.

Volcanoes

VOLCANISM is the term given to the movement of magma through the crust and its emergence as lava onto the Earth's surface. Volcanic mountains are built up by successive deposits of volcanic materials.

An ACTIVE VOLCANO is one that is currently erupting or building to an eruption. A DORMANT VOLCANO is one that is between eruptions but still shows signs of internal activity that might lead to an eruption in the future. An EXTINCT VOLCANO is said to be no longer capable of erupting. Most of the world's active volcanoes are found along the rim of the Pacific Ocean, which is also a major earthquake zone. This curving belt of active faults and volcanoes is often called the Ring of Fire. The world's best known volcanic mountains include Mount Etna in Italy and Mount Kilimanjaro in Africa. The Hawaiian Islands are actually the tops of a chain of volcanic mountains that rise from the ocean floor.

There are three types of volcanic mountains:

- Shield volcanoes are associated with quiet eruptions. Lava emerges from the vent or opening in the crater and flows freely out over the Earth's surface until it cools and hardens into a layer of igneous rock. A repeated lava flow builds this type of volcano into the largest volcanic mountain. Mauna Loa in Hawaii is the largest shield volcano on Earth.

- Cinder-cone volcanoes are associated with explosive eruptions as lava is hurled high into the air in a spray of droplets of various sizes. These droplets cool and harden into cinders and particles of ash before falling to the ground. The ash and cinder pile up around the vent to form a steep, cone-shaped hill called the cinder cone. Cinder-cone volcanoes are relatively small but may form quite rapidly.

- Composite volcanoes are those built by both lava flows and layers of ash and cinders. Mount Fuji in Japan, Mount St. Helens in the United States (Washington), and Mount Vesuvius in Italy are all famous composite volcanoes.

VOLCANISM: the movement of magma through the crust and its emergence as lava onto the Earth's surface

ACTIVE VOLCANO: one that is currently erupting or building to an eruption

DORMANT VOLCANO: one that is between eruptions but still shows signs of internal activity that might lead to an eruption in the future

EXTINCT VOLCANO: no longer capable of erupting

When lava cools, igneous rock is formed. This formation can occur either above or below ground.

INTRUSIVE ROCK: any igneous rock that was formed below the Earth's surface

EXTRUSIVE ROCK: any igneous rock that was formed at the Earth's surface

DIKES: old lava tubes formed when magma entered a vertical fracture and hardened

CALDERA: normally formed by the collapse of the top of a volcano

INTRUSIVE ROCK includes any igneous rock that was formed below the Earth's surface. Batholiths are the largest structures of intrusive rock and are composed of near-granite materials; they are the core of the Sierra Nevada Mountains. EXTRUSIVE ROCK includes any igneous rock that was formed at the Earth's surface.

DIKES are old lava tubes formed when magma entered a vertical fracture and hardened. Sometimes magma squeezes between two rock layers and hardens into a thin horizontal sheet called a sill. A laccolith is formed in much the same way as a sill, but the magma that creates a laccolith is very thick and does not flow easily. It pools and forces the overlying strata creating an obvious surface dome.

A CALDERA is normally formed by the collapse of the top of a volcano. This collapse can be caused by a massive explosion that destroys the cone and empties most, if not all, of the magma chamber below the volcano. The cone collapses into the empty magma chamber, forming a caldera.

An inactive volcano may have magma solidified in its pipe. This structure, called a volcanic neck, is resistant to erosion and today may be the only visible evidence of the past presence of an active volcano.

Rocks

There are three major subdivisions of rocks:

- Sedimentary rocks are created through a process known as lithification. It occurs when fluid sediments are transformed into solid rocks. One common process affecting sediments is compaction, when the weights of overlying materials compress and compact the deeper sediments. The compaction process leads to cementation. Cementation is when sediments are converted to sedimentary rock.

- Igneous rocks can be classified according to their texture, their composition, and the way they formed. They are made from molten rock. Molten rock is called magma. As magma cools, the elements and compounds begin to form crystals. The more slowly the magma cools, the larger the crystals grow. Rocks with large crystals are said to have a coarse-grained texture. Granite is an example of a coarse-grained igneous rock. Rocks that cool rapidly before any crystals can form have a glassy texture like obsidian, also commonly known as volcanic glass.

- Metamorphic rocks are formed by high temperatures and great pressures. The process by which the rocks undergo these changes is called metamorphism. The outcome of metamorphic changes includes deformation by extreme heat and pressure, compaction, destruction of the original characteristics of the parent rock, bending and folding while in a plastic stage, and the emergence of completely new and different minerals due to chemical reactions with heated water and dissolved minerals.

Metamorphic rocks are classified into two groups: foliated (leaflike) rocks and unfoliated rocks. Foliated rocks consist of compressed, parallel bands of minerals, which give the rocks a striped appearance. Examples of such rocks include slate, schist, and gneiss. Unfoliated rocks are not banded; examples of unfoliated rocks include quartzite, marble, and anthracite.

MINERALS are natural, nonliving solids with a definite chemical composition and a crystalline structure. ORES are minerals or rock deposits that can be mined for a profit. ROCKS are Earth materials made of one or more minerals. A ROCK FACIES is a rock group that differs from comparable rocks (as in composition, age, or fossil content).

Glaciation

About twelve thousand years ago, a vast sheet of ice covered a large part of the northern United States. This huge, frozen mass moved southward from the northern regions of Canada as several large bodies of slow-moving ice. These bodies of ice, called GLACIERS, are large masses of ice that move or flow over the land in response to gravity. Glaciers form among high mountains and in other cold regions. A time period in which glaciers advance over a large portion of a continent is called an ICE AGE.

Evidence of glacial coverage remains as abrasive grooves, large boulders from northern environments dropped in southerly locations, glacial troughs created by the rounding out of steep valleys through glacial scouring, and the remains of glacial sources called cirques that were created by frost wedging the rock at the bottom of the glacier. Remains of plants and animals typically found in warm climates that have been discovered in the moraines and outwash plains help support the theory of periods of warmth during the past ice ages.

The major ice age began about two to three million years ago. This age saw the advancement and retreat of glacial ice over millions of years. Theories relating to the origin of glacial activity include plate tectonics, through which it can be demonstrated that some continental masses, now in temperate climates, were at one time blanketed by ice and snow. Another theory involves changes in the Earth's orbit around the Sun, changes in the angle of the Earth's axis, and the wobbling of the Earth's axis. Support for the validity of this theory has come from deep-ocean research that indicates a correlation between climatic-sensitive microorganisms and the changes in the Earth's orbital status.

MINERALS: natural, non-living solids with a definite chemical composition and a crystalline structure

ORES: minerals or rock deposits that can be mined for a profit

ROCKS: Earth materials made of one or more minerals

ROCK FACIES: a rock group that differs from comparable rocks (as in composition, age, or fossil content)

GLACIERS: large masses of ice that move or flow over the land in response to gravity

ICE AGE: a time period in which glaciers advance over a large portion of a continent

There are two main types of glaciers: valley glaciers and continental glaciers. Erosion by valley glaciers is characteristic of U-shaped erosion. Valley glaciers produce sharp-peaked mountains such as the Matterhorn in Switzerland. Erosion by continental glaciers is characteristic of the movement of glaciers over mountains, leaving smoothed, rounded mountains and ridges in their paths.

Fossilization

A FOSSIL is the remains or trace of an ancient organism that has been preserved naturally in the Earth's crust. Sedimentary rocks usually are rich sources of fossil remains. Those fossils found in layers of sediment were embedded in the slowly forming sedimentary rock strata. The oldest fossils known are the traces of 3.5 billion-year-old bacteria found in sedimentary rocks. Few fossils are found in metamorphic rock, and virtually none are found in igneous rocks. The magma is so hot that any organism trapped in the magma is destroyed.

Although the fairly well preserved remains of a woolly mammoth embedded in ice were found in Russia in May 2007, the best-preserved animal remains are typically discovered in natural tar pits. When an animal accidentally falls into the tar, it becomes trapped, sinking to the bottom. Preserved bones of the saber-toothed cat have been found in tar pits.

Prehistoric insects have been found trapped in ancient amber or fossil resin that was excreted by some extinct species of pine trees. Fossil molds are the hollow spaces in a rock previously occupied by bones or shells. A fossil cast is a fossil mold that fills with sediments or minerals and later hardens, forming a cast.

Fossil tracks are the imprints in hardened mud left behind by birds or animals.

Types of Weathering

EROSION is the inclusion and transportation of surface materials by another moveable material—usually water, winds, or ice. The most important cause of erosion is running water. Streams, rivers, and tides are constantly at work removing weathered fragments of bedrock and carrying them away from their original location.

A stream erodes bedrock by the grinding action of the sand, pebbles, and other rock fragments. This grinding against each other is called abrasion. Streams also erode rocks by dissolving or absorbing their minerals. Limestone and marble are readily dissolved by streams.

DEPOSITION, also known as sedimentation, is the term for the process by which material from one area is slowly deposited into another area. This is usually due

FOSSIL: the remains or trace of an ancient organism that has been preserved naturally in the Earth's crust

Sedimentary rocks usually are rich sources of fossil remains.

EROSION: the inclusion and transportation of surface materials by another moveable material—usually water, winds, or ice

The most important cause of erosion is running water.

DEPOSITION: also known as sedimentation, the process by which material from one area is slowly deposited into another area to the movement of wind, water, or ice containing particles of matter. When the rate of movement slows down, particles filter out and remain behind, causing a buildup of matter. Note that this is a result of matter being eroded and removed from another site.

The breaking down of rocks at or near the Earth's surface is known as WEATHER-ING. Weathering breaks down these rocks into smaller and smaller pieces. There are two types of weathering: physical weathering and chemical weathering.

WEATHERING: the breaking down of rocks at or near the Earth's surface

Physical weathering is the process by which rocks are broken down into smaller fragments without undergoing any change in chemical composition. Physical weathering is mainly caused by the freezing of water, the expansion of rock, and the activities of plants and animals.

One example of physical weathering occurs through frost wedging, which is the cycle of daytime thawing and refreezing at night. This cycle causes large rock masses, especially the rocks exposed on mountaintops, to be broken into smaller pieces. Another example is the peeling away of the outer layers from a rock, which is called exfoliation. Rounded mountaintops are called exfoliation domes; they have been formed in this way.

Chemical weathering is the breaking down of rocks through changes in their chemical composition. Water, oxygen, and carbon dioxide are the main agents of chemical weathering. When water and carbon dioxide combine chemically, they produce a weak acid that breaks down rocks. An example of this is the change of feldspar in granite to clay.

Sample Test Questions and Rationale

(Average)

1. **What conditions are required to create coarse-grained igneous rocks?**

   A. High temperature and pressure

   B. Magma that cools slowly

   C. Lava that cools quickly

   D. Evaporation and cementation

Answer: B. Magma that cools slowly

Igneous rocks are formed from cooling magma and lava. Lava that cools quickly forms fine-grained or glassy igneous rocks as crystals do not have a chance to form. Magma that cools slowly forms coarse-grained igneous rocks as the crystals are given time to form.

Sample Test Questions and Rationale (cont.)

(Average)

2. **What is the main cause of the formation of mountains?**

   A. Glaciation

   B. Volcanism

   C. Orogeny

   D. Tectonic movements

Answer: D. Tectonic movements

The crust of the Earth is made up of very large plates, which move at very slow rates. When the plates collide, the surface of the Earth changes and mountains can be formed. Volcanoes also form mountains, but there are far fewer formed from the flow of magma than from the folding and faulting of tectonic plates. Orogeny is just the name given to the formation of mountains. Glaciation is the movement of large blocks of ice. It changes the landscape, but is not a cause of mountains.

SKILL 15.3 **Understands Earth history** *(e.g., origin of Earth, paleontology, the rock record)*

Earth's history extends over more than four billion years and is reckoned in terms of a scale. Paleontologists who study the history of the Earth have divided this huge period of time into four large time units called eons. Eons are divided into smaller units of time called eras. An era refers to a time interval in which particular plants and animals were dominant or present in great abundance. The end of an era is most often characterized by:

- A general uplifting of the crust

- The extinction of the dominant plants or animals

- The appearance of new life forms

Each era is divided into several smaller divisions of time called periods. Some periods are divided into smaller time units called epochs. The table below outlines these eras and periods by their major characteristics.

ERA	PERIOD	TIME	CHARACTERISTICS
Cenozoic	Quaternary	1.6 million years ago to the present	The ice age occurred, and human beings evolved.
	Tertiary	65-1.64 million years ago	Mammals and birds evolved to replace the great reptiles and dinosaurs that had just become extinct. Forests gave way to grasslands, and the climate become cooler.
Mesozoic	Cretaceous	135-65 million years ago	Reptiles and dinosaurs roamed the Earth. Most of the modern continents had split away from the large landmass, Pangaea, and many were flooded by shallow chalk seas.
	Jurassic	350-135 million years ago	Reptiles were beginning to evolve. Pangaea started to break up. Deserts gave way to forests and swamps.
	Triassic		
Paleozoic	Permian	355-250 million years ago	Continents came together to form one big landmass, Pangaea. Forests (that formed today's coal) grew on deltas around the new mountains, and deserts formed.
	Carboniferous		
	Devonian	410-355 million years ago	Continents started moving toward each other. The first land animals, such as insects and amphibians, existed. Many fish swam in the seas.
	Silurian	510-410 million years ago	Sea life flourished, and the first fish evolved. The earliest land plants began to grow around shorelines and estuaries.
	Ordovician		
	Cambrian	570-510 million years ago	No life on land, but many kinds of sea animals existed.
Precambrian	Proterozoic	Beginning of the Earth to 570 million years ago (seven-eighths of the Earth's history)	Some sort of life existed.
	Archaean		No life.

Using Geologic Evidence to Understand the Past

The process of determining the age of rocks by cataloging their composition has been outmoded since the middle 1800s. Today, a sequential history can be determined by the fossil content (principle of fossil succession) of a rock system as well as its superposition within a range of systems. This classification process was termed stratigraphy and permitted the construction of a geologic column in which rock systems are arranged in their correct chronological order.

UNIFORMITARIANISM is a fundamental concept in modern geology. It simply states that the physical, chemical, and biological laws that operated in the geologic past operate in the same way today. The forces and processes that we observe presently shaping our planet have been at work for a very long time. This idea is commonly stated as, "The present is the key to the past." CATASTROPHISM is the concept that the Earth was shaped by catastrophic events of a short-term nature.

Estimates of the Earth's age have been made possible with the discovery of radioactivity and the invention of instruments that can measure the amount of radioactivity in rocks. The use of radioactivity to make accurate determinations of Earth's age is called ABSOLUTE DATING. This process depends upon comparing the amount of radioactive material in a rock with the amount that has decayed in another element. Studying the radiation given off by atoms of radioactive elements is the most accurate method of measuring the Earth's age.

Radioactive atoms are unstable and are continuously breaking down or undergoing decay. The radioactive element that decays is called the parent element. The new element that results from the radioactive decay of the parent element is called the daughter element. The time required for one half of a given amount of a radioactive element to decay is called the half-life of that element or compound. Geologists also commonly use carbon dating to calculate the age of a fossil substance.

UNIFORMITARIANISM: states that the physical, chemical, and biological laws that operated in the geologic past operate in the same way today

CATASTROPHISM: the concept that the Earth was shaped by catastrophic events of a short-term nature

ABSOLUTE DATING: the use of radioactivity to make accurate determinations of Earth's age

Studying the radiation given off by atoms of radioactive elements is the most accurate method of measuring the Earth's age.

Sample Test Questions and Rationale

(Easy)

1. The use of radioactivity to determine the age of rocks and fossils is called which of the following?

   A. Carbon dating

   B. Absolute dating

   C. Stratigraphy

   D. Geological dating

Answer: B. Absolute dating

Carbon dating measures the relative amount of carbon-14, which is radioactive, with the amount of carbon-12. The ratio of carbon-12 and carbon-14 in an organic substance at different points in time is known. Stratigraphy is the study of rock layers.

Sample Test Questions and Rationale (cont.)

(Easy)

2. **Which of the following describes the law of superposition?**

   A. The present is the key to the past

   B. The oldest rocks in a rock unit are found on the top of the rock column

   C. The oldest rocks in a rock unit are found on the bottom of the rock column

   D. Faults that cut across rock units are younger than the units they cut across

Answer: C. The oldest rocks in a rock unit are found on the bottom of the rock column

Sediments are deposited and cemented on top of old deposits. Therefore the oldest rocks are at the bottom of a column and the youngest rocks are at the top of a column.

SKILL 15.4 **Understands Earth and the universe** *(e.g., stars and galaxies, the solar system and planets; Earth, Sun, and Moon relationships)*

Earth is the third planet away from the Sun in our solar system. Earth's numerous types of motion and states of orientation greatly affect global conditions, such as seasons, tides, and lunar phases. The Earth orbits the Sun within a period of 365 days. During this orbit, the average distance between the Earth and the Sun is 93 million miles.

The shape of the Earth's orbit around the Sun deviates from the shape of a circle only slightly. This deviation, known as the Earth's eccentricity, has a very small effect on the Earth's climate. The Earth is closest to the Sun at perihelion, occurring around January 2 of each year, and farthest from the Sun at aphelion, occurring around July 2. Because the Earth is closest to the Sun in January, the northern winter is slightly warmer than the southern winter.

Planets

There are eight established planets in our solar system: Mercury, Venus, Earth, Mars, Jupiter, Saturn, Uranus, and Neptune. For many years Pluto was an established planet in our solar system, but as of 2006, its status is being reconsidered.

The planets are divided into two groups based on distance from the Sun. The inner planets include Mercury, Venus, Earth, and Mars. The outer planets include Jupiter, Saturn, Uranus, and Neptune.

PLANETS IN THE SOLAR SYSTEM	
Mercury	The closest planet to the Sun. Its surface has craters and rocks. The atmosphere is composed of hydrogen, helium, and sodium. Mercury was named after the Roman messenger god.
Venus	Has a slow rotation when compared to Earth. Venus and Uranus rotate in opposite directions from the other planets. This opposite rotation is called retrograde rotation. The surface of Venus is not visible due to the extensive cloud cover. The atmosphere is composed mostly of carbon dioxide, while sulfuric acid droplets in the dense cloud cover give Venus a yellow appearance. Venus has a greater greenhouse effect than that observed on Earth, and the dense clouds combined with carbon dioxide trap heat. Venus was named after the Roman goddess of love.
Earth	Considered a water planet, with 70 percent of its surface covered by water. Gravity holds the masses of water in place. The different temperatures observed on Earth allow for the different states of water (solid, liquid, gas) to exist. The atmosphere is composed mainly of oxygen and nitrogen. Earth is the only planet known to support life.
Mars	Surface contains numerous craters, active and extinct volcanoes, ridges, and valleys with extremely deep fractures. Iron oxide found in the dusty soil makes the surface seem rust-colored and the skies seem pink in color. The atmosphere is composed of carbon dioxide, nitrogen, argon, oxygen, and water vapor. Mars has polar regions with ice caps composed of water as well as two satellites (moons). Mars was named after the Roman war god.
Jupiter	The largest planet in the solar system. Jupiter has sixteen moons. The atmosphere is composed of hydrogen, helium, methane, and ammonia. There are white-colored bands of clouds indicating rising gas and dark-colored bands of clouds indicating descending gases. The gas movement is caused by heat resulting from the energy of Jupiter's core. Jupiter has a strong magnetic field and a great red spot that is thought to be a hurricane-like cloud.
Saturn	The second largest planet in the solar system. Saturn has rings of ice, rock, and dust particles circling it. Its atmosphere is composed of hydrogen, helium, methane, and ammonia. It has more than twenty satellites. Saturn was named after the Roman god of agriculture.
Uranus	The third largest planet in the solar system and has retrograde revolution. Uranus is a gaseous planet. It has ten dark rings and fifteen satellites. Its atmosphere is composed of hydrogen, helium, and methane. Uranus was named after the Greek god of the heavens.
Neptune	Another gaseous planet with an atmosphere consisting of hydrogen, helium, and methane. Neptune has three rings and two satellites. It was named after the Roman sea god because its atmosphere is the same color as the seas.
Pluto	Once considered the smallest planet in the solar system, its status as a planet is now being reconsidered. Pluto's atmosphere probably contains methane, ammonia, and frozen water. Pluto has one satellite. It revolves around the Sun every 250 years. Pluto was named after the Roman god of the underworld.

The Sun and Stars

The Sun

The Sun is considered the nearest star to Earth that produces solar energy. By the process of nuclear fusion, hydrogen gas is converted to helium gas. Energy flows out of the core to the surface; radiation then escapes into space.

Parts of the Sun include:

- **The core:** The inner portion of the Sun where fusion takes place.
- **The photosphere:** Considered the surface of the Sun, it also produces **sunspots** (cool, dark areas that can be seen on the Sun's surface).
- **The chromosphere:** Hydrogen gas causes this portion to be red. Also found here are solar flares (sudden brightness of the chromosphere) and solar prominences (gases that shoot outward from the chromosphere).
- **The corona:** The transparent area of the Sun visible only during a total eclipse.

Solar radiation is energy traveling from the Sun that radiates into space. Solar flares produce excited protons and electrons that shoot outward from the chromosphere at great speeds reaching Earth. These particles disturb radio reception and also affect the magnetic field on Earth.

Stars

A star is a ball of hot, glowing gas that is hot enough and dense enough to trigger nuclear reactions, which fuel the star. In comparing the mass, light production, and size of the Sun to other stars, astronomers find that the Sun is a perfectly ordinary star. It behaves exactly the way they would expect a star of its size to behave. The main difference between the Sun and other stars is that the Sun is much closer to Earth.

> A star is a ball of hot, glowing gas that is hot enough and dense enough to trigger nuclear reactions, which fuel the star.

Most stars have masses similar to that of the Sun. The majority of stars' masses are between 0.3 to 3.0 times the mass of the Sun. Theoretical calculations indicate that in order to trigger nuclear reactions and to create its own energy—that is, to become a star—a body must have a mass greater than 7 percent of the mass of the Sun. Astronomical bodies that are less massive than this become planets or objects called brown dwarfs. The largest accurately determined stellar mass is of a star called V382 Cygni; it is twenty-seven times the mass of the Sun.

The range of brightness among stars is much larger than the range of mass. Astronomers measure the brightness of a star by measuring its magnitude and luminosity. **Magnitude** allows astronomers to rank how bright different stars appear to humans. Because of the way our eyes detect light, a lamp ten times more luminous than another lamp will appear less than ten times brighter to human eyes. This discrepancy affects the magnitude scale, as does the tradition of giving brighter stars lower magnitudes. The lower a star's magnitude, the brighter it is. Stars with negative magnitudes are the brightest of all.

Magnitude is given in terms of absolute and apparent values. Absolute magnitude is a measurement of how bright a star would appear if viewed from a set distance away. Astronomers also measure a star's brightness in terms of its luminosity. A star's absolute luminosity, or intrinsic brightness, is the total amount of energy radiated by the star per second. Luminosity is often expressed in units of watts.

MAGNITUDE STARS:
twenty-one of the brightest stars that can be seen from Earth

MAGNITUDE STARS are twenty-one of the brightest stars that can be seen from Earth. These are the first stars noticed at night. In the Northern Hemisphere, there are fifteen commonly observed first-magnitude stars.

CONSTELLATIONS:
groups, or patterns, of stars

Astronomers use groups, or patterns, of stars called **CONSTELLATIONS** as reference points to locate other stars in the sky. Familiar constellations include Ursa Major (also known as Great Bear or Big Bear) and Ursa Minor (known as Little Bear). Within Ursa Major, the smaller constellation the Big Dipper is found. Within Ursa Minor, the smaller constellation the Little Dipper is found. Different constellations appear as the Earth continues its revolution around the Sun with the seasonal changes.

GALAXIES: vast collections of stars

Vast collections of stars are defined as **GALAXIES**. Galaxies are classified as irregular, elliptical, and spiral. An irregular galaxy has no real structured appearance; most are in their early stages of life. An elliptical galaxy consists of smooth ellipses, containing little dust and gas but composed of millions or trillions of stars. Spiral galaxies are disk shaped and have extending arms that rotate around their dense centers. Earth's galaxy is the Milky Way. It is a spiral galaxy.

PULSAR: a variable radio source that emits signals in very short, regular bursts, believed to be a rotating neutron star

A **PULSAR** is defined as a variable radio source that emits signals in very short, regular bursts; it is believed to be a rotating neutron star. A **QUASAR** is defined as an object that photographs like a star but has an extremely large redshift and a variable energy output; it is believed to be the active core of a very distant galaxy.

QUASAR: an object that photographs like a star but has an extremely large redshift and a variable energy output, believed to be the active core of a very distant galaxy

BLACK HOLES are defined as objects that have collapsed to such a degree that light cannot escape from the surface; light is trapped by the intense gravitational field.

BLACK HOLES: objects that have collapsed to such a degree that light cannot escape from the surface

The forces of gravity acting on particles of gas and dust in a cloud in an area of space produce stars. This cloud is called a nebula. Particles in this cloud attract each other; as the star grows, its temperature increases. With the increased temperature, the star begins to glow. Fusion occurs in the core of the star, releasing radiant energy at the star's surface.

When hydrogen becomes exhausted in a small, or even an average star, its core will collapse and cause its temperature to rise. The released heat causes nearby gases to heat, contract, carry out fusion, and produce helium. Stars at this stage are nearing the end of their life. These stars are called red giants or super giants. A white dwarf is the dying core of a giant star. A nova is an ordinary star that experiences a sudden increase in brightness and then fades back to its original brightness. A supernova radiates even greater light energy. A neutron star is the result of mass left behind after a supernova. A black hole is a star with condensed matter and gravity so intense that light cannot escape.

Comets, Asteroids, and Meteors

Astronomers believe that rocky fragments may have been the remains of the birth of the solar system that never formed into a planet. These asteroids are found in the region between Mars and Jupiter.

COMETS are masses of frozen gases, cosmic dust, and small rocky particles. Astronomers think that most comets originate in a dense comet cloud beyond Pluto. A comet consists of a nucleus, a coma, and a tail. A comet's tail always points away from the Sun. The most famous comet, Halley's comet, is named after the person who first discovered it in 240 BCE. It returns to the skies near Earth every seventy-five to seventy-six years.

METEOROIDS are composed of particles of rock and metal of various sizes. When a meteoroid travels through the Earth's atmosphere, friction causes its surface to heat up and it begins to burn. A burning meteoroid falling through the Earth's atmosphere is called a METEOR (also known as a "shooting star").

METEORITES are meteors that strike the Earth's surface. A physical example of a meteorite's impact on the Earth's surface can be seen in Arizona; the Barringer Crater is a huge meteor crater. There are many other meteor craters throughout the world.

Oort Cloud and Kuiper Belt

The OORT CLOUD is a hypothetical spherical cloud surrounding our solar system. It extends approximately three light years or 30 trillion kilometers from the Sun. The cloud is believed to be made up of materials that were ejected from the inner solar system because of interaction with Uranus and Neptune, but are gravitation-ally bound to the Sun. It is named the Oort cloud after Jan Oort, who suggested its existence in 1950. Comets from the Oort cloud exhibit a wide range of sizes, inclinations, and eccentricities; they are often referred to as long-period comets because they have a period of greater than 200 years.

COMETS: masses of frozen gases, cosmic dust, and small rocky particles

Astronomers think that most comets originate in a dense comet cloud beyond Pluto.

METEOROIDS: composed of particles of rock and metal of various sizes

METEOR: a burning meteoroid falling through the Earth's atmosphere also known as a "shooting star"

METEORITES: meteors that strike the Earth's surface

OORT CLOUD: a hypothetical spherical cloud surrounding our solar system extending approximately three light years or 30 trillion kilometers from the Sun

KUIPER BELT: a vast population of small bodies orbiting the Sun beyond Neptune

The **KUIPER BELT** is the name given to a vast population of small bodies orbiting the Sun beyond Neptune. There are more than 70,000 of these small bodies, some with diameters larger than 100 kilometers extending outwards from the orbit of Neptune to 50AU. They exist mostly within a ring or belt surrounding the Sun. It is believed that the objects in the Kuiper Belt are primitive remnants of the earliest phases of the solar system. It is also believed that the Kuiper Belt is the source of many short-period comets (comets with periods of less than 200 years). It is a reservoir for the comets in the same way that the Oort cloud is a reservoir for long-period comets.

Occasionally, the orbit of a Kuiper Belt object will be disturbed by the interactions of the giant planets in such a way as to cause the object to cross the orbit of Neptune. It will then very likely have a close encounter with Neptune, sending it out of the solar system or into an orbit crossing those of the other giant planets or even into the inner solar system. Prevailing theory states that scattered disk objects began as Kuiper Belt objects, which were scattered through gravitational interactions with the giant planets.

It seems that the Oort cloud objects were formed closer to the Sun than the Kuiper Belt objects. Small objects formed near the giant planets would have been ejected from the solar system by gravitational encounters. Those that didn't escape entirely formed the distant Oort cloud. Small objects formed farther out had no such interactions and remained as the Kuiper Belt objects.

Origins of the Solar System and Universe

There are two main hypotheses about the origin of the solar system:

- The tidal hypothesis proposes that the solar system began with a near collision of the Sun and a large star. Some astronomers believe that as these two stars passed each other, the great gravitational pull of the large star extracted hot gases from the Sun. The mass from the hot gases started to orbit the Sun, which began to cool, then condensing into the nine planets. (Few astronomers support this hypothesis.)

- The condensation hypothesis proposes that the solar system began with rotating clouds of dust and gas. Condensation occurred in the center, forming the Sun, and the smaller parts of the cloud formed the nine planets. (This hypothesis is accepted by many astronomers.)

The two main theories to explain the origins of the universe include:

- The big bang theory, widely accepted by many astronomers, states that the universe originated from a magnificent explosion spreading mass, matter, and energy into space. Galaxies formed from this material as it cooled during the next half-billion years.

- **The steady state theory,** the least accepted theory, states that the universe is continuously being renewed. Galaxies move outward and new galaxies replace the older galaxies. Astronomers have not found any evidence to prove this theory.

The future of the universe is hypothesized by the oscillating universe hypothesis, which states that the universe will oscillate, or expand and contract. Galaxies will move away from one another and will, in time, slow down and stop. Then a gradual moving toward each other will again activate an explosion—another big bang.

Sample Test Questions and Rationale

(Easy)

1. Which of the following astronomical entities is not part of the galaxy the Sun is located in?

   A. Nebulae

   B. Quasars

   C. Pulsars

   D. Neutron stars

Answer: B. Quasars

Nebulae are visible in the night sky and are glowing clouds of dust, hydrogen, and plasma. Neutron stars are the remnants of supernovae, and pulsars are neutron stars that emit radio waves on a periodic basis. A quasar is a distant galaxy that emits large amounts of visible light and radio waves.

(Rigorous)

2. Why is winter in the Northern Hemisphere warmer than winter in the Southern Hemisphere?

   A. The angle of incidence of the Sun's rays upon the Earth is greater in the Northern Hemisphere

   B. There is a greater concentration of greenhouse gases in the Northern Hemisphere

   C. The perihelion occurs in January

   D. There is more water in the Northern Hemisphere

Answer: C. The perihelion occurs in January.

The Earth's orbit around the Sun is not a circle with the Sun in the center. The Earth is closer to the Sun in January and further from the Sun in July. This is not the main cause of seasons. When there is winter in the Northern Hemisphere there is summer in the Southern Hemisphere. Seasons are caused by the tilt of the Earth's axis of rotation. The point where the Earth is closest to the Sun is called the perihelion and the point where the Earth is farthest from the Sun is called the aphelion. The northern winter is only slightly warmer than the southern winter.

> ## SKILL 15.5 Understands Earth patterns, cycles, and change

Seasons

The rotation axis of the Earth is not perpendicular to the orbital (ecliptic) plane. The axis of the Earth is tilted 23.45 degrees from the perpendicular; the tilt of this axis is known as the obliquity of the ecliptic, and is mainly responsible for the four seasons of the year by influencing the intensity of solar rays received by the Northern and Southern hemispheres.

The four seasons—spring, summer, fall, and winter—are extended periods of characteristic average temperature, rainfall, storm frequency, and vegetation growth or dormancy. The effect of the Earth's tilt on climate is best demonstrated at the solstices, the two days of the year when the Sun is farthest from the Earth's equatorial plane. At the summer solstice (June), the Earth's tilt on its axis causes the Northern Hemisphere to lean toward the Sun, while the Southern Hemisphere leans away. Consequently, the Northern Hemisphere receives more intense rays from the Sun and experiences summer during this time, while the Southern Hemisphere experiences winter. At the winter solstice (December), it is the Southern Hemisphere that leans toward the Sun and thus experiences summer. Spring and fall are produced by varying degrees of the same leaning toward or away from the Sun.

Tides

The orientation of and gravitational interaction between the Earth and the moon are responsible for the ocean tides that occur on Earth. The term tide refers to the cyclic rise and fall of large bodies of water. Gravitational attraction is defined as the force of attraction between all bodies in the universe. At the location on Earth closest to the moon, the gravitational attraction of the moon draws seawater toward the moon in the form of a tidal bulge. On the opposite side of the Earth, another tidal bulge forms in the direction away from the moon because at this point, the moon's gravitational pull is the weakest.

SPRING TIDES are the especially strong tides that occur when the Earth, Sun, and moon are in line, allowing both the Sun and the moon to exert gravitational force on the Earth, thereby increasing tidal bulge height. These tides occur during the full moon and the new moon. NEAP TIDES are especially weak tides occurring when the gravitational forces of the moon and the Sun are perpendicular to one another. These tides occur during quarter moons.

SPRING TIDES: occuring during the full and new moon, the especially strong tides that occur when the Earth, Sun, and moon are in line, allowing both the Sun and the moon to exert gravitational force on the Earth, thereby increasing tidal bulge height

NEAP TIDES: occuring during quarter moons, especially weak tides during which the gravitational forces of the moon and the Sun are perpendicular to one another

Phases of the Moon

The Earth's orientation in relation to the solar system is also responsible for our perception of the phases of the moon. While the Earth orbits the Sun within a period of 365 days, the moon orbits the Earth every twenty-seven days. As the moon circles the Earth, its shape in the night sky appears to change. The changes in the appearance of the moon from the Earth are known as LUNAR PHASES.

These phases vary cyclically according to the relative positions of the moon, the Earth, and the Sun. At all times, half of the moon is facing the Sun; thus, it is illuminated by reflecting the Sun's light. As the moon orbits the Earth and the Earth orbits the Sun, the half of the moon that faces the Sun changes. However, the moon is in synchronous rotation around the Earth, meaning that nearly the same side of the moon faces the Earth at all times. This side is referred to as the near side of the moon. Lunar phases occur as the Earth and moon orbit the Sun and the fractional illumination of the moon's near side changes.

When the Sun and moon are on opposite sides of the Earth, observers on Earth perceive a full moon, meaning the moon appears circular because the entire illuminated half of the moon is visible. As the moon orbits the Earth, the moon "wanes" as the amount of the illuminated half of the moon that is visible from Earth decreases. A gibbous moon is between a full moon and a half moon, or between a half moon and a full moon. When the Sun and the moon are on the same side of Earth, the illuminated half of the moon is facing away from Earth, and the moon appears invisible. This lunar phase is known as the new moon. The time between full moons is approximately 29.53 days.

LUNAR PHASES: the changes in the appearance of the moon from the Earth

PHASES OF THE MOON	
New Moon	The moon is invisible or the first signs of a crescent appear
Waxing Crescent	The right crescent of the moon is visible
First Quarter	The right quarter of the moon is visible
Waxing Gibbous	Only the left crescent is not illuminated
Full Moon	The entire illuminated half of the moon is visible
Waning Gibbous	Only the right crescent of the moon is not illuminated
Last Quarter	The left quarter of the moon is illuminated
Waning Crescent	Only the left crescent of the moon is illuminated

SCIENCE

Viewing the moon from the Southern Hemisphere causes these phases to occur in the opposite order.

Sample Test Question and Rationale

(Rigorous)

1. Which of the following facts of physics best explains the cause of tides?

   A. The density of water is less than the density of rock

   B. The force of gravity follows the inverse square law

   C. Centripetal acceleration causes water on Earth to bulge

   D. The gravitational force of the moon on Earth's oceans

Answer: B. The force of gravity follows the inverse square law

The main cause of lunar tides is that the moon's gravitational force is greater on water near the moon than on the other side of Earth. This causes the bulge of water. Earth's rotation causes the location of the bulge to change. Centripetal acceleration causes Earth's water to bulge and affects tides caused by the Sun's gravity, however, the effect is minor.

COMPETENCY 16
LIFE SCIENCE

> **SKILL 16.1 Understands the structure and function of living systems** *(e.g., living characteristics and cells, tissues and organs, life processes)*

The organization of living systems builds by levels from small to increasingly larger and more complex. All living things, from cells to ecosystems, have the same requirements to sustain life.

Life is organized from simple to complex in the following ways: Organelles make up cells. Cells make up tissues, and tissues make up organs. Groups of organs make up organ systems. Organ systems work together to provide life for an organism.

Several characteristics identify living versus nonliving things:

- **Living things are made of cells:** They grow, respond to stimuli and are capable of reproduction

- **Living things must adapt to environmental changes or perish**

- **Living things carry on metabolic processes:** They use and make energy

All organic life has a common element: carbon. Carbon is recycled through the ecosystem through both biotic and abiotic means. It is the link between biological processes and the chemical makeup of life.

Prokaryotic and Eukaryotic Cells

The cell is the basic unit of all living things. The two types of cells are prokaryotic and eukaryotic.

Prokaryotic cells consist only of bacteria and blue-green algae. Bacteria were most likely the first cells; they date back in the fossil record 3.5 billion years. These cells are grouped together because of the following characteristics:

- They have no defined nucleus or nuclear membrane. The DNA and ribosomes float freely within the cell.

- They have a thick cell wall. This is for protection, to give shape, and to keep the cell from bursting.

- The cell walls contain amino sugars (glycoproteins). Penicillin works by disrupting the cell wall, which is bad for the bacteria but does not harm the host.

- Some have a capsule made of polysaccharides that make them sticky.

- Some have a pilus, which is a protein strand. This also allows for attachment of the bacteria and may be used for sexual reproduction (conjugation).

- Some have flagella for movement.

Eukaryotic cells are found in protists, fungi, plants, and animals. Some features of eukaryotic cells include the following:

- They are usually larger than prokaryotic cells.

- They contain many organelles, which are membrane-bound areas for specific cell functions.

- They contain a cytoskeleton that provides a protein framework for the cell.

- They contain cytoplasm, which supports the organelles and contains the ions and molecules necessary for cell function.

> *The cell is the basic unit of all living things.*

Parts of eukaryotic cells

1. **Nucleus:** The brain of the cell. The nucleus contains:

    – **Chromosomes:** DNA, RNA, and proteins tightly coiled to conserve space while providing a large surface area.

    – **Chromatin:** The loose structure of chromosomes. Chromosomes are called chromatin when the cell is not dividing.

    – **Nucleoli:** Where ribosomes are made. These are seen as dark spots in the nucleus.

    – **Nuclear membrane:** Contains pores that let RNA out of the nucleus. The nuclear membrane is continuous with the endoplasmic reticulum, which allows the membrane to expand or shrink if needed.

2. **Ribosomes:** The site of protein synthesis. Ribosomes may be free floating in the cytoplasm or attached to the endoplasmic reticulum. There may be up to a half million ribosomes in a cell, depending on how much protein is made by the cell.

3. **Endoplasmic reticulum:** These are folded and provide a large surface area. They are the "roadway" of the cell and allow for transport of materials. The lumen of the endoplasmic reticulum helps to keep materials out of the cytoplasm and headed in the right direction. The endoplasmic reticulum is capable of building new membrane material. There are two types:

    – **Smooth endoplasmic reticulum:** Contain no ribosomes on their surface.

    – **Rough endoplasmic reticulum:** Contain ribosomes on their surface. This form of endoplasmic reticulum is abundant in cells that make many proteins, as in the pancreas, which produces many digestive enzymes.

4. **Golgi complex or Golgi apparatus:** This structure is stacked to increase surface area. The Golgi complex functions to sort, modify, and package molecules that are made in other parts of the cell. These molecules are either sent out of the cell or to other organelles within the cell.

5. **Lysosomes:** Found mainly in animal cells. These contain digestive enzymes that break down food, substances not needed, viruses, damaged cell components, and eventually the cell itself. It is believed that lysosomes are responsible for the aging process.

6. **Mitochondria:** Large organelles that make ATP to supply energy to the cell. Muscle cells have many mitochondria because they use a great deal of

energy. The folds inside the mitochondria are called cristae. They provide a large surface where the reactions of cellular respiration occur. Mitochondria have their own DNA and are capable of reproducing themselves if a greater demand is made for additional energy. Mitochondria are found only in animal cells.

7. Plastids: Found in photosynthetic organisms only. They are similar to the mitochondria due to their double membrane structure. They also have their own DNA and can reproduce if increased capture of sunlight becomes necessary. There are several types of plastids:

   – Chloroplasts: Green in color, they function in photosynthesis. They are capable of trapping sunlight.

   – Chromoplasts: Make and store yellow and orange pigments. They provide color to leaves, flowers, and fruits.

   – Amyloplasts: Store starch and are used as a food reserve. They are abundant in roots like potatoes.

8. Cell wall: Found in plant cells only, composed of cellulose and fibers. It is thick enough for support and protection, yet porous enough to allow water and dissolved substances to enter. Cell walls are cemented to each other.

9. Vacuoles: Hold stored food and pigments. Vacuoles are very large in plants. This allows them to fill with water in order to provide turgor pressure. Lack of turgor pressure causes a plant to wilt.

10. Cytoskeleton: Composed of protein filaments attached to the plasma membrane and organelles. They provide a framework for the cell and aid in cell movement. They constantly change shape and move about. Three types of fibers make up the cytoskeleton:

   – Microtubules: Largest of the three, they are made up of cilia and flagella for locomotion. Flagella grow from a basal body. Some examples are sperm cells and tracheal cilia. Centrioles are also composed of microtubules. They form the spindle fibers that pull the cell apart into two cells during cell division. Centrioles are not found in the cells of higher plants.

   – Intermediate filaments: Smaller than microtubules but larger than microfilaments. They help the cell keep its shape.

   – Microfilaments: Smallest of the three, they are made of actin and small amounts of myosin (as in muscle cells). They function in cell movement such as cytoplasmic streaming, endocytosis, and ameboid movement. This structure pinches the two cells apart after cell division, forming two cells.

Sample Test Questions and Rationale

(Average)

1. Which of the following is not a property that eukaryotes have and prokaryotes do not have?

   A. Nucleus

   B. Ribosomes

   C. Chromosomes

   D. Mitochondria

   Answer: B. Ribosomes

   Prokaryotes do not have a nuclear membrane and the DNA is not packed into chromosomes. Mitochondria are organelles that produce power and are not in the smaller, simpler cell. Ribosomes are the sites where cells assemble proteins.

(Rigorous)

2. What cell organelle contains the cell's stored food?

   A. Vacuoles

   B. Golgi apparatus

   C. Ribosome

   D. Lysosome

   Answer: A. Vacuoles

   In a cell, the subparts are called organelles. Of these, the vacuoles hold stored food (and water and pigments). The Golgi apparatus sorts molecules from other parts of the cell; the ribosomes are sites of protein synthesis; and the lysosomes contain digestive enzymes.

SKILL 16.2 Understands reproduction and heredity *(e.g., growth and development, patterns of inheritance of traits, molecular basis of heredity)*

Reproductive System

Sexual reproduction greatly increases diversity due to the many combinations possible through meiosis and fertilization. **GAMETOGENESIS** is the production of the sperm and egg cells. Spermatogenesis begins at puberty in the male. One spermatozoa produces four sperm. The sperm mature in the seminiferous tubules located in the testes. Oogenesis, the production of egg cells, is usually complete by the birth of a female. Egg cells are not released until menstruation begins at puberty. Meiosis forms one ovum with all the cytoplasm and three polar bodies, which are reabsorbed by the body. The ovum are stored in the ovaries and released each month from puberty to menopause.

> **GAMETOGENESIS:** the production of the sperm and egg cells

Path of the sperm

Sperm are stored in the seminiferous tubules in the testes where they mature. Mature sperm are found in the epididymis, located on top of the testes. After ejaculation, the sperm travel up the vas deferens where they mix with semen made in the prostate and seminal vesicles; they then travel out the urethra.

Path of the egg

Eggs are stored in the ovaries. Ovulation releases the egg into the fallopian tubes, which are ciliated to move the egg along. Fertilization normally occurs in the fallopian tube. If pregnancy does not occur, the egg passes through the uterus and is expelled through the vagina during menstruation. Levels of progesterone and estrogen stimulate menstruation. In the event of pregnancy, hormonal levels are affected by the implantation of a fertilized egg, so menstruation does not occur.

Pregnancy

If fertilization occurs, the zygote implants in about two to three days in the uterus. Implantation promotes secretion of human chorionic gonadotropin (HCG). This is what is detected in pregnancy tests. The HCG keeps the level of progesterone elevated to maintain the uterine lining in order to feed the developing embryo until the umbilical cord forms. Labor is initiated by oxytocin, which causes labor contractions and dilation of the cervix. Prolactin and oxytocin cause the production of milk.

Cellular Reproduction

The purpose of cell division is to provide growth and repair in body (somatic) cells and to replenish or create sex cells for reproduction. There are two forms of cell division:

- Mitosis is the division of somatic cells
- Meiosis is the division of sex cells (eggs and sperm)

MAJOR DIFFERENCES BETWEEN MITOSIS AND MEIOSIS	
Mitosis	**Meiosis**
Division of somatic cell	Division of sex cells
Two cells result from each division	Four cells or polar bodies result from each division
Chromosome number is identical	Chromosome number is half the number of parent cells
Division is for cell growth and repair	Recombinations provide genetic diversity

Some terms to know:

- Gamete: Sex cell or germ cell; eggs and sperm

- Chromatin: Loose chromosomes; this state is found when the cell is not dividing

- Chromosome: Tightly coiled, visible chromatin; this state is found when the cell is dividing

- Homologues: Chromosomes that contain the same information—they are of the same length and contain the same genes

- Diploid: Two in number; diploid chromosomes are a pair of chromosomes (somatic cells)

- Haploid: One in number; haploid chromosomes are half of a pair (sex cells)

Mitosis

The cell cycle is the life cycle of the cell. It is divided into two stages: interphase and mitotic division (when the cell is actively dividing).

Interphase is divided into three steps:

1. G1 Period (growth): The cell is growing and metabolizing

2. S Period (synthesis): New DNA and enzymes are being made

3. G2 Period (growth): New proteins and organelles are being made to prepare for cell division

The mitotic stage consists of the stages of mitosis and the division of the cytoplasm. The stages of mitosis and their events are as follows. Be sure to know the correct order of steps (IPMAT).

1. Interphase: Chromatin is loose, chromosomes are replicated, and cell metabolism is occurring. Interphase is technically not a stage of mitosis.

2. Prophase: Once the cell enters prophase, it proceeds through the following steps continuously, without stopping. The chromatin condenses to become visible chromosomes. The nucleolus disappears and the nuclear membrane breaks apart. Mitotic spindles form, which will eventually pull the chromosomes apart. They are composed of microtubules. The cytoskeleton breaks down and the spindles are pushed to the poles or opposite ends of the cell by the action of centrioles.

3. Metaphase: Kinetechore fibers attach to the chromosomes, which causes the chromosomes to line up in the center of the cell (think middle for metaphase).

4. **Anaphase**: Centromeres split in half and homologous chromosomes separate. The chromosomes are pulled to the poles of the cell, with identical sets at either end.

5. **Telophase**: There are two nuclei with a full set of DNA identical to the parent cell. The nucleoli become visible and the nuclear membrane reassembles. A cell plate is visible in plant cells, whereas a cleavage furrow is formed in animal cells. The cell is pinched into two cells. Cytokinesis, or division, of the cytoplasm and organelles occurs.

Meiosis

Meiosis consists of the same five stages as mitosis, but is repeated in order to reduce the chromosome number by one half. This way, when the sperm and egg join during fertilization, the haploid number is reached. The steps of meiosis are:

- **Meiosis I**: The major function is to replicate chromosomes; cells remain diploid.

- **Prophase I**: Replicated chromosomes condense and pair with homologues. This forms a tetrad. Crossing over (the exchange of genetic material between homologues to further increase diversity) occurs during Prophase I.

- **Metaphase I**: Homologous sets attach to spindle fibers after lining up in the middle of the cell.

- **Anaphase I**: Sister chromatids remain joined and move to the poles of the cell.

- **Telophase I**: Two new cells are formed and the chromosome number is still diploid.

- **Meiosis II**: The major function is to reduce the chromosome number in half.

- **Prophase II**: Chromosomes condense.

- **Metaphase II**: Spindle fibers form again, sister chromatids line up in center of cell, centromeres divide, and sister chromatids separate.

- **Anaphase II**: Separated chromosomes move to opposite ends of cell.

- **Telophase II**: Four haploid cells form for each original sperm germ cell. One viable egg cell gets all the genetic information and three polar bodies form with no DNA. The nuclear membrane reforms and cytokinesis occurs.

Mutations

During these very intricate steps, mistakes do happen. Inheritable changes in DNA are called **MUTATIONS**. Mutations may be errors in replication or a

MUTATIONS: inheritable changes in DNA

spontaneous rearrangement of one or more segments by factors like radioactivity, drugs, or chemicals. The amount of the change is not as critical as where the change is. Mutations may occur on somatic or sex cells. Usually changes on sex cells are more dangerous since they contain the basis of all information for the developing offspring.

Mutations are not always bad. They are the basis of evolution, and if they make a more favorable variation that enhances the organism's survival, then they are beneficial. However, mutations may also lead to abnormalities, birth defects, and even death.

There are several types of mutations. Here are a few examples. First, suppose a normal sequence was as follows:

Normal   **A B C D E F**

Here are a few types of mutations:

- **Duplication** (one gene is repeated):   A B C C D E F
- **Inversion** (a segment of the sequence is flipped around):   A E D C B F
- **Deletion** (a gene is left out):   A B C E F
- **Insertion, or translocation** (a segment from another place on the DNA is inserted in the wrong place):   A B C R S D E F
- **Breakage** (a piece is lost):   A B C (DEF is lost)

Nondisjunction occurs during meiosis when chromosomes fail to separate properly. One sex cell may get both genes and another may get none. Depending on the chromosomes involved, this may or may not be serious. Offspring end up with either an extra chromosome or missing one. An example of nondisjunction is Down syndrome, in which three of chromosome 21 are present.

Genetics

Gregor Mendel is recognized as the father of genetics. His work in the late 1800s is the basis of our knowledge of genetics. Although unaware of the presence of DNA or genes, Mendel realized there were factors (now known as genes) that were transferred from parents to their offspring. Mendel worked with pea plants; he fertilized the plants himself, keeping track of subsequent generations. His findings led to the Mendelian laws of genetics. Mendel found that two "factors" governed each trait, one from each parent. Traits or characteristics came in several forms, known as alleles. For example, the trait of flower color had white alleles and purple alleles.

Mendel established three laws:

- **Law of dominance:** In a pair of alleles, one trait may cover up the allele of the other trait. Example: Brown eyes are dominant (over blue eyes).

- **Law of segregation:** Only one of the two possible alleles from each parent is passed on to the offspring. (During meiosis, the haploid number ensures that half the sex cells get one allele and half get the other.)

- **Law of independent assortment:** Alleles sort independently of each other. (Many combinations are possible, depending on which sperm ends up with which egg. Compare this to the many combinations of hands possible when dealing a deck of cards.)

Punnet squares are used to show the possible ways that genes combine and indicate probability of the occurrence of a certain genotype or phenotype. One parent's genes are put at the top of the box and the other parent's at the side of the box. Genes combine on the square just like numbers that are added in addition tables we learned in elementary school. Below is an example of a **monohybrid cross**, which is a cross using only one trait—in this case, a trait labeled *g*.

Punnet Square

	G	g
G	GG	Gg
g	Gg	gg

In a **dihybrid cross**, sixteen gene combinations are possible, as each cross has two traits.

Some definitions to know:

- **Dominant:** The stronger of two traits. If a dominant gene is present, it will be expressed. It is shown by a capital letter.

- **Recessive:** The weaker of two traits. In order for the recessive gene to be expressed, there must be two recessive genes present. It is shown by a lower case letter.

- **Homozygous (purebred):** Having two of the same genes present; an organism may be homozygous dominant with two dominant genes or homozygous recessive with two recessive genes.

- **Heterozygous (hybrid):** Having one dominant gene and one recessive gene. Due to the law of dominance, the dominant gene will be expressed.

- Genotype: The genes the organism has. Genes are represented with letters. AA, Bb, and tt are examples of genotypes.

- Phenotype: How the trait is expressed in an organism. Blue eyes, brown hair, and red flowers are examples of phenotypes.

- Incomplete dominance: Neither gene masks the other; a new phenotype is formed. For example, red flowers and white flowers may have equal strength. A heterozygote (Rr) would have pink flowers. If a problem occurs with a third phenotype, incomplete dominance is occurring.

- Codominance: Genes may form new phenotypes. The ABO blood grouping is an example of codominance. A and B are of equal strength and O is recessive. Therefore, Type A blood may have the genotypes of AA or AO, Type B blood may have the genotypes of BB or BO, Type AB blood has the genotype A and B, and Type O blood has two recessive O genes.

- Linkage: Genes that are found on the same chromosome usually appear together unless crossing over has occurred in meiosis (e.g., blue eyes and blonde hair commonly occur together).

- Lethal alleles: These are usually recessive due to the early death of the offspring. If a 2:1 ratio of alleles is found in offspring, a lethal gene combination may be the reason. Some examples of lethal alleles include sickle cell anemia, Tay-Sachs disease, and cystic fibrosis. In most cases, the coding for an important protein is affected.

- Inborn errors of metabolism: These occur when the protein affected is an enzyme. Examples include PKU (phenylketonuria) and albinism.

- Polygenic characters: Many alleles code for a phenotype. There may be as many as twenty genes that code for skin color. This is why there is such a variety of skin tones. Another example is height. A couple of medium height may have very tall offspring.

- Sex-linked traits: The Y chromosome found only in males (XY) carries very little genetic information, whereas the X chromosome found in females (XX) carries very important information. Since men have no second X chromosome to cover up a recessive gene, the recessive trait is expressed more often in men. Women need the recessive gene on both X chromosomes to show the trait. Examples of sex-linked traits include hemophilia and color blindness.

- Sex-influenced traits: Traits are influenced by the sex hormones. Male-pattern baldness is an example of a sex-influenced trait. Testosterone influences the expression of the gene. Most men lose their hair due to this trait.

Sample Test Questions and Rationale

(Average)

1. At what stage in mitosis does the chromatin become chromosomes?

    A. Telophase

    B. Anaphase

    C. Prophase

    D. Metaphase

    Answer: C. Prophase

    Prophase is the beginning of mitosis. In metaphase fibers attach to chromosomes and in anaphase the chromosomes separate. In telophase the cells divide.

(Average)

2. Meiosis starts with a single cell and ends with which of the following?

    A. Two diploid cells

    B. Two haploid cells

    C. Four diploid cells

    D. Four haploid cells

    Answer: D. Four haploid cells

    The single cell that begins the creation of a gamete has a full set of chromosomes in matched pairs. This is called a diploid cell. After the first division there are two haploid cells. After the second division, there are four haploid cells.

SKILL **Understands change over time in living things** *(e.g., life cycles,*
16.3 *mutations, adaptations and natural selection)*

Charles Darwin defined the theory of natural selection in the mid-1800s. Through the study of finches on the Galapagos Islands, Darwin theorized that nature selects the traits that are advantageous to the organism. Organisms that do not possess the desirable trait die, and do not pass on their genes. Those more fit to survive get the opportunity to reproduce, thus increasing that gene in the population.

Darwin listed four principles to define natural selection:

1. The individuals in a certain species vary from generation to generation

2. Some of the variations are determined by the genetic makeup of the species

3. More individuals are produced than will survive

4. Some genes allow for better survival of an animal

Causes of Evolution

Certain factors increase the chances of variability in a population, thus leading to evolution. Factors that increase variability include mutations, sexual reproduction, immigration, and large population. Factors that decrease variation include natural selection, emigration, small population, and random mating.

Sexual selection

Genes that happen to come together determine the makeup of the gene pool. Animals that use mating behaviors may be successful or unsuccessful. An animal that lacks attractive plumage or has a weak mating call will not attract the female, thereby eventually limiting that gene in the gene pool. Mechanical isolation, where sex organs do not fit the female, has an obvious disadvantage.

Sample Test Question and Rationale

(Rigorous)

1. **Which of the following is a correct explanation for scientific evolution?**

   A. Giraffes need to reach higher leaves to eat, so their necks stretch. The giraffe babies are then born with longer necks. Eventually, there are more long-necked giraffes in the population.

   B. Giraffes with longer necks are able to reach more leaves, so they eat more and have more babies than other giraffes. Eventually, there are more long-necked giraffes in the population.

   C. Giraffes want to reach higher for leaves to eat, so they release enzymes into their bloodstream, which in turn causes fetal development of longer-necked giraffes. Eventually, there are more long-necked giraffes in the population.

   D. Giraffes with long necks are more attractive to other giraffes, so they get the best mating partners and have more babies. Eventually, there are more long-necked giraffes in the population.

Answer: B. Giraffes with longer necks are able to reach more leaves, so they eat more and have more babies than other giraffes. Eventually, there are more long-necked giraffes in the population.

Organisms with a life/reproductive advantage will produce more offspring. Over many generations, this changes the proportions in the population. In any case, it is impossible for a stretched neck or a fervent desire to result in biologically mutated babies. Although there are traits that are naturally selected because of mate attractiveness and fitness, this is not the primary situation here, so answer B is the best choice.

ANIMAL COMMUNICATION is defined as any behavior by one animal that affects the behavior of another animal. Animals use body language, sound, and smell to communicate. Perhaps the most common type of animal communication is the presentation or movement of distinctive body parts. Many animal species reveal or conceal body parts to communicate with potential mates, predators, and prey.

> **ANIMAL COMMUNICATION:** any behavior by one animal that affects the behavior of another animal

In addition, many species communicate with sound. Examples of vocal communication include the mating "songs" of birds and frogs and warning cries of monkeys. Many animals also release scented chemicals called pheromones and secrete distinctive odors from specialized glands to communicate with other animals. Pheromones are important in reproduction and mating, and glandular secretions of long-lasting smell alert animals to the presence of others.

Ecological and behavioral factors affect the interrelationships among organisms in many ways. Two important ecological factors are environmental conditions and resource availability.

There are four important types of organismal behavior:

1. Competitive: In any system, organisms compete with other species for scarce resources. Organisms also compete with members of their own species for mates and territory. Many competitive behaviors involve rituals and dominance hierarchies. Rituals are symbolic activities that often settle disputes without undue harm. For example, dogs bare their teeth, erect their ears, and growl to intimidate competitors. A dominance hierarchy, or "pecking order," organizes groups of animals, simplifying interrelationships, conserving energy, and minimizing the potential for harm in a community.

2. Instinctive: Instinctive, or innate, behavior is common to all members of a given species; it is genetically preprogrammed. Environmental differences do not affect instinctive behaviors. For example, baby birds of many types and species beg for food by raising their heads and opening their beaks.

3. Territorial: Many animals act aggressively to protect their territory from other animals. Animals protect territories for use in feeding, mating, and the rearing of young.

4. Mating: Mating behaviors are very important interspecies interactions. The search for a mate with which to reproduce is an instinctive behavior. Mating interrelationships often involve ritualistic and territorial behaviors that are competitive.

Environmental conditions such as climate influence organismal interrelationships by changing the dynamic of the ecosystem. Changes in climate (such as moisture levels and temperature) can alter the environment, changing the characteristics that are advantageous. For example, an increase in temperature will favor those organisms that can tolerate the temperature change. Thus, those organisms gain a competitive advantage. In addition, the availability of necessary resources influences interrelationships. For example, when necessary resources are scarce, interrelationships are more competitive than when resources are abundant.

Behavior may be innate or learned. INNATE BEHAVIOR is defined as behavior that is inborn or instinctual. An environmental stimulus (such as the length of day or temperature) results in a behavior. Hibernation among some animals is an innate behavior. LEARNED BEHAVIOR is any behavior that is modified due to past experience.

> **INNATE BEHAVIOR:** behavior that is inborn or instinctual

> **LEARNED BEHAVIOR:** behavior that is modified due to past experience

Basic Life Functions

Members of the five different kingdoms of the classification system of living organisms often differ in their basic life functions. Here we compare and analyze how members of the five kingdoms obtain nutrients, excrete waste, and reproduce.

Bacteria

Bacteria are prokaryotic, single-celled organisms that lack cell nuclei. The different types of bacteria obtain nutrients in a variety of ways. Most bacteria absorb nutrients from the environment through small channels in their cell walls and membranes (chemotrophs) while some perform photosynthesis (phototrophs). Chemoorganotrophs use organic compounds as energy sources while chemolithotrophs can use inorganic chemicals. Depending on the type of metabolism and energy source, bacteria release a variety of waste products (e.g., alcohols, acids, carbon dioxide) to the environment through diffusion.

All bacteria reproduce through binary fission (asexual reproduction), producing two identical cells. Bacteria reproduce very rapidly, dividing or doubling every twenty minutes in optimal conditions. Asexual reproduction does not allow for genetic variation, but bacteria achieve genetic variety by absorbing DNA from ruptured cells and conjugating or swapping chromosomal or plasmid DNA with other cells.

Animals

Animals are multicellular, eukaryotic organisms. All animals obtain nutrients by eating food (ingestion). Different types of animals derive nutrients from eating plants, other animals, or both. Animal cells perform digestion that converts food molecules, mainly carbohydrates and fats, into energy. The excretory systems of animals, like animals themselves, vary in complexity. Simple invertebrates eliminate waste through a single tube, while complex vertebrates have a specialized system of organs that process and excrete waste.

Most animals, unlike bacteria, exist in two distinct sexes. Members of the female sex give birth or lay eggs. Some less-developed animals can reproduce asexually. For example, flatworms can divide in two, and some unfertilized insect eggs can develop into viable organisms. Most animals reproduce sexually through various mechanisms. For example, many aquatic animals reproduce by external fertilization of eggs, while mammals reproduce by internal fertilization. More-developed animals possess specialized reproductive systems and cycles that facilitate reproduction and promote genetic variation.

Plants
Plants, like animals, are multicellular, eukaryotic organisms. Plants obtain nutrients from the soil through their root systems and convert sunlight into energy through photosynthesis. Many plants store waste products in vacuoles or organs (e.g., leaves, bark) that are discarded. Some plants also excrete waste through their roots.

More than half of the plant species reproduce by producing seeds from which new plants grow. Depending on the type of plant, flowers or cones produce seeds. Other plants reproduce by spores, tubers, bulbs, buds, and grafts. The flowers of flowering plants contain their reproductive organs. Pollination is the joining of male and female gametes that is often facilitated by movement of wind or animals.

Fungi
Fungi are eukaryotic, mostly multicellular organisms. All fungi are heterotrophs, obtaining nutrients from other organisms. More specifically, most fungi obtain nutrients by digesting and absorbing nutrients from dead organisms. Fungi secrete enzymes outside of their bodies to digest organic material and then absorb the nutrients through their cell walls.

Most fungi can reproduce asexually and sexually. Different types of fungi reproduce asexually by mitosis, budding, sporification, or fragmentation. The sexual reproduction of fungi is different from the sexual reproduction of animals. The two mating types of fungi are plus and minus, not male and female. The fusion of hyphae, the specialized reproductive structure in fungi, between plus and minus types, produces and scatters diverse spores.

Protists

Protists are eukaryotic, single-celled organisms. Most protists are heterotrophic, obtaining nutrients by ingesting small molecules and cells and digesting them in vacuoles. All protists reproduce asexually by either binary or multiple fission. Like bacteria, protists achieve genetic variation by exchange of DNA through conjugation.

Sample Test Question and Rationale

(Easy)

1. **Which is not a characteristic of all living organisms?**

   A. Sexual reproduction

   B. Ingestion

   C. Synthesis

   D. Respiration

Answer: A. Sexual reproduction

Only certain organisms reproduce sexually, that is, by mixing DNA. Single-celled organisms generally reproduce by cell division. Ingestion means taking nutrients from outside the cell wall. Synthesis means creating new cellular material. Respiration means generating energy by combining oxygen or some other gas with material in the cell.

SKILL 16.5 Understands unity and diversity of life, adaptation, and classification

> **TAXONOMY:** the science of classification

Carolus Linnaeus is called the father of taxonomy. **TAXONOMY** is the science of classification. Linnaeus based his system on morphology, the study of structure. Later, evolutionary relationships (phylogeny) were also used to sort and group species.

The modern classification system uses binomial nomenclature. This consists of a two-word name for every species. The genus is the first part of the name and the species is the second part. Notice, in the levels explained below, that Homo sapiens is the scientific name for humans. Starting with the kingdom, the groups get smaller and more alike as one moves down the levels in the classification of humans.

Kingdom	Animalia
Phylum	Chordata
Subphylum	Vertebrata

Table continued on next page

Class	Mammalia
Order	Primate
Family	Hominidae
Genus	Homo
Species	Sapiens

Species are defined by the ability to successfully reproduce with members of their own kind.

The Five Kingdoms of Living Organisms

Living organisms are divided into five major kingdoms:

- Monera
- Protista
- Fungi
- Plantae
- Animalia

Kingdom Monera

This kingdom includes bacteria and blue-green algae; these are prokaryotic, unicellular organisms with no true nucleus.

Bacteria are classified according to their morphology (shape). Bacilli are rod shaped, cocci are round, and spirillia are spiral shaped. The gram stain is a staining procedure used to identify bacteria. Gram-positive bacteria pick up the stain and turn purple. Gram-negative bacteria do not pick up the stain and are pink in color.

Methods of locomotion

Flagellates have a flagellum; ciliates have cilia; and ameboids move through use of pseudopodia.

Methods of reproduction

Binary fission is simply dividing in half and is asexual. All new organisms are exact clones of the parent. Sexual modes provide more diversity. Bacteria can reproduce sexually through conjugation, where genetic material is exchanged.

Methods of obtaining nutrition

Photosynthetic organisms, or producers, convert sunlight to chemical energy, while consumers, or heterotrophs, eat other living things. Saprophytes are consumers that live off dead or decaying material.

Kingdom Protista

This kingdom includes eukaryotic, unicellular organisms; some are photosynthetic, and some are consumers. Microbiologists use methods of locomotion, reproduction, and how the organism obtains its food to classify protista.

Kingdom Fungi

Organisms in this kingdom are eukaryotic, multicellular, absorptive consumers, and contain a chitin cell wall.

Kingdom Plantae

This kingdom contains nonvascular plants and vascular plants.

Nonvascular plants

Small in size, these plants do not require vascular tissue (xylem and phloem) because individual cells are close to their environment. The nonvascular plants have no true leaves, stems, or roots.

- Division Bryophyta: Mosses and liverworts; these plants have a dominant gametophyte generation. They possess rhizoids, which are root-like structures. Moisture in their environment is required for reproduction and absorption.

Vascular plants

The development of vascular tissue enables these plants to grow in size. Xylem and phloem allow for the transport of water and minerals up to the top of the plant, as well as for the transport of food manufactured in the leaves to the bottom of the plant. All vascular plants have a dominant sporophyte generation.

- Division Lycophyta: Club mosses; these plants reproduce with spores and require water for reproduction.

- Division Sphenophyta: Horsetails; also reproduce with spores. These plants have small, needle-like leaves and rhizoids. They require moisture for reproduction.

- Division Pterophyta: Ferns; they reproduce with spores and flagellated sperm. These plants have a true stem and need moisture for reproduction.

- **Gymnosperms:** The word means "naked seed." These were the first plants to evolve with seeds, which made them less dependent on water for reproduction. Their seeds can travel by wind; pollen from the male is also easily carried by the wind. Gymnosperms have cones that protect the seeds.

- **Division Cycadophyta:** Cycads; these plants look like palms with cones.

- **Divison Ghetophyta:** Desert dwellers.

- **Division Coniferophyta:** Pines; these plants have needles and cones.

- **Divison Ginkgophyta:** The ginkgo is the only member of this division.

Angiosperms (division Anthophyta)

The largest group in the plant kingdom. Plants in this kingdom are the flowering plants that produce true seeds for reproduction.

Kingdom Animalia

Annelida

This phylum includes the segmented worms. The Annelida have specialized tissue. The circulatory system is more advanced in these worms; it is a closed system with blood vessels. The nephridia are their excretory organs. They are hermaphroditic, and each worm fertilizes the other upon mating. They support themselves with a hydrostatic skeleton and have circular and longitudinal muscles for movement.

Mollusca

This phylum includes clams, octopi, and soft-bodied animals. These animals have a muscular foot for movement. They breathe through gills, and most are able to make a shell for protection from predators. They have an open circulatory system, with sinuses bathing the body regions.

Arthropoda

This phylum includes insects, crustaceans, and spiders; this is the largest group of the animal kingdom. Phylum Arthropoda accounts for about 85 percent of all the animal species. Animals in this phylum possess an exoskeleton made of chitin. They must molt to grow. Insects, for example, go through four stages of development. They begin as an egg, hatch into a larva, form a pupa, then emerge as an adult. Arthropods breathe through gills, trachea, or book lungs. Movement varies, with members being able to swim, fly, and crawl. There is a division of labor among the appendages (legs, antennae, etc.). This is an extremely successful phylum, with members occupying diverse habitats.

Echinodermata

This phylum includes sea urchins and starfish; these animals have spiny skin. Their habitat is marine. They have tube feet for locomotion and feeding.

Chordata

This phylum includes all animals with a notocord or a backbone. The classes in this phylum include Agnatha (jawless fish), Chondrichthyes (cartilage fish), Osteichthyes (bony fish), Amphibia (frogs and toads; gills that are replaced by lungs during development), Reptilia (snakes, lizards; the first to lay eggs with a protective covering), Aves (birds; warm-blooded with wings consisting of a particular shape and composition designed for flight), and Mammalia (warm-blooded animals with body hair who bear their young alive and possess mammary glands for milk production).

Sample Test Question and Rationale

(Easy)

1. Taxonomy classifies species into genera (plural of genus) based on similarities. Species are subordinate to genera. The most general, or highest, taxonomical group is the kingdom. Which of the following is the correct order of the other groups from highest to lowest?

   A. Class → order → family → phylum

   B. Phylum → class → family → order

   C. Phylum → class → order → family

   D. Order → phylum → class → family

Answer: C. Phylum → class → order → family

In the case of the domestic dog, the genus (Canis) includes wolves, the family (Canidae) includes jackals and coyotes, the order (Carnivore) includes lions, the class (Mammals) includes mice, and the phylum (Chordata) includes fish.

SKILL 16.6 Understands the interdependence of organisms (e.g., ecosystems, populations, communities)

Ecology is the study of organisms: where they live and their interactions with the environment. A population is a group of the same species in a specific area. A community is a group of populations residing in the same area. Communities that are ecologically similar in relation to temperature, rainfall, and the species that live there are called biomes.

BIOMES	
Marine	Covers 75 percent of the Earth. This biome is organized by the depth of the water. The intertidal zone is located from the tide line to the edge of the water. The littoral zone is from the water's edge to the open sea. It includes coral reef habitats and is the most densely populated area of the marine biome. The open sea zone is divided into the epipelagic zone and the pelagic zone. The epipelagic zone receives more sunlight and has a larger number of species. The ocean floor is called the benthic zone and is populated with bottom feeders.
Tropical Rain Forest	Temperature is constant (25°C), and rainfall exceeds 200 cm per year. Located around the area of the equator, the rain forest has abundant, diverse species of plants and animals.
Savanna	Temperatures range from 0 to 25°C, depending on the location. Rainfall is from 90 to 150 cm per year. Plants include shrubs and grasses. The savanna is a transitional biome between the rain forest and the desert.
Desert	Temperatures range from 10 to 38°C. Rainfall is under 25 cm per year. Plant species include xerophytes and succulents. Lizards, snakes, and small mammals are common animals.
Temperate	Deciduous forest temperatures range from -24 to 38°C. Rainfall is from 65 to 150 cm per year. Deciduous trees are common, as are deer, bear, and squirrels.
Taiga	Temperatures range from -24 to 22°C. Rainfall is from 35 to 40 cm per year. Taiga is located far north and far south of the equator, close to the poles. Plant life includes conifers and plants that can withstand harsh winters. Animals include weasels, mink, and moose.
Tundra	Temperatures range from -28 to 15°C. Rainfall is limited, ranging from 10 to 15 cm per year. The tundra is located even farther north and south than the taiga. Common plants include lichens and mosses. Animals include polar bears and musk ox.
Polar or Permafrost	Temperatures range from -40 to 0°C. It rarely gets above freezing. Rainfall is below 10 cm per year. Most water is bound up as ice. Life is limited.

Succession is defined as an orderly process of replacing a community that has been damaged or has begun where no life previously existed. Primary succession occurs after a community has been totally wiped out by a natural disaster or where life never existed before, as in a flooded area. Secondary succession takes place in communities that were once flourishing but were disturbed by some force, either human or natural, but not totally stripped. A climax community is a community that is established and flourishing.

Definitions of Feeding Relationships

- Parasitism: When two species occupy a similar place, but the parasite benefits from the relationship while the host is harmed.

- **Commensalism:** When two species occupy a similar place and neither species is harmed or benefits from the relationship.

- **Mutualism (symbiosis):** When two species occupy a similar place and both species benefit from the relationship.

- **Competition:** When two species occupy the same habitat or eat the same food.

- **Predation:** When animals eat other animals. The animals they feed on are called the prey. Population growth depends upon competition for food, water, shelter, and space. The number of predators determines the number of prey, which in turn affects the number of predators.

- **Carrying capacity:** The total amount of life a habitat can support. Once the habitat runs out of food, water, shelter, or space, the carrying capacity decreases and then restabilizes.

Ecological Problems

Nonrenewable resources are fragile and must be conserved for use in the future. Humankind's impact on the environment and knowledge of conservation will control our future. The following are just some of the ways in which the Earth's ecology is altered by human interaction:

- **Biological magnification:** Chemicals and pesticides accumulate along the food chain. Tertiary consumers have more accumulated toxins than animals at the bottom of the food chain.

- **Simplification of the food web:** Three major crops feed the world— rice, corn, and wheat. Planting these foods in abundance wipes out habitats and pushes animals residing there into other habitats, causing overpopulation or extinction.

- **Fuel sources:** Strip mining and the overuse of oil reserves have depleted these resources. At the current rate of consumption, the only way to guarantee our future fuel sources is conservation or alternate fuel sources.

- **Pollution:** Although technology gives us many advances, pollution is a side effect of production. Waste disposal and the burning of fossil fuels have polluted our land, water, and air. Global warming and acid rain are two results of the burning of hydrocarbons and sulfur.

- **Global warming:** Rainforest depletion and the use of fossil fuels and aerosols have caused an increase in carbon dioxide production. This leads to a decrease in the amount of oxygen, which is directly proportional to the amount of ozone. As the ozone layer depletes, more heat enters our

LIFE SCIENCE

atmosphere and is trapped. This causes an overall warming effect, which may eventually melt polar ice caps and cause a rise in water levels or changes in climate that will affect weather systems worldwide.

- Endangered species: Construction of homes to house people has caused the destruction of habitats for other animals, leading to their extinction.

- Overpopulation: The human race is still growing at an exponential rate. Carrying capacity has not been met due to our ability to use technology to produce more food and housing. However, space and water cannot be manufactured; eventually, our nonrenewable resources will reach a crisis state. Our overuse affects every living thing on this planet.

Sample Test Questions and Rationale

(Easy)

1. Which of the following describes the interaction between community members when one species feeds off another species but does not kill it immediately?

    A. Parasitism

    B. Predation

    C. Commensalism

    D. Mutualism

Answer: A. Parasitism

Predation occurs when one species kills another species. In mutualism, both species benefit. In commensalism one species benefits without the other being harmed.

(Average)

2. Which of the following is the most accurate definition of a nonrenewable resource?

    A. A nonrenewable resource is never replaced once used

    B. A nonrenewable resource is replaced on a timescale that is very long relative to human life spans

    C. A nonrenewable resource is a resource that can only be manufactured by humans

    D. A nonrenewable resource is a species that has already become extinct

Answer: B. A nonrenewable resource is replaced on a timescale that is very long relative to human life spans

Renewable resources are those that are renewed, or replaced, in time for humans to use more of them. Examples include fast-growing plants, animals, or oxygen gas. (Note that while sunlight is often considered a renewable resource, it is actually a nonrenewable but extremely abundant resource.) Nonrenewable resources are those that renew themselves only on very long timescales, usually geologic timescales. Examples include minerals, metals, or fossil fuels.

TEACHER CERTIFICATION STUDY GUIDE   275

COMPETENCY 17
PHYSICAL SCIENCE

> **SKILL 17.1** **Understands the physical and chemical properties and structure of matter** *(e.g., changes of states, mixtures and solutions, atoms and elements)*

Matter

Everything in our world is made up of matter, whether it is a rock, a building, an animal, or a person. Matter is defined by its characteristics: It takes up space and it has mass.

MASS: a measure of the amount of matter in an object

MASS is a measure of the amount of matter in an object. Two objects of equal mass will balance each other on a simple balance scale no matter where the scale is located. For instance, two rocks with the same amount of mass that are in balance on Earth will also be in balance on the moon. They will feel heavier on the Earth than on the moon because of the gravitational pull of the Earth. Therefore, although the two rocks have the same mass, they will have different weight.

WEIGHT: the measure of the Earth's pull of gravity on an object

WEIGHT is the measure of the Earth's pull of gravity on an object. It can also be defined as the pull of gravity between other bodies. The units of weight measurement commonly used are the pound (English measure) and the kilogram (metric measure).

VOLUME: the amount of cubic space that an object occupies

In addition to mass, matter also has the property of volume. **VOLUME** is the amount of cubic space that an object occupies. Volume and mass together give a more exact description of an object. Two objects may have the same volume, but different mass, or the same mass but different volumes.

DENSITY: the mass of a substance contained per unit of volume

For instance, consider two cubes that are each one cubic centimeter, one made from plastic and one from lead. They have the same volume, but the lead cube has more mass. The measure that we use to describe the cubes takes into consideration both the mass and the volume. **DENSITY** is the mass of a substance contained per unit of volume. If the density of an object is less than the density of a liquid, the object will float in the liquid. If the object is denser than the liquid, then the object will sink.

Density is stated in grams per cubic centimeter (g/cm^3), where the gram is the standard unit of mass. To find an object's density, you must measure its mass and its volume. Then divide the mass by the volume ($D = m/V$).

To discover an object's density, first use a balance scale to find its mass. Then calculate its volume. If the object is a regular shape, you can find the volume by multiplying the length, width, and height together. However, if it is an irregular shape, you can find the volume by seeing how much water it displaces. Measure the water in the container before and after the object is submerged. The difference is the volume of the object.

SPECIFIC GRAVITY is the ratio of the density of a substance to the density of water. For instance, the specific density of one liter of alcohol is calculated by comparing its mass (0.81 kg) to the mass of one liter of water (1 kg):

$$\frac{\text{mass of 1 L alcohol}}{\text{mass of 1 L water}} = \frac{0.81 \text{ kg}}{1.00 \text{ kg}} = 0.81$$

SPECIFIC GRAVITY: the ratio of the density of a substance to the density of water

Physical and Chemical Properties of Matter

Physical and chemical properties of matter describe the appearance or behavior of a substance. A physical property can be observed without changing the identity of a substance. For instance, you can describe the color, mass, shape, and volume of a book. Chemical properties describe the ability of a substance to be changed into new substances. Baking powder goes through a chemical change as it changes into carbon dioxide gas during the baking process.

Matter constantly changes. A physical change is a change that does not produce a new substance. The freezing and melting of water is an example of physical change. A chemical change (or chemical reaction) is any change of a substance into one or more other substances. Burning materials turn into smoke; a seltzer tablet fizzes into gas bubbles. The phase of matter (solid, liquid, or gas) is identified by its shape and volume.

A solid has a definite shape and volume. A liquid has a definite volume, but no shape. A gas has no shape or volume because it will spread out to occupy the entire space of whatever container it is in. While plasma is really a type of gas, its properties are so unique that it is considered a unique phase of matter.

Plasma is a gas that has been ionized, meaning that at least one electron has been removed from some of its atoms. Plasma shares some characteristics with gas, specifically, the high kinetic energy of its molecules. Thus, plasma exists as a diffuse "cloud," though it sometimes includes tiny grains (this is called dusty plasma). What most distinguishes plasma from gas is that it is electrically conductive and exhibits a strong response to electromagnetic fields. This property is a consequence of the charged particles that result from the removal of electrons from the molecules in the plasma.

Energy is the ability to cause changes in matter. Applying heat to a frozen liquid changes it from solid back to liquid. Continue heating it and it will boil and give off steam, a gas. Evaporation is the change in phase from liquid to gas. Condensation is the change in phase from gas to liquid.

Composition of Matter

An **ELEMENT** is a substance that cannot be broken down into other substances. To date, scientists have identified 109 elements: 89 are found in nature and 20 are synthetic.

An **ATOM** is the smallest particle of an element that retains the properties of that element. All of the atoms of a particular element are the same. The atoms of each element are different from the atoms of other elements. Elements are assigned an identifying symbol of one or two letters. The symbol for oxygen is O; it stands for one atom of oxygen. However, because oxygen atoms in nature are joined together in pairs, the symbol O_2 represents oxygen.

This pair of oxygen atoms is a molecule. A **MOLECULE** is the smallest particle of a substance that can exist independently and still have all of the properties of that substance. A molecule of most elements is made up of one atom. However, oxygen, hydrogen, nitrogen, and chlorine molecules are made of two atoms each.

A **COMPOUND** is made of two or more elements that have been chemically combined. Atoms join together when elements are chemically combined. The result is that the elements lose their individual identities; the compound that they become has different properties.

We use a formula to show the elements of a chemical compound. A chemical formula is a shorthand way of showing what is in a compound through symbols and subscripts. The letter symbols let us know what elements are involved and the number subscript indicates how many atoms of each element are involved. No subscript is used if there is only one atom involved. For example, carbon dioxide is made up of one atom of carbon (C) and two atoms of oxygen (O_2), so the formula would be represented as CO_2.

Substances can combine without a chemical change. A mixture is any combination of two or more substances in which the substances keep their own properties. A fruit salad is a mixture (so is an ice cream sundae, although you might not recognize each part if it is stirred together). Colognes and perfumes are other examples. You may not readily recognize the individual elements; however, they can be separated.

Compounds and mixtures are similar in that they are made up of two or more substances. However, they have the opposite characteristics, as shown in the table:

ELEMENT: a substance that cannot be broken down into other substances

ATOM: the smallest particle of an element that retains the properties of that element

MOLECULE: the smallest particle of a substance that can exist independently and still have all of the properties of that substance

COMPOUND: two or more elements that have been chemically combined

Compounds	Made up of one kind of particle Formed during a chemical change Broken down only by chemical changes Properties are different from their parts Have a specific amount of each ingredient
Mixtures	Made up of two or more particles Not formed by a chemical change Can be separated by physical changes Properties are the same as their parts Do not have a definite amount of each ingredient.

Common compounds are acids, bases, salts, and oxides. These are classified according to their characteristics.

Atoms

The nucleus is the center of the atom. The positive particles inside the nucleus are called protons. The mass of a proton is about 2,000 times the mass of an electron. The number of protons in the nucleus of an atom is called the atomic number. All atoms of the same element have the same atomic number.

Neutrons are another type of particle in the nucleus. Neutrons and protons have about the same mass, but neutrons have no charge. Neutrons were discovered because scientists observed that not all atoms in neon gas have the same mass. They had identified isotopes. Isotopes of an element have the same number of protons in the nucleus, but have different masses. Neutrons explain the difference in mass.

The mass of matter is measured against a standard mass such as the gram. Scientists measure the mass of an atom by comparing it to that of a standard atom. The result is relative mass. The relative mass of an atom is its mass expressed in terms of the mass of the standard atom. The isotope of the element carbon is the standard atom. It has six (6) neutrons and is called carbon-12. It is assigned a mass of 12 atomic mass units (amu). Therefore, the ATOMIC MASS UNIT (AMU) is the standard unit for measuring the mass of an atom. It is equal to the mass of a carbon atom.

The mass number of an atom is the sum of its protons and neutrons. In any element, there is a mixture of isotopes, some having slightly more or slightly fewer protons and neutrons. The atomic mass of an element is an average of the mass numbers of its atoms.

ATOMIC MASS UNIT (AMU): the standard unit for measuring the mass of an atom, equal to the mass of a carbon atom

The following table summarizes the terms used to describe atomic nuclei:

TERM	EXAMPLE	MEANING	CHARACTERISTIC
Atomic Number	No. of protons (p)	Same for all atoms of a given element	Carbon (C) Atomic number = 6 (6p)
Mass Number	No. of protons + no. of neutrons (p + n)	Changes for different isotopes of an element	C-12 (6p + 6n) C-13 (6p + 7n)
Atomic Mass	Average mass of the atoms of the element	Usually not a whole number	Atomic mass of carbon equals 12.011

Each atom has an equal number of electrons (negative) and protons (positive). Therefore, atoms are neutral. Electrons orbiting the nucleus occupy energy levels that are arranged in order and the electrons tend to occupy the lowest energy level available. A stable electron arrangement is an atom that has all of its electrons in the lowest possible energy levels.

Each energy level holds a maximum number of electrons. However, an atom with more than one level does not hold more than eight electrons in its outermost shell.

LEVEL	NAME	MAXIMUM NUMBER OF ELECTRONS
First	K shell	2
Second	L shell	8
Third	M shell	18
Fourth	N shell	32

This can help to explain why chemical reactions occur. Atoms react with each other when their outer levels are unfilled. When atoms either exchange or share electrons with each other, these energy levels become filled and the atom becomes more stable.

As an electron gains energy, it moves from one energy level to a higher energy level. The electron cannot leave one level until it has enough energy to reach the next level. Excited electrons are electrons that have absorbed energy and have moved farther from the nucleus.

Electrons can also lose energy. When they do, they fall to a lower level. However, they can only fall to the lowest level that has room for them. This explains why atoms do not collapse.

Sample Test Questions and Rationale

(Easy)

1. Which of the following statements about the density of a substance is true?

   A. It is a chemical property

   B. It is a physical property

   C. It does not depend on the temperature of the substance

   D. It is a property only of liquids and solids

   Answer: B. It is a physical property

   The density of a substance is the mass of an object made of the substance divided by the object's volume. Chemical properties involve chemical reactions. Densities of substances generally decrease with higher temperatures.

(Easy)

2. A type of mixture in which one substance is suspended in another is called what?

   A. Heterogeneous

   B. A colloid

   C. A solution

   D. Homogeneous

   Answer: C. A solution

   Colloids are mixtures in which one substance is evenly dispersed in another. Most colloids exist somewhere between a heterogeneous and a homogeneous mixture.

SKILL 17.2 **Understands forces and motions** *(e.g., types of motion, laws of motion, forces and equilibrium)*

DYNAMICS is the study of the relationship between motion and the forces affecting motion. Force causes motion. Surfaces that touch each other have a certain resistance to motion. This resistance is friction. Some principles of friction include:

- The materials that make up the surfaces will determine the magnitude of the frictional force

- The frictional force is independent of the area of contact between the two surfaces

> **DYNAMICS:** the study of the relationship between motion and the forces affecting motion

- The direction of the frictional force is opposite to the direction of motion
- The frictional force is proportional to the normal force between the two surfaces in contact

Static friction describes the force of friction of two surfaces that are in contact but do not have any motion relative to each other, such as a block sitting on an inclined plane. Kinetic friction describes the force of friction of two surfaces in contact with each other when there is relative motion between the surfaces.

When an object moves in a circular path, a force must be directed toward the center of the circle in order to keep the motion going. This constraining force is called centripetal force. Gravity is the centripetal force that keeps a satellite circling the Earth.

ELECTRICAL FORCE is the force between two charged objects and is described by Coulomb's law. Coulomb's law shows that like charges repel each other (for example, two positive charges) and unlike charges attract each other (for example, a positive and a negative charge) and that the size of the force varies inversely as a square of the distance between the 2 charged objects.

There is something of a mystery as to how objects affect each other when they are not in mechanical contact. Newton wrestled with the concept of "action-at-a-distance" (as electrical force is now classified) and eventually concluded that it was necessary for there to be some form of ether, or intermediate medium, which made it possible for one object to transfer force to another. We now know that no ether exists. It is possible for objects to exert forces on one another without any medium to transfer the force. From our fluid notion of electrical forces, however, we still associate forces as being due to the exchange of something between the two objects. The electrical field force acts between two charges, in the same way that the gravitational field force acts between two masses.

Magnetic force occurs when magnetized items interact with other items in specific ways. If a magnet is brought close enough to a ferromagnetic material (that is not magnetized itself) the magnet will strongly attract the ferromagnetic material regardless of orientation. Both the north and south pole of the magnet will attract the other item with equal strength. In opposition, diamagnetic materials weakly repel a magnetic field. This occurs regardless of the north-south orientation of the field. Paramagnetic materials are weakly attracted to a magnetic field. This occurs regardless of the north-south orientation of the field. Calculating the attractive or repulsive magnetic force between two magnets is, in the general case, an extremely complex operation, as it depends on the shape, magnetization, orientation, and separation of the magnets.

In the nuclear force, the protons in the nucleus of an atom are positively charged. If protons interact, they are usually pushed apart by the electromagnetic

ELECTRICAL FORCE:
the force between two charged objects described by Coulomb's law: that like charges repel each other, unlike charges attract each other, and the size of the force varies inversely as a square of the distance between the two charged objects

force. However, when two or more nuclei come very close together, the nuclear force comes into play. The nuclear force is a hundred times stronger than the electromagnetic force, so the nuclear force may be able to "glue" the nuclei together to allow fusion to happen. The nuclear force is also known as the strong force. The nuclear force keeps together the most basic of elementary particles, the quarks. Quarks combine to form the protons and neutrons in the atomic nucleus.

The **FORCE OF GRAVITY** is the force by which the Earth, moon, or other massively large object attracts another object toward itself. By definition, this is the weight of the object. All objects on Earth experience a force of gravity that is directed "downward" toward the center of the Earth. The force of gravity on Earth is always equal to the weight of the object as found by the equation:

> **FORCE OF GRAVITY:** the force at which the Earth, moon, or other massively large object attracts another object toward itself

Fgrav = m × g where $g = 9.8 \frac{m}{s^2}$ (on Earth) and m = mass (in kg)

Newton's Laws of Motion

Newton's first law of motion is also called the law of inertia. It states that an object at rest will remain at rest, and an object in motion will remain in motion at a constant velocity unless acted upon by an external force.

Newton's second law of motion states that if a net force acts on an object, it will cause the acceleration of the object. The relationship between force and motion is force equals mass times acceleration (F = ma).

Newton's third law of motion states that for every action there is an equal and opposite reaction. Therefore, if an object exerts a force on another object, that second object exerts an equal and opposite force on the first.

Sample Test Questions and Rationale

(Easy)

1. **A pendulum has _____ at the top of its swinging arc.**

   A. maximum kinetic energy

   B. maximum potential energy

   C. maximum total energy

   D. minimum potential energy

Answer: B. maximum potential energy

Potential energy is the stored energy. Kinetic energy is the energy of motion. Potential energy maxes out at the top of the arc while kinetic energy maxes out at the bottom of the arc.

Sample Test Questions and Rationale (cont.)

(Rigorous)

2. **Which statement best explains why a balance scale is used to measure both weight and mass?**

   A. The weight and mass of an object are identical concepts

   B. The force of gravity between two objects depends on the mass of the two objects

   C. Inertial mass and gravitational mass are identical

   D. A balance scale compares the weight of two objects

Answer: C. Inertial mass and gravitational mass are identical

The mass of an object is a fundamental property of matter and is measured in kilograms. The weight is the force of gravity between Earth and an object near Earth's surface and is measured in newtons or pounds. Newton's second law ($F = ma$) and the universal law of gravity ($F = G \frac{m_{earth}\, m}{d^2}$) determine the weight of an object. The mass in Newton's second law is called the inertial mass and the mass in the universal law of gravity is called the gravitational mass. The two kinds of masses are identical.

SKILL 17.3 **Understands energy** *(e.g., forms of energy, transfer and conservation of energy, simple machines)*

The kinetic theory states that matter consists of molecules that possess kinetic energies in continual random motion. The state of matter (solid, liquid, or gas) depends on the speed of the molecules and the amount of kinetic energy the molecules possess. The molecules of solid matter merely vibrate, allowing strong intermolecular forces to hold the molecules in place. The molecules of liquid matter move freely and quickly, and the molecules of gaseous matter move randomly and at high speeds.

Matter changes state when energy is added or taken away.

Matter changes state when energy is added or taken away. The addition of energy, usually in the form of heat, increases the speed and kinetic energy of the component molecules. Faster-moving molecules more readily overcome the intermolecular attractions that maintain the form of solids and liquids. In conclusion, as the speed of molecules increases, matter changes state from solid to liquid to gas (melting and evaporation).

As matter loses heat energy to the environment, the speed of the component molecules decreases. Intermolecular forces have greater impact on slower-moving molecules. Thus, as the speed of molecules decreases, matter changes from gas to liquid to solid (condensation and freezing).

Heat and Temperature

Heat and temperature are different physical quantities. Heat is a measure of energy. Temperature is the measure of how hot (or cold) a body is with respect to a standard object.

Two concepts are important in the discussion of temperature changes. Objects are in thermal contact if they can affect each other's temperatures. Set a hot cup of coffee on a desktop. The two objects are in thermal contact with each other and will begin affecting each other's temperatures. The coffee will become cooler and the desktop warmer. Eventually, they will have the same temperature. When this happens, they are in thermal equilibrium.

We cannot rely on our sense of touch to determine temperature because the heat from a hand may be conducted more efficiently by certain objects than others, making them feel colder. Thermometers are used to measure temperature. In thermometers, a small amount of mercury in a capillary tube will expand when heated. The thermometer and the object whose temperature it is measuring are put in contact long enough for them to reach thermal equilibrium. The temperature can then be read from the thermometer scale.

Three temperature scales are used:

- Celsius: The freezing point of water is set at 0 and the steam (boiling) point is 100. The interval between the two is divided into 100 equal parts called degrees Celsius.

- Fahrenheit: The freezing point of water is 32 degrees and the boiling point is 212. The interval between is divided into 180 equal parts called degrees Fahrenheit.

- Temperature readings can be converted from one to the other as follows:

  Fahrenheit to Celsius   **Celsius to Fahrenheit**
  $$C = \frac{5}{9}(F - 32) \qquad F = \left(\frac{9}{5}\right)C + 32$$

- Kelvin: The Kelvin scale has degrees the same size as the Celsius scale, but the zero point is moved to the triple point of water. Water inside a closed vessel is in thermal equilibrium in all three states (ice, water, and vapor) at 273.15 degrees Kelvin. This temperature is equivalent to .01 degrees Celsius. Because the degrees are the same in the two scales, temperature changes are the same in Celsius and Kelvin.

- Temperature readings can be converted from Celsius to Kelvin:

  Celsius to Kelvin   **Kelvin to Celsius**
  $$K = C + 273.15 \qquad C = K - 273.15$$

The heat capacity of an object is the amount of heat energy it takes to raise the temperature of the object by one degree.

Heat capacity (C) per unit mass (m) is called specific heat (c):

$$c = \frac{C}{m} = \frac{Q}{m}$$

There are a number of ways that heat is measured. In each case, the measurement is dependent upon raising the temperature of a specific amount of water by a specific amount. These conversions of heat energy and work are called the mechanical equivalent of heat.

A CALORIE is the amount of energy it takes to raise one gram of water one degree Celsius.

A KILOCALORIE is the amount of energy it takes to raise one kilogram of water by one degree Celsius. Food calories are kilocalories.

In the International System of Units (SI), the calorie is equal to 4.184 joules.

A British thermal unit (BTU) = 252 calories = 1.054 kJ.

Heat transfer

Heat energy that is transferred into or out of a system is HEAT TRANSFER. The temperature change is positive for a gain in heat energy and negative when heat is removed from the object or system.

The formula for heat transfer is $Q = mc\triangle T$ where Q is the amount of heat energy transferred, m is the amount of substance (in kilograms), c is the specific heat of the substance, and $\triangle T$ is the change in temperature of the substance. It is important to assume that the objects in thermal contact are isolated and insulated from their surroundings.

If a substance in a closed container loses heat, then another substance in the container must gain heat.

A calorimeter uses the transfer of heat from one substance to another to determine the specific heat of the substance. When an object undergoes a change of phase it goes from one physical state (solid, liquid, or gas) to another. For instance, water can go from liquid to solid (freezing) or from liquid to gas (boiling). The heat that is required to change from one state to the other is called latent heat.

The heat of fusion is the amount of heat it takes to change from a solid to a liquid or the amount of heat released during the change from liquid to solid.

The heat of vaporization is the amount of heat it takes to change from a liquid to a gaseous state.

CALORIE: the amount of energy it takes to raise one gram of water one degree Celsius

KILOCALORIE: the amount of energy it takes to raise one kilogram of water by one degree Celsius

HEAT TRANSFER: heat energy that is transferred into or out of a system

Heat is transferred in three ways:

- Conduction: Heat travels through the heated solid. The transfer rate is the ratio of the amount of heat per amount of time it takes to transfer heat from one area of an object to another. For example, if you place an iron pan on a flame, the handle will eventually become hot. How fast the handle gets too hot to handle is a function of the amount of heat and how long it is applied. Because the change in time is in the denominator of the function, the shorter the amount of time it takes to heat the handle, the greater the transfer rate.

- Convection: Heat transported by the movement of a heated substance. Warmed air rising from a heat source such as a fire or electric heater is a common example of convection. Convection ovens make use of circulating air to more efficiently cook food.

- Radiation: Heat transfer as the result of electromagnetic waves. The Sun warms the Earth by emitting radiant energy.

An example of all three methods of heat transfer occurs in a thermos bottle or dewar flask. The bottle is constructed of double walls of Pyrex glass that have a space in between. Air is evacuated from the space between the walls and the inner wall is silvered. The lack of air between the walls lessens heat loss by convection and conduction. The heat inside is reflected by the silver, cutting down heat transfer by radiation. Hot liquids remain hotter and cold liquids remain colder for longer periods of time.

Laws of thermodynamics

The relationship between heat, forms of energy, and work (mechanical, electrical, etc.) are the laws of thermodynamics. These laws deal strictly with systems in thermal equilibrium and not those within the process of rapid change or in a state of transition. Systems that are nearly always in a state of equilibrium are called reversible systems.

The first law of thermodynamics is a restatement of conservation of energy. The change in heat energy supplied to a system (Q) is equal to the sum of the change in the internal energy (U) and the change in the work done by the system against internal forces.

$$\triangle Q = \triangle U + \triangle W$$

The second law of thermodynamics is stated in two parts:

1. No machine is 100 percent efficient. It is impossible to construct a machine that only absorbs heat from a heat source and performs an equal amount of work because some heat will always be lost to the environment.

2. Heat cannot spontaneously pass from a colder to a hotter object. An ice cube sitting on a hot sidewalk will melt into a little puddle, but it will never spontaneously cool and form the same ice cube. Certain events have a preferred direction called the arrow of time.

ENTROPY: the measure of how much energy or heat is available for work

ENTROPY is the measure of how much energy or heat is available for work. Work occurs only when heat is transferred from hot to cooler objects. Once this is done, no more work can be extracted. The energy is still being conserved, but it is not available for work as long as the objects are the same temperature. Theory has it that, eventually, all things in the universe will reach the same temperature. If this happens, energy will no longer be usable.

Sample Test Questions and Rationale

(Easy)

1. The transfer of heat by electromagnetic waves is called:

   A. Conduction

   B. Convection

   C. Phase change

   D. Radiation

Answer: D. Radiation

Heat transfer via electromagnetic waves (which can occur even in a vacuum) is called radiation. Heat can also be transferred by direct contact (conduction), by fluid current (convection), and by matter changing phase, but these are not relevant here.

(Average)

2. Which statement could be described as the first law of thermodynamics?

   A. No machine can convert heat energy to work with 100 percent efficiency

   B. Energy is neither created nor destroyed

   C. Thermometers can be used to measure temperatures

   D. Heat flows from hot objects to cold objects

Answer: B. Energy is neither created nor destroyed

The first law of thermodynamics is considered to be a statement of the conservation of energy. Answers A and D are statements of the second law of thermodynamics. Answer C is not a law of thermodynamics.

> SKILL **Understands interactions of energy and matter** (e.g., electricity, 17.4 magnetism, sound)

The law of conservation of energy states that energy is neither created nor destroyed. Thus, energy changes form when energy transactions occur in nature. Because the total energy in the universe is constant, energy continually transitions between forms. For example, an engine burns gasoline, converting the chemical energy of the gasoline into mechanical energy; a plant converts radiant energy of the Sun into chemical energy found in glucose; and a battery converts chemical energy into electrical energy.

CHEMICAL REACTIONS are the interactions of substances that result in chemical changes and changes in energy. Chemical reactions involve changes in electron motion as well as the breaking and forming of chemical bonds. Reactants are the original substances that interact to form distinct products. Endothermic chemical reactions consume energy while exothermic chemical reactions release energy with product formation. Chemical reactions occur continually in nature and are also induced by humans for many purposes.

> **CHEMICAL REACTION:** the interactions of substances that result in chemical changes and changes in energy

Nuclear reactions, or atomic reactions, are reactions that change the composition, energy, or structure of atomic nuclei. Nuclear reactions change the number of protons and neutrons in the nucleus. The two main types of nuclear reaction are fission (splitting of nuclei) and fusion (joining of nuclei). Fusion reactions are exothermic, releasing heat energy. Fission reactions are endothermic, absorbing heat energy. Fission of large nuclei (e.g., uranium) releases energy because the products of fission undergo further fusion reactions. Fission and fusion reactions can occur naturally, but are usually recognized as manufactured events. Particle acceleration and bombardment with neutrons are two methods of inducing nuclear reactions.

The law of conservation can also be applied to physical and biological processes. For example, when a rock is weathered, it does not just lose pieces. Instead it is broken down into its composite minerals, many of which enter the soil. Biology takes advantage of decomposers to recycle decaying material. Since energy is neither created nor destroyed, we know it must change form. An animal may die, but its body will be consumed by other animals or decay into the ecosystem. Either way, it enters another form and the matter still exists—it was not destroyed.

Sample Test Question and Rationale

(Average)

1. The following are examples of chemical reactions EXCEPT:

   A. Melting ice into water

   B. Dissolving a seltzer tablet in water

   C. Using a fire-cracker

   D. Burning a piece of plastic

Answer: A. Melting ice into water

When you melt ice there is no chemical reaction. Ice and water have the same chemical makeup. A chemical reaction requires a change in the chemical components of matter.

COMPETENCY 18
SCIENCE IN PERSONAL AND SOCIAL PERSPECTIVES

SKILL 18.1 **Knows about personal health** *(e.g., nutrition, communicable diseases, substance abuse)*

Overview of Systems in the Human Body

The function of the skeletal system is support. Vertebrates have an endo-skeleton, with muscles attached to bones. Skeletal proportions are controlled by area-to-volume relationships. Body size and shape is limited due to the forces of gravity. Surface area is increased to improve efficiency in all organ systems.

The function of the muscular system is movement. There are three types of muscle tissue. Skeletal muscle is voluntary. Skeletal muscles are attached to bones. Smooth muscle is involuntary. It is found in organs and enables functions such as digestion and respiration. Cardiac muscle is a specialized type of smooth muscle.

The neuron is the basic unit of the nervous system. It consists of an axon, which carries impulses away from the cell body; the dendrite, which carries impulses toward the cell body; and the cell body, which contains the nucleus. Synapses are spaces between neurons. Chemicals called neurotransmitters are found close to the synapse. The myelin sheath, composed of Schwann cells, covers the neurons and provides insulation.

The function of the digestive system is to break down food and absorb it into the bloodstream, where it can be delivered to all cells of the body for use in cellular respiration. As animals evolved, digestive systems changed from simple absorption to a system with a separate mouth and anus, capable of allowing the animal to become independent of a host.

The respiratory system functions in the gas exchange of oxygen (needed) and carbon dioxide (waste). It delivers oxygen to the bloodstream and picks up carbon dioxide for release out of the body. Simple animals diffuse gases from and to their environment. Gills allow aquatic animals to exchange gases in a fluid medium by removing dissolved oxygen from the water. Lungs maintain a fluid environment for gas exchange in terrestrial animals.

The function of the circulatory system is to carry oxygenated blood and nutrients to all cells of the body and return carbon dioxide waste to be expelled from the lungs. Animals evolved from an open system to a closed system with vessels leading to and from the heart.

Nutrition and Exercise

The components of nutrition are:

- Carbohydrates: The main source of energy (glucose) in the human diet. There are two types: simple and complex. Complex carbohydrates have greater nutritional value because they take longer to digest, contain dietary fiber, and do not excessively elevate blood sugar levels. Common sources of carbohydrates are fruits, vegetables, grains, dairy products, and legumes.

- Proteins: Necessary for growth, development, and cellular function. The body breaks down consumed protein into component amino acids for future use. Major sources of protein are meat, poultry, fish, legumes, eggs, dairy products, and grains.

- Fats: A concentrated energy source and important component of the human body. The types of fats are saturated, monounsaturated, and polyunsaturated. Polyunsaturated fats are the healthiest because they may lower cholesterol levels, while saturated fats increase cholesterol levels. Common sources of saturated fats include dairy products, meat, coconut oil, and palm oil. Common sources of unsaturated fats include nuts, most vegetable oils, and fish.

- Vitamins and minerals: Organic substances that the body requires in small quantities for proper functioning. People acquire vitamins and minerals in their diets and in supplements. Important vitamins include A, B, C, D, E, and K. Important minerals include calcium, phosphorus, magnesium, potassium, sodium, chlorine, and sulfur.

- Water: Makes up 55–75 percent of the human body. Essential for most bodily functions. Acquired through foods and liquids.

Nutritional requirements vary from person-to-person. General guidelines for meeting adequate nutritional needs are:

- No more than 30 percent of total caloric intake from fats (preferably 10 percent from saturated fats, 10 percent from monounsaturated fats, and 10 percent from polyunsaturated fats)

- No more than 15 percent of total caloric intake from protein (complete)

- *At least* 55 percent of total caloric intake from carbohydrates (mainly complex carbohydrates)

Exercise and diet help maintain proper body weight by equalizing caloric intake and caloric output.

Regular exercise improves overall health. Benefits of regular exercise include a stronger immune system; stronger muscles, bones, and joints; reduced risk of premature death; reduced risk of heart disease; improved psychological well-being; and weight management. The health risk factors improved by physical activity include cholesterol levels, blood pressure, stress-related disorders, heart disease, weight and obesity disorders, early death, certain types of cancer, musculoskeletal problems, mental health, and susceptibility to infectious diseases.

Sample Test Question and Rationale

(Average)

1. **Which of the following is the main source of energy in the diet?**

   A. Vitamins

   B. Minerals

   C. Water

   D. Carbohydrates

Answer: D. Carbohydrates

The components of nutrition are carbohydrates, proteins, fats, vitamins, minerals, and water. Carbohydrates are the main source of energy (glucose) in the human diet. Common sources of carbohydrates are fruits, vegetables, grains, dairy products, and legumes.

SKILL 18.2 Understands science as a human endeavor, process, and career

Science is tentative. By definition, it is about humans searching for information by making educated guesses. It must be replicable. Another scientist must be able to achieve the same results under the same conditions at a later time. The term empirical means that a phenomenon must be assessed through tests and observations. Science changes over time. Science is limited by available technology. An example of this would be the relationship of the discovery of the cell and the invention of the microscope. As our technology improves, more hypotheses will become theories and possibly laws.

Science is also limited by the data that can be collected. Data may be interpreted differently on different occasions. The limitations of science cause explanations to be changed as new technologies emerge. New technologies gather previously unavailable data and enable us to build upon current theories with new information.

The Nature of Science

The nature of science mainly consists of three important things:

1. **The scientific world view:** It is possible to understand this highly organized world and its complexities with the help of the latest technology. Scientific ideas are subject to change. After repeated experiments, a theory is established, but this theory can be changed or supported in the future. Only laws that occur naturally do not change. Scientific knowledge may not be discarded but can be modified (e.g., Albert Einstein didn't discard Newtonian principles but modified them in his theory of relativity). Also, science can't answer all of our questions. We can't find answers to questions related to our beliefs, moral values, and norms.

2. **Scientific inquiry:** Scientific inquiry starts with a simple question. This simple question leads to information gathering and an educated guess otherwise known as a hypothesis. To prove the hypothesis, an experiment has to be conducted, which yields data and the conclusion. All experiments must be repeated at least twice to get reliable results. Thus, scientific inquiry leads to new knowledge or the verification of established theories. Science requires proof or evidence. Science is dependent on accuracy, not bias or prejudice. In science, there is no place for preconceived ideas or premeditated results. By using their senses and modern technology, scientists will be able to get reliable information. Science is a combination of logic and imagination. A scientist needs to think and imagine and be able to reason.

3. **Scientific enterprise:** Science is a complex activity involving various people and places. A scientist may work alone or in a laboratory, in a classroom, or almost anywhere. Most of the time, it is a group activity requiring the social skills of cooperation, communication of results or findings, consultations, and discussions. Science demands a high degree of communication to governments, funding authorities, and the public.

Science explains, reasons, and predicts. These three actions are interwoven and inseparable. While reasoning is absolutely important for science, there should be no bias or prejudice. Science is not authoritarian because it has been shown that scientific authority can be wrong. No one can determine or make decisions for others on any issue.

Science is a process of checks and balances. It is expected that scientific findings will be challenged, and in many cases retested. Often, one experiment will be the beginning point for another. While bias does exist, the use of controlled experiments and an awareness on the part of the scientist can go far to ensure a sound experiment. Even if the science is well done, it may still be questioned. It is through this continual search that hypotheses develop into theories and sometimes become laws. It is also through this search that new information is discovered.

Science as a career

Society is not the same as it used to be even twenty-five years ago. Technology has changed our lifestyles, our behavior, our ethical and moral thinking, our economy, and our career opportunities.

Science is an interesting, innovative, and thoroughly enjoyable subject. Science careers are challenging and stimulating, and the possibilities for scientific careers are endless.

Why do people choose careers in science? This is a very important question. The reasons are manifold and may include:

- A passion for science

- A desire to experiment and gain knowledge

- A desire to contribute to society's betterment

- An inquiring mind

- Wanting to work on a team

There are a number of opportunities in science. For the sake of ease and convenience, they are grouped under various categories.

- Biological sciences: The study of living organisms and their life cycles, medicinal properties, and the like

  - Botanist

  - Microbiologist

- Physical science: The study of matter and energy

  - Analytical chemist

  - Biochemist

  - Chemist

  - Physicist

- Earth science: The study of the Earth, its changes over the years, and natural disasters such as earthquakes and hurricanes

  - Geologist

  - Meteorologist

- Oceanographer

- Seismologist

- Volcanologist

- **Space science:** The study of space, the universe, and planets

  - Astrophysicist

  - Space scientist

- **Forensic science:** The solving of crimes using various techniques

  - Forensic pathologist

- **Medical science:** Science with practical applications in the care and cure of diseases

  - Biomedical scientist

  - Clinical scientist

- **Agricultural science:** The use of science to grow and improve upon crops

  - Agriculturist

  - Agricultural service industry worker

  - Agronomist

  - Veterinary science worker

Sample Test Question and Rationale

(Average)

1. **All of the following professions are classified under Earth science EXCEPT:**

   A. Geologist

   B. Meteorologist

   C. Seismologist

   D. Biochemist

Answer: D. Biochemist

Geologists, meteorologists, and seismologists all work with phenomena that are related to the Earth. A biochemist deals with living objects.

COMPETENCY 19
SCIENCE AS INQUIRY AND SCIENCE PROCESSES

> **SKILL Understands science as inquiry** *(e.g., questioning, gathering data, drawing*
> **19.1** *reasonable conclusions)*

Science can be defined as a body of knowledge that is systematically derived from study, observations, and experimentation. Its goal is to identify and establish principles and theories that can be applied to solve problems. Pseudoscience, on the other hand, is a belief that is not warranted. There is no scientific methodology or application involved in pseudoscience. Classic examples of pseudoscience include witchcraft, alien encounters, or any topics that are explained by hearsay.

Scientific inquiry starts with observation.

Scientific inquiry starts with observation. Observation is an important skill by itself, as it leads to experimentation and communicating the experimental findings to the public. After observation, a question is formed, which starts with *why* or *how*. To answer these questions, experimentation is necessary. Between observation and experimentation there are three more important steps: gathering information (or researching the problem), forming a hypothesis, and designing the experiment.

The design of an experiment is very important since it involves identifying a control, constants, independent variables, and dependent variables. A control is something we compare our results with at the end of the experiment. It is like a reference. Constants are the factors that are kept the same in an experiment to get reliable results. Independent variables are factors we change in an experiment. Dependent variables are the changes that arise from the experiment. It is important to bear in mind that there should be more constants than variables to obtain reproducible results in an experiment.

After the experiment is done, it is repeated and results are graphically presented. The results are then analyzed and conclusions drawn. After the conclusion is drawn, the final step is communication. It is the responsibility of scientists to share the knowledge they obtain through their research. In this age, much emphasis is put on the form and the method of communication. The conclusions must be communicated by clearly describing the information using accurate data and visual presentations like graphs (bar/line/pie), tables/charts, diagrams, artwork, and other appropriate media. Modern technology should be used whenever necessary. The method of communication must be suitable to the audience.

Written communication is as important as oral communication. This is essential for submitting research papers to scientific journals, newspapers, and other magazines.

Planning and Conducting Investigations

The scientific method

The scientific method is the basic process behind science. It involves several steps, beginning with hypothesis formulation and working through to the conclusion:

1. **Posing a question:** Although many discoveries happen by chance, the standard thought process of a scientist begins with forming a question to research. The more limited the question, the easier it is to set up an experiment to answer it.

2. **Forming a hypothesis:** Once the question is formulated, researchers should take an educated guess about the answer to the problem or question. This "best guess" is the hypothesis.

3. **Doing the test:** To make a test fair, data from an experiment must have a variable or a condition that can be changed, such as temperature or mass. A good test will try to manipulate as few variables as possible to see which variable is responsible for the result. This requires a second example of a control. A control is an extra setup in which all the conditions are the same except for the variable being tested.

4. **Observing and recording the data:** Reporting the data should include the specifics of how measurements were calculated. For example, a graduated cylinder needs to be read with proper procedures. For beginning students, technique must be part of the instructional process so as to give validity to the data.

5. **Drawing a conclusion:** After recording data, compare your data with the data of other groups. A conclusion is the judgment derived from the data results.

Graphs and lab reports

Graphs utilize numbers to demonstrate patterns. The patterns offer a visual representation, making it easier to draw conclusions.

Normally, knowledge is integrated in the form of a lab report. A report has many sections. It should include a specific title that tells exactly what is being studied. The abstract is a summary of the report written at the beginning of the paper. The purpose should always be defined to state the problem. The purpose should include the hypothesis (educated guess) of what is expected from the outcome of the experiment. The entire experiment should relate to this problem.

It is important to describe exactly what was done to prove or disprove a hypothesis. A control is necessary to prove that the results occurred from the changed conditions and would not have happened normally. Only one variable should be manipulated at a time. Observations and results of the experiment, including all results from data, should be recorded. Drawings, graphs, and illustrations should be included to support information. Observations are objective, whereas analysis and interpretation are subjective. A conclusion should explain why the results of the experiment either proved or disproved the hypothesis.

A **SCIENTIFIC THEORY** is an explanation of a set of related observations based on a proven hypothesis. A **SCIENTIFIC LAW** usually lasts longer than a scientific theory and has more experimental data to support it.

SCIENTIFIC THEORY: an explanation of a set of related observations based on a proven hypothesis

SCIENTIFIC LAW: usually lasts longer than a scientific theory and has more experimental data to support it.

Gathering and Using Data to Draw Reasonable Conclusions

Whenever scientists begin an experiment or project, they must decide what pieces of data they are going to collect. This data can be qualitative or quantitative. Scientists use a variety of methods to gather and analyze this data. These methods include storing the data in a table or analyzing the data using a graph. Scientists also make notes of their observations (what they see, hear, smell, etc.), throughout the experiment. Scientists are then able to use the data and observations to make inferences and draw conclusions about a question or problem.

Several steps should be followed in the interpretation and evaluation of data:

1. Apply critical analysis and thinking strategies, asking questions about the accuracy of the data and the procedures of the experiment and procurement of the data.

2. Determine the importance of information and its relevance to the essential question. Any experiment may produce a plethora of data, not all of which is necessary to consider when analyzing the hypothesis. The useful information must then be separated into component parts.

3. Make inferences, identify trends, and interpret data.

4. Determine the most appropriate method of communicating these inferences and conclusions to the intended audience.

Sample Test Questions and Rationale

(Rigorous)

1. In an experiment measuring the growth of bacteria at different temperatures, what is the independent variable?

   A. Number of bacteria

   B. Growth rate of bacteria

   C. Temperature

   D. Size of bacteria

   Answer: C. Temperature

   To answer this question, recall that the independent variable in an experiment is the entity that is changed by the scientist in order to observe its effects (the dependent variable). In this experiment, temperature is changed in order to measure growth of bacteria. Note that number of bacteria is the dependent variable, and neither growth rate nor size of bacteria is directly relevant to the question.

(Average)

2. Which is the correct order of scientific methodology?
   1. Collecting data
   2. Planning a controlled experiment
   3. Drawing a conclusion
   4. Hypothesizing a result
   5. Revisiting a hypothesis to answer a question

   A. 1, 2, 3, 4, 5

   B. 4, 2, 1, 3, 5

   C. 4, 5, 1, 3, 2

   D. 1, 3, 4, 5, 2

   Answer: B. 4, 2, 1, 3, 5: Hypothesizing a result, planning a controlled experiment, collecting data, drawing a conclusion, and revisiting a hypothesis to answer a question.

   The scientific method is a very structured way to create valid theories and laws. All methodologies must follow this specific, linear plan.

SKILL 19.2 **Understands how to use resource and research material in science**

Professional journals provide core information about scientific research. Popular magazines focused on science also provide summaries of research as well as everyday translations of interesting scientific research. Many newspapers report on scientific endeavors; some publish a special section on science news. All of these sources are useful to teachers and students of science. However, much information utilized in the classroom comes from texts specifically designed for particular grade levels.

While a certain amount of information will always be presented in lecture form or using traditional written materials (i.e., textbooks), there are also many alternative resources available for teaching science at the elementary level. Several examples are listed below:

Hands-on Experiments and Games

Some simple experiments in the life and environmental sciences may be appropriate for elementary-level students. For instance, they might examine samples of pond water under a microscope or assist with the dissection of plants or lower animals. Students can also model environmental scenarios, perhaps pretending to be either predatory or prey animals. Such interactive experiences help students visualize principles explained elsewhere and help them become more involved with the subject matter.

Software and Simulations

When hands-on experiments are costly, complicated, dangerous, or otherwise not possible, students may benefit from software programs that simulate them. Multimedia software packages can be used to expose students to the sounds of the life forms and the environmental settings they are studying.

Natural History Museums, Zoos, and Wildlife Preserves

Visits to facilities that aim to spread information about the life and environmental sciences, such as museums and zoos, can be an exciting change from classroom learning. Wildlife preserves and similar facilities often provide educational opportunities and allow students to observe living things in their native environments.

Professional Scientists and State/National Government Employees

Research scientists and other professionals may be a good resource to teach students more about certain subjects. This is especially true when they can present demonstrations or invite students to their labs or other places of work. In some cases an agency such as the Department of Natural Resources, Environmental Protection Agency, or state Extension Service may also be a resource.

The following Web site lists many publishers of multimedia software packages:

http://www.educational-software-directory.net/science/

These Web sites list resources for science teachers:

- *http://sciencepage.org/teachers.htm*
- *http://www.nbii.gov/portal/server.pt?open=512&objID=236&mode=2&cached=true*
- *http://www.biologycorner.com/*

Sample Test Question and Rationale

(Rigorous)

1. Adequate resource materials in science:

    A. Should be limited to scientific journals

    B. Are often difficult for teachers to find

    C. Come from a variety of sources and are written at different learning levels

    D. Are rarely found in the average library

Answer: C. Come from a variety of sources and are written at different learning levels

Resources for science classes can come from many places, including materials generated in the classroom from experiments. Scientific journal articles and many texts and references in the school library are appropriate, along with science textbooks and magazine articles, to name a few.

The following concepts and processes are generally recognized as common to all
scientific disciplines:

1. Systems, order, and organization: Because the natural world is
   so complex, the study of science involves the organization of items into
   smaller groups based on interaction or interdependence. These groups are
   called systems. Examples of organization are the periodic table of elements
   and the five-kingdom classification scheme for living organisms. Examples
   of systems are the solar system, the cardiovascular system, Newton's laws of
   force and motion, and the laws of conservation. Order refers to the behavior
   and measurability of organisms and events in nature. The arrangement of
   planets in the solar system and the life cycle of bacterial cells are examples of
   order.

2. Evidence, models, and explanation: Scientists use evidence and
   models to form explanations of natural events. Models are miniatur-
   ized representations of a larger event or system. Evidence is anything that
   furnishes proof.

3. Constancy, change, and measurement: Constancy and
   change describe the observable properties of natural organisms and events.
   Scientists use different systems of measurement to observe change and
   constancy. For example, the freezing and melting points of given substances
   and the speed of sound are the same under constant conditions. Growth,
   decay, and erosion are all examples of natural changes.

4. Evolution and equilibrium: Evolution is the process of change
   over a long period of time. While biological evolution is the most common
   example, one can also classify technological advancement, changes in the
   universe, and changes in the environment as evolution.

5. Equilibrium is the state of balance between opposing forces of change.
   Homeostasis and ecological balance are examples of equilibrium.

6. Form and function: Form and function are properties of organisms
   and systems that are closely related. The function of an object usually dictates its form, and the form of an object usually facilitates its function. For
   example, the form of the heart (e.g., muscle and valves) allows it to perform
   its function of circulating blood through the body.

Structure and Function Model

The function of different systems in organisms from bacteria to humans dictates system structure. The basic principle that "form follows function" applies to all organismal systems. We will discuss a few examples to illustrate this principle. Keep in mind that we can relate the structure and function of all organismal systems.

Mitochondria, subcellular organelles present in eukaryotic cells, provide energy for cell functions. Much of the energy-generating activity takes place in the mito-chondrial membrane. To maximize this activity, the mitochondrial membrane has many folds to pack a relatively large amount of membrane into a small space.

Bacterial cells maintain a high surface area-to-volume ratio to maximize contact with the environment and to allow for the exchange of nutrients and waste products. Bacterial cells achieve this high ratio by maintaining a small internal volume by cell division.

The cardiovascular system of animals has many specialized structures that help to achieve the function of delivering blood to all parts of the body. The heart has four chambers for the delivery and reception of blood. The blood vessels vary in size to accommodate the necessary volume of blood. For example, vessels near the heart are large to accommodate large amounts of blood, and vessels in the extremities are very small to limit the amount of blood delivered.

The structure of the skeletal systems of different animals varies based on the animal's method of movement. For example, the honeycombed structure of bird bones provides a lightweight skeleton of great strength to accommodate flight. The bones of the human skeletal system are dense, strong, and aligned in such a way as to allow walking on two legs in an upright position.

Sample Test Question and Rationale

(Rigorous)

1. Identify the correct sequence of organization of living things from lower to higher order:

   A. Cell, organelle, organ, tissue, system, organism

   B. Cell, tissue, organ, organelle, system, organism

   C. Organelle, cell, tissue, organ, system, organism

   D. Organelle, tissue, cell, organ, system, organism

Answer: C. Organelle, cell, tissue, organ, system, organism

Organelles are parts of the cell; cells make up tissue, which makes up organs. Organs work together in systems (e.g., the respiratory system), and the organism is the living thing as a whole.

SAMPLE TEST

SAMPLE TEST
LANGUAGE ARTS

(Average) (Skill 1.1)

1. Which of the following represents a popular method of teaching students to read?

   I. Literacy
   II. Memorization
   III. Phonics
   IV. Whole language

   A. II and III only

   B. I and II only

   C. III and IV only

   D. I only

(Average) (Skill 1.2)

2. Children are taught phonological awareness when they are taught all but which concept?

   A. The sounds made by the letters

   B. The correct spelling of words

   C. The sounds made by various combinations of letters

   D. The ability to recognize individual sounds in words

(Easy) (Skill 1.3)

3. Which of the following indicates that a student is a fluent reader?

   A. Reads texts with expression or prosody

   B. Reads word-to-word and haltingly

   C. Must intentionally decode a majority of the words

   D. In a writing assignment, sentences are poorly organized structurally

(Rigorous) (Skill 1.4)

4. All of the following are true about vocabulary instruction EXCEPT:

   A. There is a need for direct instruction of vocabulary items required for a specific text

   B. Vocabulary learning is effective when it entails rote memorization

   C. Computer technology can be used effectively to help teach vocabulary

   D. Vocabulary can be acquired through incidental learning

(Rigorous) (Skill 1.5)

5. Effective reading comprehension requires:

   A. Identifying all words automatically

   B. Knowing at least 50 percent of the words within a given text

   C. Both A and B

   D. Neither A nor B

(Average) (Skill 1.6)

6. Which of the following is NOT a characteristic of a fable?

   A. Animals that feel and talk like humans

   B. Happy solutions to human dilemmas

   C. Teaches a moral or standard for behavior

   D. Illustrates specific peoples or groups without directly naming them

(Average) (Skill 1.7)

7. **Alliteration is a poetic device where:**

   A. The words used (pow, zap, eek) evoke meaning by their sounds

   B. The final consonant sounds are the same, but the vowels are different.

   C. The vowel sound in a word matches the vowel sound in a nearby word, but the surrounding consonant sounds are different (for example, June and Tune)

   D. The initial sound of a word, beginning with either a consonant or a vowel, is repeated in succession (for example, people who pen poetry)

(Average) (Skill 1.8)

8. **A euphemism is:**

   A. A direct comparison of two things

   B. An indirect comparison of two things

   C. A deliberate exaggeration for effect

   D. The substitution of an agreeable term for one that might offend

(Rigorous) (Skill 14.2)

9. **Which of the following is NOT an effective way to compile research sources?**

   A. Analyze the applicability and validity of the massive amounts of information in cyberspace

   B. Discern authentic sources of information from the mass collections of Web sites and information databases available

   C. Bookmark Web sites of interest and cut and paste relevant information onto word documents for citation and reference

   D. Avoid using large search engines like Google and Yahoo to minimize the amount of irrelevant, unauthentic sources and save a lot of research time

(Rigorous) (Skill 2.1)

10. **Which sentence is NOT punctuated correctly?**

    A. The more he knew about her, the less he wished he had known

    B. Ellen daydreamed about getting out of the rain, taking a shower and eating a hot dinner

    C. The veterinarian, not his assistant, would perform the delicate surgery

    D. His thorough, though esoteric, scientific research could not easily be understood by high school students

(Rigorous) (Skill 2.2)

11. **Which is NOT a true statement concerning an author's literary style?**

    A. Style can be through word choice

    B. Style may vary across genres

    C. Style can be affected by sentence structure

    D. Style is the expression of the author's attitude toward his/her subject

(Average) (Skill 2.3)

12. **The most important step for the writer in the writing process is:**

    A. Prewriting

    B. Researching

    C. Drafting

    D. Revising

(Rigorous) (Skill 2.4)

13. Which stage of writing development would be most accurate for the following text:

"Bobbie n me playd games at hr moms house. We ate sereal n toest."

A. Emergent writer

B. Developing writer

C. Beginning writer

D. Expanding writer

(Average) (Skill 2.5)

14. A sentence that contains one independent clause with one subject and one predicate best describes:

A. Simple sentence

B. Compound sentence

C. Complex sentence

D. Compound complex sentence

(Rigorous) (Skill 2.6)

15. All of the following are true about the topic sentence of a paragraph EXCEPT:

A. It is more general than the other sentences

B. It usually covers one single idea

C. In question form, all the other sentences answer it

D. It could be in any position in the paragraph

(Rigorous) (Skill 3.1)

16. Students should practice all of the following when speaking orally EXCEPT:

A. Students should look at a spot on the back wall or at notes

B. Students should vary the pitch of their voice

C. Students should maintain a straight but not stiff posture

D. Students should use gestures they would use when speaking to a friend

(Average) (Skill 3.2)

17. Which of the following methods will help students learn good listening skills?

A. Have students write down questions to ask the speaker

B. Have students critique the speaker's public speaking skills

C. Have students participate in a discussion.

D. Have students practice following complex directions.

(Average) (Skill 3.3)

18. Which of the following would NOT be useful in developing students' ability to view images to enhance their literacy skills?

A. Describe a picture in a book in great detail

B. Cutting out pictures in magazines to tell a story

C. Drawing self-portraits

D. Identifying billboards in their environment that reflect a certain theme

(Average) (Skill 3.4)

19. Ms. Chomski is presenting a new story to her class of first graders. In the story, a family visits their grandparents where they all gather around a record player and listen to music. Many students do not understand what a record player is, especially some children for whom English is not their first language. Which of the following would Ms. Chomski be best to do?

   A. Discuss what a record player is with her students

   B. Compare a record player with a CD player

   C. Have students look up record player in a dictionary

   D. Show the students a picture of a record player

(Rigorous) (Skill 1.1)

20. All of the following are true about schemata EXCEPT:

   A. Used as a basis for literary response

   B. Structures that represent concepts stored in our memories

   C. A generalization that is proven with facts

   D. Used together with prior knowledge for effective reading comprehension

(Easy) (Skill 1.2)

21. To decode is to:

   A. Construct meaning

   B. Sound out a printed sequence of letters

   C. Use a special code to decipher a message

   D. None of the above

(Rigorous) (Skill 1.5)

22. Which of the following is NOT a strategy of teaching reading comprehension?

   A. Summarization

   B. Utilizing graphic organizers

   C. Manipulating sounds

   D. Having students generate questions

(Average) (Skill 1.6)

23. The children's literature genre came into its own in the:

   A. Seventeenth century

   B. Eighteenth century

   C. Nineteenth century

   D. Twentieth century

(Average) (Skill 1.7)

24. Assonance is a poetic device where:

   A. The vowel sound in a word matches the same sound in a nearby word, but the surrounding consonant sounds are different

   B. The initial sounds of a word, beginning either with a consonant or a vowel, are repeated in close succession

   C. The words used evoke meaning by their sounds

   D. The final consonant sounds are the same, but the vowels are different

(Easy) (Skill 2.2)

25. A student has written a paper with the following characteristics: written in first person; characters, setting, and plot; some dialogue; and events organized in chronological sequence with some flash-backs. In what genre has the student written?

   A. Expository writing

   B. Narrative writing

   C. Persuasive writing

   D. Technical writing

(Rigorous) (Skill 2.1)

26. The following words are made plural correctly EXCEPT:

   A. Radios

   B. Bananas

   C. Poppies

   D. Tomatos

(Average) (Skill 2.3)

27. All of the following are true about writing an introduction EXCEPT:

   A. It should be written last

   B. It should lead the audience into the discourse

   C. It is the point of the paper

   D. It can take up a large percentage of the total word count

(Average) (Skill 2.6)

28. Topic sentences, transition words, and appropriate vocabulary are used by writers to:

   A. Meet various purposes

   B. Organize a multi-paragraph essay

   C. Express an attitude on a subject

   D. Explain the presentation of ideas

(Average) (Skill 2.3)

29. Which of the following is NOT a technique of prewriting?

   A. Clustering

   B. Listing

   C. Brainstorming

   D. Proofreading

MATHEMATICS

(Average) (Skill 4.1)

30. Deductive reasoning is:

   A. The process of finding a pattern from a group of examples

   B. The process of arriving at a conclusion based on other statements that are known to be true.

   C. Both A and B

   D. Neither A nor B

(Easy) (Skill 5.1)

31. 4,087,361: What number represents the ten-thousands place?

    A. 4

    B. 6

    C. 0

    D. 8

(Rigorous) (Skill 5.2)

32. Which of the following is an irrational number?

    A. .36262626262…

    B. 4

    C. 8.2

    D. -5

(Average) (Skill 5.3)

33. The order of mathematical operations is done in the following order:

    A. Simplify inside grouping characters such as parentheses, brackets, square root, fraction bar, etc.; multiply out expressions with exponents; do multiplication or division, from left to right; do addition or subtraction, from left to right

    B. Do multiplication or division, from left to right; simplify inside grouping characters such as parentheses, brackets, square root, fraction bar, etc.; multiply out expressions with exponents; do addition or subtraction, from left to right

    C. Simplify inside grouping characters such as parentheses, brackets, square root, fraction bar, etc.; do addition or subtraction, from left to right; multiply out expressions with exponents; do multiplication or division, from left to right

    D. None of the above

(Easy) (Skill 5.4)

34. What is the greatest common factor of 16, 28, and 36?

    A. 2

    B. 4

    C. 8

    D. 16

(Easy) (Skill 5.5)

35. The mass of a cookie is closest to:

    A. 0.5 kg

    B. 0.5 grams

    C. 15 grams

    D. 1.5 grams

(Average) (Skill 5.6)

36. An item that sells for $375 is put on sale at $120. What is the percent of decrease?

    A. 25%

    B. 28%

    C. 68%

    D. 34%

(Average) (Skill 6.1)

37. Find the coordinates of intersection point for the lines described by the equations below.

    $y = 3x - 7$ $y = -2x + 1$

    A. (1, 2)

    B. (-1.6, 2.2)

    C. (1.6, 2)

    D. (1.6, -2.2)

(Rigorous) (Skill 6.2)

38. What is the value of the following expression?

$$\frac{15 - 24(1 - 0.8)}{-5 + 8}$$

   A. -24.6

   B. -3.6

   C. 3.4

   D. 13.4

(Rigorous) (Skill 6.3)

39. An equation in the form $\frac{a}{b}x = c$ is solved by multiplying both sides by $\frac{b}{a}$. Which of the following statements explains why?
   I. The product of multiplicative inverses is 1
   II. The solution must be in the form $1x$ = some number
   III. Use of the multiplicative inverse cancels the factor $\frac{a}{b}$ to zero

   A. I and II

   B. II and III

   C. I and III

   D. I, II, and III

(Rigorous) (Skill 6.4)

40. Which of the following statements are always true?
   I. The square of a negative number is a whole number
   II. The quotient of two integers is a rational number
   III. Fractions are rational numbers
   IV. Decimals are rational numbers

   A. I

   B. II and III

   C. II and IV

   D. II, III, and IV

(Average) (Skill 6.5)

41. What is the solution set of the following inequality?

$$-5(2x - 1) \geq 6x - 5$$

   A. $x \leq 0$

   B. $x \geq 0$

   C. $x \leq \frac{5}{8}$

   D. $x \geq \frac{5}{8}$

(Average) (Skill 6.6)

42. A boat travels 30 miles upstream in three hours. It makes the return trip in one and a half hours. What is the speed of the boat in still water?

   A. 10 mph

   B. 15 mph

   C. 20 mph

   D. 30 mph

(Rigorous) (Skill 7.1)

43. Three-dimensional figures in geometry are called:

   A. Solids

   B. Cubes

   C. Polygons

   D. Blocks

(Average) (Skill 7.2)

44. Which of the following polygons will not tessellate a plane?

   A. Obtuse triangle

   B. Parallelogram

   C. Regular hexagon

   D. Regular octagon

(Average) (Skill 7.3)

45. If a right triangle has legs with the measurements of 3 cm and 4 cm, what is the measure of the hypotenuse?

A. 6 cm

B. 1 cm

C. 7 cm

D. 5 cm

(Average) (Skill 8.1)

46. What conclusion can be drawn from the graph below?

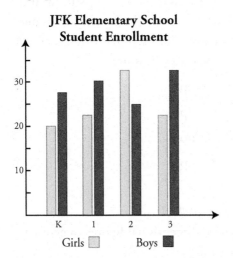

JFK Elementary School
Student Enrollment

A. The number of students in first grade exceeds the number in second grade

B. There are more boys than girls in the entire school

C. There are more girls than boys in the first grade

D. Third grade has the greatest number of students.

(Average) (Skill 8.2)

47. Suppose you have a bag of marbles that contains 2 red marbles, 5 blue marbles, and 3 green marbles. If you replace the first marble chosen, what is the probability you will choose 2 green marbles in a row?

A. $\frac{2}{5}$

B. $\frac{9}{100}$

C. $\frac{9}{10}$

D. $\frac{3}{5}$

(Rigorous) (Skill 8.3)

48. How many different five-letter words (not necessarily dictionary words) can be formed from the first 10 letters of the alphabet, assuming no letter is repeated?

A. 5

B. 252

C. 30,240

D. 3,628,800

(Rigorous) (Skill 8.4)

49. Given the following numbers, find the median: 25, 18, 16, 45, 10, 27

A. 21.5

B. 25

C. 18

D. There is no median

(Average) (Skill 5.2)

50. Which of the following terms most accurately describes the set of numbers below?

$$\{3, \sqrt{16}, \pi°, 6, \tfrac{28}{4}\}$$

A. Rationals

B. Irrationals

C. Complex

D. Whole numbers

(Average) (Skill 5.3)

51. Calculate the value of the following expression.

$$(\tfrac{6}{3} + 1 \times 5)^2 \times (\tfrac{1}{7}) + (3 \times 2 - 1)$$

A. 6

B. 10

C. 12

D. 294

(Rigorous) (Skill 5.4)

52. What is the LCM of 6, 7, and 9?

A. 14

B. 42

C. 126

D. 378

(Average) (Skill 5.6)

53. The final cost of an item (with sales tax) is $8.35. If the sales tax is 7%, what was the pretax price of the item?

A. $7.80

B. $8.00

C. $8.28

D. $8.93

(Average) (Skill 6.2)

54. Which property justifies the following manipulation?

$$x^2 - 3y \rightarrow -3y + x^2$$

A. Associative

B. Commutative

C. Distributive

D. None of the above

(Average) (Skill 6.3)

55. Which of the following is an example of a multiplicative inverse?

A. $x^2 - x^2 = 0$

B. $(y - 3)^0 = 1$

C. $\tfrac{1}{e^{3z}} e^{3z} = 1$

D. $f^2 = \tfrac{1}{g}$

(Rigorous) (Skill 6.6)

56. Two farmers are buying feed for animals. One farmer buys eight bags of grain and six bales of hay for $105, and the other farmer buys three bags of grain and nine bales of hay for $69.75. How much is a bag of grain?

A. $4.50

B. $9.75

C. $14.25

D. $28.50

(Average) (Skill 7.3)

57. What is the area of the shaded region below, where the circle has a radius r?

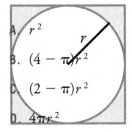

A. r^2

B. $(4 - \pi)r^2$

C. $(2 - \pi)r^2$

D. $4\pi r^2$

(Rigorous) (Skill 8.2)

58. A bag contains four red marbles and six blue marbles. If three selections are made without replacement, what is the probability of choosing three red marbles?

A. $\frac{3}{10}$

B. $\frac{8}{125}$

C. $\frac{1}{30}$

D. $\frac{1}{60}$

(Average) (Skill 8.3)

59. How many different three-card hands can be drawn from a standard deck of 52 playing cards?

A. 156

B. 2,704

C. 22,100

D. 140,608

SOCIAL STUDIES

(Rigorous) (Skill 9.1)

60. What are two factors that can generate and affect landforms?

A. Observing a plateau at various scales

B. Erosion and deposition

C. The presence of oceans, lakes, seas, and canals

D. The dry nature of some plateaus

(Easy) (Skill 9.2)

61. _____ is the southernmost continent in the world.

A. Australia

B. New Zealand

C. The Arctic

D. Antarctica

(Rigorous) (Skill 9.3)

62. Human bones found during construction near an American Civil War battlefield would most likely be delivered to which of the following for study?

A. The Department of Veterans Affairs

B. A state medical examiner

C. A homicide detective

D. An anthropologist

(Average) (Skill 9.4)

63. States that are near the Rocky Mountains, such as Montana, have exceptional trout fishing because of which of the following:

   A. Lakes in mountain regions have warm water that trout enjoy

   B. Mountain regions are the only places that have large numbers of the aquatic insects trout like to eat

   C. There are fewer people in these areas, so the fishing pressure is light

   D. Trout thrive in the cold, clean rivers found in mountainous regions

(Average) (Skill 10.1)

64. Our present day alphabet comes from which of the following:

   A. Cuneiform

   B. The Greek alphabet

   C. Hieroglyphic writing

   D. Hebrew Scriptures

(Rigorous) (Skill 10.2)

65. The cold war involved which two countries who both emerged as world powers?

   A. China and Japan

   B. United States and the Soviet Union

   C. England and Brazil

   D. Afghanistan and the United States

(Rigorous) (Skill 10.3)

66. Cultural diffusion is:

   A. The process that individuals and societies go through in changing their behavior and organization to cope with social, economic and environmental pressures

   B. The complete disappearance of a culture

   C. The exchange or adoption of cultural features when two cultures come into regular direct contact

   D. The movement of cultural ideas or materials between populations independent of the movement of those populations

(Rigorous) (Skill 11.1)

67. The economic activities of the Middle Atlantic colonies included:

   A. Manufacturing

   B. Fishing

   C. Iron mining

   D. Melting pots

(Average) (Skill 11.2)

68. All of the following were causes of the American Revolution EXCEPT:

   A. The Tea Act of 1773

   B. The Stamp Act

   C. The colonists were forced to house English troops

   D. The colonists wanted more schools

(Easy) (Skill 11.3)

69. **The belief that the United States should control all of North America was called:**

A. Westward Expansion

B. Pan Americanism

C. Manifest Destiny

D. Nationalism

(Average) (Skill 11.4)

70. **What happened to weapons and technology during World War II?**

A. They remained about the same as in World War I

B. They saw dramatic changes in terms of new equipment and new technology

C. These areas suffered because radar had not yet been invented

D. Weapons, like submarines, remained very primitive

(Rigorous) (Skill 11.5)

71. **After a string of Republican Presidents, the American public elected Franklin D. Roosevelt on a promise to do what?**

A. Provide relief to citizens

B. Focus on recovering the economy

C. Reforming the economic system

D. All of the above

(Average) (Skill 12.1)

72. **A communistic government is:**

A. A government that is ruled by one individual or a small group of individuals

B. A government with a legislature, usually involving a multiplicity of political parties and often coalition politics

C. A political system characterized by the ideology of class conflict and revolution and that the product of all the people is shared by each and every person.

D. A political system that values conflict and revolution with a central political control that allows for private ownership of the means of production

(Average) (Skill 12.2)

73. **The Constitution of the United States:**

A. Is an unwritten constitution

B. Is a precise, formal, written document

C. Does not allow states to be sovereign in their own affairs

D. Can be amended on the vote of two-thirds of the states

(Rigorous) (Skill 12.3)

74. **All of the following are rights that are granted by the Bill of Rights EXCEPT:**

A. Freedom of religion

B. No cruel or unusual punishment allowed

C. Right for a free education

D. Security from the quartering of troops in homes

(Rigorous) (Skill 13.1)

75. **What is a market?**

    A. A place where people buy groceries

    B. The mechanism that brings buyers and sellers in contact with each other

    C. A stock exchange or a commodity futures exchange

    D. The process of supply and demand

(Rigorous) (Skill 13.2)

76. **The following are factors of production EXCEPT:**

    A. Labor

    B. Entrepreneurship

    C. Land

    D. Income

(Average) (Skill 13.3)

77. **The United States has which type of economy:**

    A. A market economy

    B. A centrally planned economy

    C. A market socialist economy

    D. None of the above

(Average) (Skill 14.1)

78. **The literature that exists in a particular field of historical study is often called:**

    A. The historiography

    B. The bibliography

    C. The histology

    D. The faculty

(Average) (Skill 14.2)

79. **Which of the following is a primary source document?**

    A. A book recounting the events surrounding the 1932 kidnapping of aviator Charles Lindbergh's son

    B. A newspaper story about the Wall Street Crash of 1987

    C. The text of Franklin Roosevelt's address to Congress of December 8, 1941, requesting a declaration of war against Japan

    D. A movie dramatizing the life of a fictional family who are living in Poland during the German invasion of 1939

(Rigorous) (Skill 14.3)

80. **Which of the following is an example of a historical concept?**

    A. Capitalism

    B. Racism

    C. Globalization

    D. All of the above

(Average) (Skill 9.1)

81. **Denver is called the "mile-high city" because it is:**

    A. Located approximately one mile above the plains of eastern Colorado

    B. Located exactly one mile above the base of Cheyenne Mountain

    C. Located approximately one mile above sea level

    D. The city with the tallest buildings in Colorado

(Average) (Skill 9.2)

82. The great plains in the United States are an excellent place to grow corn and wheat for all of the following reasons except:

   A. Rainfall is abundant and the soil is rich

   B. The land is mostly flat and easy to cultivate

   C. The human population is modest in size, so there is plenty of space for large farms

   D. The climate is semitropical

(Rigorous) (Skill 10.1)

83. What is the "Pax Romana"?

   A. Long period of peace enabling free travel and trade, spreading people, cultures, goods, and ideas all over the world

   B. A period of war where the Romans expanded their empire

   C. The Roman government

   D. A time where the government was overruled

(Average) (Skill 11.1)

84. English and Spanish colonists took what from Native Americans?

   A. Land

   B. Water rights

   C. Money

   D. Religious beliefs

(Rigorous) (Skill 11.3)

85. How did manufacturing change in the early 1800s?

   A. The electronics industry was born

   B. Production moved from small shops or homes into factories

   C. Industry benefited from the Federal Reserve Act

   D. The timber industry was hurt when Theodore Roosevelt set aside 238 million acres of federal lands to be protected from development

(Rigorous) (Skill 11.3)

86. The post World-War II years in the United States saw the emergence of the largest consumer culture in the world. What was not a benefit of this culture?

   A. Improved working conditions in third world countries

   B. Improved American economy

   C. Improved global economy

   D. Improved standard of living in the United States

(Average) (Skill 12.1)

87. The U.S. House of Representatives has

   A. 100 members

   B. 435 members

   C. Three branches

   D. A president and a vice-president

(Easy) (Skill 13.1)

88. Which of the following terms best describes the international nature of commerce today?

    A. Industrialization

    B. Laissez-faire

    C. Globalization

    D. Autarky

(Rigorous) (Skill 14.1)

89. What is a major drawback to using maps in social studies?

    A. They provide a solid foundation for social science studies

    B. They quickly convey complex information

    C. They reflect a great variety of knowledge

    D. They must be understood to be of value

(Average) (Skill 14.2)

90. An example of something that is not a primary source is:

    A. The published correspondence between Winston Churchill and Franklin D. Roosevelt during World War II

    B. Martin Gilbert's biography of Winston Churchill

    C. The diary of Field Marshal Sir Alan Brooke, the head of the British Army during World War II

    D. Franklin D. Roosevelt's handwritten notes from the World War II era

SCIENCE

(Easy) (Skill 15.1)

91. Which of the following layers comprises the Earth's plates?

    A. Mesosphere

    B. Troposphere

    C. Asthensophere

    D. Lithosphere

(Average) (Skill 15.2)

92. What conditions are required to create coarse grained igneous rocks?

    A. High temperature and pressure

    B. Magma that cools slowly

    C. Lava that cools quickly

    D. Evaporation and cementation

(Easy) (Skill 15.3)

93. The use of radioactivity to determine the age of rocks and fossils is called which of the following?

    A. Carbon dating

    B. Absolute dating

    C. Stratigraphy

    D. Geological dating

(Easy) (Skill 15.4)

94. Which of the following astronomical entities is not part of the galaxy the Sun is located in?

    A. Nebulae

    B. Quasars

    C. Pulsars

    D. Neutron stars

(Rigorous) (Skill 15.5)

95. Which of the following facts of physics best explains the cause of tides?

    A. The density of water is less than the density of rock

    B. The force of gravity follows the inverse square law

    C. Centripetal acceleration causes water on Earth to bulge

    D. The gravitational force of the Moon on Earth's oceans

(Average) (Skill 16.1)

96. Which of the following is not a property that eukaryotes have and prokaryotes do not have?

    A. Nucleus

    B. Ribosomes

    C. Chromosomes

    D. Mitochondria

(Average) (Skill 16.2)

97. At what stage in mitosis does the chromatin become chromosomes?

    A. Telophase

    B. Anaphase

    C. Prophase

    D. Metaphase

(Rigorous) (Skill 16.3)

98. Which of the following is a correct explanation for scientific evolution?

    A. Giraffes need to reach higher leaves to eat, so their necks stretch. The giraffe babies are then born with longer necks. Eventually, there are more long-necked giraffes in the population.

    B. Giraffes with longer necks are able to reach more leaves, so they eat more and have more babies than other giraffes. Eventually, there are more long-necked giraffes in the population.

    C. C. Giraffes want to reach higher for leaves to eat, so they release enzymes into their bloodstream, which in turn causes fetal development of longer-necked giraffes. Eventually, there are more long-necked giraffes in the population.

    D. Giraffes with long necks are more attractive to other giraffes, so they get the best mating partners and have more babies. Eventually, there are more long-necked giraffes in the population.

(Easy) (Skill 16.4)

99. Which is not a characteristic of living organisms?

    A. Sexual reproduction

    B. Ingestion

    C. Synthesis

    D. Respiration

(Easy) (Skill 16.5)

100. Taxonomy classifies species into genera (plural of genus) based on similarities. Species are subordinate to genera. The most general or highest taxonomical group is the kingdom. Which of the following is the correct order of the other groups from highest to lowest?

A. Class → order → family → phylum

B. Phylum → class → family → order

C. Phylum → class → order → family

D. Order → phylum → class → family

(Easy) (Skill 16.6)

101. Which of the following describes the interaction between community members when one species feeds of another species but does not kill it immediately?

A. Parasitism

B. Predation

C. Commensalism

D. Mutualism

(Easy) (Skill 17.1)

102. Which of the following statements about the density of a substance is true?

A. It is a chemical property

B. It is a physical property

C. It does not depend on the temperature of the substance

D. It is a property only of liquids and solids

(Rigorous) (Skill 17.2)

103. Which statement best explains why a balance scale is used to measure both weight and mass?

A. The weight and mass of an object are identical concepts

B. The force of gravity between two objects depends on the mass of the two objects

C. Inertial mass and gravitational mass are identical

D. A balance scale compares the weight of two objects

(Easy) (Skill 17.3)

104. The transfer of heat by electromagnetic waves is called:

A. Conduction

B. Convection

C. Phase change

D. Radiation

(Average) (Skill 17.4)

105. The following are examples of chemical reactions EXCEPT:

A. Melting ice into water

B. Dissolving a seltzer tablet in water

C. Using a fire-cracker

D. Burning a piece of plastic

(Average) (Skill 18.1)

106. Which of the following is the main source of energy in the diet?

A. Vitamins

B. Minerals

C. Water

D. Carbohydrates

(Average) (Skill 18.2)

107. All of the following professions are classified under 'earth sciences' EXCEPT:

A. Geologist

B. Meteorologist

C. Seismologist

D. Biochemist

(Rigorous) (Skill 19.1)

108. In an experiment measuring the growth of bacteria at different temperatures, what is the independent variable?

A. Number of bacteria

B. Growth rate of bacteria

C. Temperature

D. Size of bacteria

(Rigorous) (Skill 19.2)

109. Adequate resource materials in science:

A. Should be limited to scientific journals

B. Are often difficult for teachers to find

C. Come from a variety of sources and are written at different learning levels

D. Rarely are found in the average library

(Rigorous) (Skill 19.3)

110. Identify the correct sequence of organization of living things from lower to higher order:

A. Cell, Organelle, Organ, Tissue, System, Organism

B. Cell, Tissue, Organ, Organelle, System, Organism

C. Organelle, Cell, Tissue, Organ, System, Organism

D. Organelle, Tissue, Cell, Organ, System, Organism

(Average Rigor) (Skill 15.2)

111. What is the main cause of the formation of mountains?

A. Glaciation

B. Volcanism

C. Orogeny

D. Tectonic movements

(Easy) (Skill 15.3)

112. Which of the following describes the law of superposition?

A. The present is the key to the past

B. The oldest rocks in a rock unit are found on the top of the rock column

C. The oldest rocks in a rock unit are found on the bottom of the rock column

D. Faults that cut across rock units are younger than the units they cut across

(Rigorous) (Skill 15.4)

113. Why is winter in the Northern Hemisphere warmer than winter in the Southern Hemisphere?

A. The angle of incidence of the Sun's rays upon the earth is greater in the Northern Hemisphere

B. There is a greater concentration of greenhouse gases in the Northern Hemisphere

C. The perihelion occurs in January.

D. There is more water in the Northern Hemisphere

(Rigorous) (Skill 16.1)

114. What cell organelle contains the cell's stored food?

    A. Vacuoles

    B. Golgi Apparatus

    C. Ribosome

    D. Lysosome

(Average) (Skill 16.2)

115. Meiosis starts with a single cell and ends with which of the following?

    A. Two diploid cells

    B. Two haploid cells

    C. Four diploid cells

    D. Four haploid cells

(Average) (Skill 16.6)

116. Which of the following is the most accurate definition of a nonrenewable resource?

    A. A nonrenewable resource is never replaced once used

    B. A nonrenewable resource is replaced on a timescale that is very long relative to human life spans

    C. A nonrenewable resource is a resource that can only be manufactured by humans

    D. A nonrenewable resource is a species that has already become extinct

(Easy) (Skill 17.1)

117. A type of mixture where one substance is suspended in another is called what?

    A. Heterogeneous

    B. A colloid

    C. A solution

    D. Homogeneous

(Easy) (Skill 17.2)

118. A pendulum has _____ at the top of its swinging arc.

    A. maximum kinetic energy

    B. maximum potential energy

    C. maximum total energy

    D. minimum potential energy

(Average) (Skill 17.3)

119. Which statement could be described as the first law of thermodynamics?

    A. No machine can convert heat energy to work with 100 percent efficiency

    B. Energy is neither created nor destroyed

    C. Thermometers can be used to measure temperatures

    D. Heat flows from hot objects to cold objects

(Average) (Skill 19.1)

120. Which is the correct order of scientific methodology?

    1. Collecting data
    2. Planning a controlled experiment
    3. Drawing a conclusion
    4. Hypothesizing a result
    5. Revisiting a hypothesis to answer a question

    A. 1,2,3,4,5

    B. 4,2,1,3,5

    C. 4,5,1,3,2

    D. 1,3,4,5,2

ANSWER KEY								
1. C	15. B	29. D	43. A	57. B	71. D	85. B	99. A	113. C
2. B	16. A	30. B	44. D	58. C	72. C	86. A	100. C	114. A
3. A	17. D	31. D	45. D	59. C	73. B	87. B	101. A	115. D
4. B	18. C	32. A	46. B	60. B	74. C	88. C	102. B	116. B
5. D	19. D	33. A	47. B	61. D	75. B	89. D	103. C	117. C
6. D	20. C	34. B	48. C	62. D	76. D	90. B	104. D	118. B
7. D	21. A	35. C	49. A	63. D	77. A	91. D	105. A	119. B
8. D	22. C	36. C	50. D	64. B	78. A	92. B	106. D	120. B
9. D	23. A	37. D	51. C	65. B	79. C	93. B	107. D	
10. B	24. A	38. C	52. C	66. D	80. D	94. B	108. C	
11. D	25. B	39. A	53. A	67. C	81. C	95. B	109. C	
12. D	26. D	40. B	54. A	68. D	82. D	96. B	110. C	
13. B	27. C	41. C	55. C	69. C	83. A	97. C	111. D	
14. A	28. B	42.B	56. B	70. B	84. A	98. B	112. C	

RIGOR TABLE	
Rigor level	Questions
Easy 25%	3, 21, 26, 31, 34, 35, 61, 69, 88, 91, 93, 94, 99, 100, 101, 102, 104, 112, 117, 118
Average Rigor 50%	1, 2, 6, 7, 8, 12, 14, 17, 18, 19, 23, 24, 27, 28, 29, 30, 33, 36, 37, 41, 42, 44, 45, 46, 47, 50, 51, 53, 54, 55, 57, 59, 63, 64, 68, 70, 72, 73, 77, 78, 79, 81, 82, 84, 87, 90, 92, 96, 97, 105, 106, 107, 111, 115, 116, 119, 120
Rigorous 50%	4, 5, 9, 10, 11, 13, 15, 16, 20, 22, 25, 32, 38, 39, 40, 43, 48, 49, 52, 56, 58, 60, 62, 65, 66, 67, 71, 74, 75, 76, 83, 85, 86, 89, 95, 98, 103, 108, 109, 110, 113, 114

CONSTRUCTED RESPONSE SAMPLE QUESTIONS

Reading Essay

Megan is a third grade student in your classroom. Megan is very quiet and shy particularly when she is asked to read aloud or speak in front of the whole class. When you listen to Megan read out loud alone, you notice that she often mumbles her way through words she does not automatically recognize. To get a better understanding of Megan's skills, you pulled Megan aside to read a portion of the current story out loud to you. Before asking Megan to read, you asked her to make a prediction about the story. Megan's prediction was very accurate and showed a deep schema from which to draw and a solid ability to make predictions. You completed a running record on Megan and found the following errors in Megan's reading of one paragraph:

Words in the Story	How Megan Read These Words
can't	cannot
reasoned	rasined
the	*skipped by Megan*
reach	retch
aboard	abode
preserve	pressure

At the end of the portion you had Megan read aloud, Megan's accuracy was eighty-eight percent. Then you asked Megan to finish reading the story silently. When you called her back to retell the story, she had several misunderstandings of the information in the story. She also had difficulty with answering literal questions correctly. Megan's parents have approached you and have requested a conference with you to discuss Megan's progress in reading so far this year.

1. Examine the information presented and make a list of Megan's strengths and weaknesses in the area of reading.

2. Develop an instructional plan of action that you could share with Megan's parents at the conference to address areas of weakness Megan is displaying in reading. Be sure to include specific objectives, goals, and activities that you and her parents can implement to ensure Megan makes the necessary progress in reading to end the year on grade level.

Reading Response

Megan demonstrates areas of strength and weakness. They are:

- Strengths:
  - Shows a strong knowledge of beginning and ending sounds
  - Applies concepts of consonant blends and digraphs
  - Consistently applies rules of syllabication
  - Excellent background knowledge
  - Good comprehension skills
- Areas to consider for improvement:
  - Medial vowel sounds (particularly vowel pairs)
  - Reading through the whole word
  - Applying meaning to sentence level reading

Plan for Action

Rationale

Megan appears to have a lot of background knowledge that she can utilize to make meaning of the passages she is reading. However, she is making many errors in her reading which is causing her to misunderstand what she has read. If her reading accuracy increases, her comprehension skills should be appropriate.

Focus area

In particular, Megan seems to be struggling with the specific phonics skill of vowel sounds. This can be seen in the errors she made in the words *reach, reasoned, aboard,* and *pressure.* At this point, the fact that Megan skipped the word the or read the contraction as its compound word equivalent is not affecting her comprehension. Therefore, I would leave these errors for a later time period.

Megan's goal

When presented with third grade level materials, Megan will increase her accuracy from her current level of eighty-eight percent to an independent level of ninety-five percent by the end of third grade.

Instructional Strategies

1. Megan will participate in a making words activity to address her phonics difficulties. In this activity, Megan will use letters and letter patterns to build words that become larger and larger. This strategy will allow Megan to use the phonics skills she has mastered in shorter words and see how adding new letters, or even syllables, changes the rules and what sounds the letters make. Daily practice of this sequential phonics activity will provide Megan with the foundational skills to read through the entire word and identify the correct vowel sounds in words.

2. When Megan is reading and miscalls a word, the teacher will use two prompts to help Megan begin to apply her new skills. The first prompt will be: *Does that make sense?* The use of this prompt will allow Megan to realize that the purpose of reading is to understand and that reading needs to make sense. The use of this prompt can be followed with the following prompt: *What sounds do the letters make?* While these prompts will not correct all of the errors Megan may make, they are a starting point to help Megan begin to address her areas which are in need of improvement. Megan's parents can utilize these same prompts at home when she is reading to them, thus providing Megan with continuity and additional practice with reading daily.

Math Essay

A school uses fraction tiles to introduce students to the concept of fractions. Students learn, for example, how to line up five $\frac{1}{5}$ tiles to get one. They also learn to use different tiles (e.g., $\frac{1}{3}, \frac{1}{6}, \frac{1}{4}, \frac{1}{4}$) to match the length of the 1 tile. Most children love this activity and learn very soon to line up the tiles correctly. Surprisingly, when the children move to higher grades they find it very difficult to do problems with equivalent fractions and addition and subtraction of fractions.

1. Why do you think students are unable to retain the learning they are supposed to have gained through the use of fraction tiles?

2. Suggest three strategies teachers can use with the manipulatives activity to improve student performance in higher grades.

Math Response

1. Learning theories based on Piaget's stages of development from concrete to abstract suggest the use of manipulatives and other relatively concrete representations to introduce a concept before moving on to more symbolic and abstract forms. The use of fraction tiles for introducing fractions, therefore, is a strategy solidly based in accepted educational practice. One important point that teachers sometimes overlook, however, is the need to build bridges from the concrete to the abstract. If the fraction tiles and the relationships between them are not linked to the higher level symbolic concepts they are supposed to represent, the activity will end up being all about tiles and students will be unable to apply their learning elsewhere. This is very likely the reason students in this example are not able to retain their learning. Even though they are able to line

up the tiles perfectly, they do not realize that this represents an operation (addition) performed on the fractions and a relationship (equality) between them and the whole.

2. The following strategies will be useful in bridging the concrete tile activity with symbolic fraction relationships:

   – Make it clear that when students place fraction tiles side by side they are adding the fractions that the tiles represent. Also, when they match up the tiles in two rows, they are setting up a relationship of equivalence between the two.

   – When students are comfortable with the use of tiles, introduce the actual symbols (e.g., +, −, =) that they will use later to represent relationships between fractions. Let them use both in parallel for a while so that they see the connection.

   – In addition to tiles, introduce other manipulatives and visual representations (e.g., a circle divided into fractions) so that they are comfortable moving between representations and do not associate fraction concepts rigidly with just the tiles.

Teachers can also consider the use of virtual manipulatives that are often very flexible in their use, can be modified, and allow one to superpose symbols on top of concrete representations.

Science Essay

Science is based on knowledge gained from the five senses. Examples of observations are: *the sky is blue* (sight), *sandpaper is rough* (touch), *sugar is sweet* (taste), *bananas smell like bananas* (smell), and *clapping hands makes a loud noise* (hearing). Other kinds of knowledge are inferences and predictions. What would be the instructional objective, lesson motivation, and student activities in a lesson about observations?

Science Response

The instructional objective is that students will be able to make observations and identify the sense with which the observation is associated. A motivation should give students an incentive or reason to be interested in the lesson. Relating the lesson to their personal lives is an effective method. Students know that they different subjects they are learning different subjects: reading, science, math. Ask the class what it means to learn and if there are different kinds of knowledge?

The lesson can be developed by eliciting from the class the observations that can be made of a candle:

1. The candle is white (sight)

2. It feels waxy (touch)

3. It has no odor (smell)

4. It is shaped like a tube (sight)

Possible activities would be to have the students write down a certain number of observations about a plant and for each observation state the sense that was used. Also, observations could be made about a stick of gum: before chewing, during chewing, and after chewing.

Social Science Essay

You are a fifth grade teacher. The reading/language arts curriculum used in your classroom dominates more than half of the school day. The math curriculum encompasses almost the other half of the school day. Because of the extreme importance placed on standardized tests, the resulting AIP and AYP scores, and how they affect the school's funding, the district has labeled items in the curriculums as "nonnegotiable." These nonnegotiable items leave very little room in the school day for science and social studies curriculum.

The sixth grade teachers at the local middle school have voiced numerous concerns regarding how unprepared the incoming sixth graders are for social studies and science and how they have to spend at least the first month of the school year teaching the students social studies and science skills to be able to start the sixth grade curriculum. These teachers are frustrated and angry that required state standards are being overlooked at the elementary school level, which leaves students unprepared for the middle school curriculum.

After meeting as a grade level, you have volunteered to create a plan for teaching social studies to the students. Knowing that you cannot eliminate any of the nonnegotiable language arts and math items, you can only find thirty minutes of time one day a week to teach social studies to your fifth graders.

Develop an instructional plan to teach social studies within the thirty minute time slot one day a week. Be sure to include specific objectives, goals, and activities for one unit of study.

Social Science Response

Initial steps

To begin, I will research the fifth grade and sixth grade social studies state standards and create a list of common themes between the two grade levels. Given my time constraints in the classroom, I will then list these common themes in order of importance per subject to ensure that the most important standards are taught to my fifth grade students. After creating this list and sharing it with my fellow fifth grade teachers, I will meet with at least one sixth grade teacher at the local middle school to discuss the list and share my plan of action. I will stay in contact with the sixth grade teachers throughout the year regarding our progress with the fifth grade social studies curriculum.

Instructional plan

One common theme stated in the state standards between the two grade levels is for students to analyze the geographic, political, economic, religious, and social structures of a settlement or civilization. Being that the fifth grade teachers will only have thirty minutes once a week for social studies, we will give each month a theme using the above commonality in the standards (i.e., in August we will teach geography of a settlement; in September we will teach politics of a settlement; in October we will teach Economy of a settlement; in November we will teach religion of a settlement; and in December we will teach society of a settlement). The remainder of the year's lessons (January through May) will focus on at least two of the components (e.g., geography and politics) until, by the end of the year, the fifth graders will have analyzed all five components and so will be prepared for that standard in sixth grade. The idea is to increase the higher learning/thinking skills by building upon prior knowledge and background information. Each month as a new theme is introduced; teachers will connect it to the prior month's theme until, by the end of the year, students are able to make connections among all five components of the standard.

Here is a detailed plan for August:

Geography of a settlement

- **Week 1:** Introduce important vocabulary to front load the lesson. Divide the class into teams of three to four students (smaller teams if there are more vocabulary words) and assign each team one vocabulary word. Using a piece of cardstock, each team will be responsible for defining the word, using the word in a sentence, creating an illustration for the word, and giving examples of the word. After all teams have completed this activity, they will share their word with the class. All of the pieces of cardstock containing the vocabulary information will be stapled together to create an Illustrated Dictionary and left on display in the classroom for reference.

- **Week 2:** This week's activity will revolve around reading material from the textbook about the geography of a settlement. An instructional strategy that can be used during the reading is "Talk to the Text." As students read a copy of the text, they complete the following steps.

    1. Box, circle, underline, or star difficult words

    2. Draw arrows from nouns to pronouns (or between ideas) as the relationship becomes clear

    3. Write brief notes in the margins near hard to understand sentences and paragraphs

    This strategy is followed by a class discussion driven by teacher- and student-driven questions

- **Week 3:** This week can be similar to the previous week if there is more text that needs to be read and/or discussion that needs to be completed. If this is not the case, students will complete journal writing about what they've learned about this theme. The journal writing will include a description of the theme and how it relates to the specific settlement of study, predictions of how varying geographical features would affect other areas of settlement, and an explanation of what they would consider to be the ideal area in which to settle.

- **Week 4:** This week's activity will serve as an assessment. This could be an assessment take from the textbook. Another idea for an assessment could be to have the students work in teams of four to create a settlement and outline how the geography and climate influences the way they adjust to the environment. This could include explanations or drawings to explain the location of the settlement, the structures that exist, or how food and clothing are obtained.

CPSIA information can be obtained
at www.ICGtesting.com
Printed in the USA
BVOW07s1101110717

489054BV00006B/35/P